D0794057

Herbert Hoover

and the Reconstruction Finance Corporation, 1931-1933

Herbert Hoover

AND THE

Reconstruction Finance Corporation,

1931-1933

JAMES STUART OLSON

The Iowa State University Press, *Ames, Iowa*

James Stuart Olson, assistant professor of history at Sam Houston State University, Huntsville, Texas, holds the B.A. degree from Brigham Young University and the M.A. and Ph.D. degrees from the State University of New York at Stony Brook. Besides this book, he is author of several articles published in the journals of his field.

© 1977 The Iowa State University Press
Ames, Iowa 50010. All rights reserved

Composed and printed by
The Iowa State University Press

First edition, 1977

Library of Congress Cataloging in Publication Data

Olson, James Stuart, 1946-
    Herbert Hoover and the Reconstruction Finance
Corporation, 1931-1933.

    Bibliography: p.
    Includes index.
    1.   Reconstruction Finance Corporation.
2.   Hoover, Herbert Clark, Pres. U.S., 1874-1964.
3.   Depressions—1929—United States. I. Title.
HG3729.U404   332.7′06′173   76-57944
ISBN 0-8138-0880-4

To Al Mehr

who lived through it
and who crystallized some ideas

C O N T E N T S

PREFACE

FORTY years after leaving the White House, Herbert Hoover remains one of the most controversial figures in the history of American politics. For two generations historians and politicians have drawn cursory and often convenient conclusions about his role in national life; conservatives have canonized him, liberals vilified him, and more recently some New Leftists have tried to restore his reputation. His life is still an enigma, and he is either despised or held in high regard by older Americans and ignored as a high-collared irrelevancy by the young. Although his political career by itself justifies historical analysis, much of his personal philosophy and approach to national problems is particularly germane to modern America.

This study evaluates the administration of Herbert Hoover by concentrating on the Reconstruction Finance Corporation. During the course of research and writing, three objectives have been kept in mind. From the beginning I wanted to fill a gap in contemporary scholarship. The RFC, despite the billions of dollars it released into the economy and the wide variety of programs it administered, has been virtually ignored by historians. A number of competent scholars, including Richard Hofstadter, William Leuchtenburg, Arthur Schlesinger, Jr., Paul Conkin, Harris Warren, Carl Degler, Albert Romasco, Thomas Cochran, Susan Estabrook Kennedy, Joan Hoff Wilson, and William Appleman Williams, have acknowledged the importance of the Reconstruction Finance Corporation to the Hoover and the Roosevelt administrations. But except for one article by Gerald D. Nash ("Herbert Hoover and the Origins of the Reconstruction Finance Corporation"), which attempted to locate the origins of the agency, and an analysis of the RFC railroad loans by Herbert Spero (*Reconstruction Finance Corporation Loans to Railroads, 1932-1937*), the RFC has not received a systematic examination. In this book I have described RFC operations, analyzed its failure to bring an end to the depression, and attempted to assess its significance in American life by explaining why it ultimately occupied center stage in the dramatic ordeal of Herbert Hoover.

I have also attempted to examine the prevailing scholarly interpretation of President Hoover's political philosophy. Until recently, historians considered that philosophy to be Hoover's greatest shortcoming, arguing that his ideological opposition to a strong central government prevented him from dealing with the Great Depression.

For years the historiography of the Hoover administration followed simple ideological lines, with both critics and supporters of Hoover agreeing that he was generally a laissez-faire president. One group of anti-Roosevelt historians looked on Hoover as the embodiment of classical economics, the last man who tried to save America from the federal government.[1] Another group of historians also believed that Hoover was a laissez-faire president, but they criticized him as a hopeless reactionary wedded to an anachronistic political philosophy. Because of "American Individualism," they argued, Hoover was unable to deal effectively with the Great Depression and unwilling to see the imperative need for intervention by the federal government.[2]

But I have concluded that Hoover's philosophy played only a minor role in the failure of the Reconstruction Finance Corporation to revive the economy. The RFC was actually incapacitated by political controversy, economic miscalculation, and the inability to assess correctly the severity of the depression.

Finally, I have shown how the relationship between the Hoover administration and the New Deal is a transition rather than a watershed. Every contemporary American historian realizes that the New Deal vastly expanded the power and scope of the federal government, but recent research into the Hoover presidency has gradually revised the older consensus that the New Deal was a total break with the past—a radical departure in the history of public policy.

In recent years a more balanced view of Hoover has emerged. Historians have for the most part transcended the older debate in which conservatives and liberals either praised or condemned Hoover for being a laissez-faire ideologue. Collectively, more recent accounts have argued that Hoover was a compassionate man deeply troubled by the decline of the economy, he was willing to use the federal government to deal with the depression, and his policies in many ways foreshadowed the New Deal.[3]

In an ironic twist of the traditional approach to Hoover, some New Left historians have taken a new look at the laissez-faire issue. In *The Contours of American History* (New York, 1961), William Appleman Williams argues that Hoover resisted federal intervention into the economy because he realized the vicious potential of the corporate state and preferred to solve the country's problems through private activities. Here we have a believer in a limited "state" praising Hoover for not moving uncritically toward a corporate or statist society. On the other hand, Murray Rothbard, in *America's Great Depression* (Princeton, 1963), argues that it was Hoover who actually destroyed the laissez-faire philosophy by directly injecting the federal government into the economy. In this instance, we have a historian who believes in classical economics criticizing Hoover for leading the nation in the opposite direction.

I have tried to show how the Reconstruction Finance Corporation played a critical role in the transition from voluntary efforts to end the depression to federal management of the economy. Rather than being totally alien to the New Deal, the Hoover administration actually foreshadowed many of the programs that President Roosevelt and the Democratic Congress later adopted.

I am indebted to a number of individuals who assisted me in this project. My high school teacher, Lee Cooper, first ignited my interest in politics and economics, and Professor H. Carlton Marlow of Brigham Young University introduced me to twentieth century U.S. history. Professor David Burner of the State University of New York at Stony Brook was generous with his time and insight—over the past five years he has read and reviewed this manuscript many times, and he has been consistently patient, courteous, and critical. His own work on Herbert Hoover inspired this study. Jeanne MacDonald of the National Archives and Robert Wood of the Herbert Hoover Presidential Library guided me through the respective collections. Paul Culp of the Sam Houston State University Library located a number of important microfilmed sources. Dr. John Payne of Sam Houston State University meticulously read the manuscript for style and content and offered many helpful suggestions; I am especially thankful for his assistance. Charles Hoffman, Eric Lampard, Hugh Cleland, Bo Barron Stow, F. Reed Johnson, Thomas Camfield, Richard Yasko, and Joseph M. Rowe read portions of the manuscript and saved me from a number of errors. I would like to express my gratitude to Jim and Julia Olson, Al and Vivian Mehr, and Paul and Ann Bottino, who on many occasions during my research and writing graciously housed me, and to my colleagues at Sam Houston State University who have provided me with a pleasant and enriched atmosphere in which to work and live.

Herbert Hoover

and the Reconstruction Finance Corporation, 1931-1933

1

Instability in the Money
Market: 1920s

THROUGHOUT much of the nineteenth century, independence, individuality, and resistance to authority played prominent roles in the development of American institutions. The "yeoman" farmers, dominant figures in the early economy, were proud and self-reliant men who worshipped individualism and aggressively asserted their independence from commercial and urban interest groups. Their dogma exerted a profound and eventually crippling influence on the country's financial system. Unlike other industrial nations, the United States commercial banking system consisted of thousands of individual banks lacking any effective central direction. Except for the Second Bank of the United States and several large banks in the East, American finance reflected the agrarian ideology: it was democratic, decentralized, and hostile to all forms of concentrated economic power.

Not surprisingly, the dominant figures of that time were also suspicious of centralized political power. A powerful laissez-faire philosophy, nurtured by the teachings of the classical economists and Whiggish suspicions about the nature of political power, had developed by the early 1800s. Although laissez-faire never really existed in the United States, it did maintain a philosophical vitality long after the Industrial Revolution had undermined its economic legitimacy.[1] Agrarian interests in early America vigorously resisted the power of the federal government.

In addition to these economic and political suspicions, the agrarian community reserved a special antipathy for banks, bankers, and paper currency. Wildcat currency, worthless bank stock, exorbitant interest rates, and the frequent specie raids by competing banks deepened its antagonism. More radical members of the agrarian community, especially during the Jacksonian era, favored the elimination of all banking companies. By the 1840s, many western states had prohibited the establishment of commercial banks.[2]

As the economy of early America expanded, a new class of entrepreneurs emerged. They exploited agrarian sentiments and the laissez-faire philosophy in order to escape the economic restraints imposed on them by conservative, established business groups in the Northeast. They attacked monopoly in the name of competition and government in the name of liberty, and with the laissez-faire ideology they hoped to democratize the business community and guarantee their own access to power and wealth.[3] Sensing and sharing this hostility, President Jackson canonized their philosophy by conducting a successful assault on the Second Bank of the United States, depriving the country of its only semblance of central banking.[4]

After forging a tenuous alliance with the antimonopoly, entrepreneurial interests of the country, the antibank Democrats sponsored a compromise system known as "free banking." Beginning in New York in the late 1830s, free banking quickly became an American trademark. Most states passed free banking laws that permitted any group meeting a simple list of financial requirements to organize a bank. Small, single-office institutions, operating independently of each other and of the federal government, proliferated throughout the country, and the financial structure gradually evolved into a single-unit banking system.[5] Free banking financially institutionalized laissez-faire, justified the creation of hundreds of banks, and destroyed for years the Hamiltonian belief in federal supervision of the banking system.

During the next seventy-five years, despite the National Banking Act of 1863 and the Federal Reserve Act of 1913, the financial system continued its disorderly expansion. By 1920 banking in the United States had become a haphazard mix of competing institutions. In addition to over 30,000 separate commercial banks, thousands of savings banks, building and loan associations, investment companies, private banks, industrial banks, credit unions, and finance companies complicated the picture. Marked by instability and irregularity, the money market consisted of nearly 50,000 separate units, almost all serving limited constituencies.[6]

The number of banks at the beginning of the 1920s far exceeded the nation's credit requirements. In rural areas especially, state banking authorities had been far too liberal in granting bank charters. Many communities with fewer than five hundred people had two or more banks that competed for the same clientele, and not surprisingly, they failed to earn enough from their assets to survive. Suspensions occurred most often in states with low population-bank ratios. The country was alarmingly "overbanked," particularly in rural communities, and the United States was about to reap the disastrous harvest of the free banking system.[7]

Rural banks suffered from other problems as well. Besides undercapitalization and lack of sound management, demographic changes severely weakened them. Urban growth was depopulating the countryside at the same time that the automobile was making it more convenient for people to shop and bank in the larger towns and cities. During the 1920s the urban center finally eclipsed the smaller community as the main focus of financial activity. Equally serious for rural banks was the rise of chain and mail-order department stores that drove country stores out of business and caused the banks to lose some of their best customers. In the face of increased competition among themselves, rural banks slowly lost their clientele to more heavily populated areas.[8]

Also, the agricultural depression of the 1920s devastated thousands of country banks. With the revival of European agriculture and the postwar collapse of the international market for American produce, most farm prices in the United States fell to the lowest levels in years. Many rural banks failed because they had completely committed themselves to the local farm economy. Huge mortgages for wartime acreage expansion and the severe decline in land values during the early 1920s left many farmers too poor to get credit from local banks. Consequently, long before the onset of the Great Depression, the rural credit structure had begun to collapse. Between 1921 and 1929 more than five thousand small-town banks suspended operations. Unable to convert their assets into cash, these banks were caught in a long-term liquidity crisis that damaged the rest of the economy and eroded public faith in the entire financial system. Nearly four thousand other banks, finding their assets deflated and their capital impaired, merged with more stable institutions.[9] These suspensions and mergers were disturbing omens for the future, since any general decline in the economy would further depress the value of bank assets and dissipate whatever confidence the public still possessed. The prosperity of the twenties was deceptively superficial, since the country's chronically weak financial system bordered on insolvency, jeopardizing the health of the entire economy.

But the weaknesses of rural banks and the general surplus of credit institutions were not the only problems facing the American economy in the 1920s. The entire money market was undergoing a series of changes that would eventually leave it totally unprepared to withstand any serious economic stress.

Ironically, on the surface the economy appeared stable; the decade was one of rapid growth with the GNP increasing from about $70 billion in 1922 to $100 billion in 1929, and the wholesale price index remained essentially unchanged after 1923.[10] During the same period the total assets of the country's financial intermediaries increased from $98 billion to over $167 billion. Commercial bank assets grew from $47 billion to $67 billion; mutual savings banks increased their holdings from nearly $7 billion in 1922 to $10 billion in 1929; life insurance companies doubled their assets during the decade from $8.7 billion to over $17 billion; and building and loan associations, profiting from the booming construction industry, tripled their holdings from $2.8 billion to $7.4 billion.[11] Most business, government, and private financial leaders in the United States were optimistic about the future of the economy and predicted that a new era of permanent prosperity was arriving.[12] Theirs was a pleasant and abiding faith, based on understandable hopes and a genuine sense of security, but it was also a naive belief whose superficiality would shortly be exposed.

The most critical dimension of the 1920s economy involved the investment mania in the securities and real estate markets. Business profits rose throughout the decade, and much of the accompanying purchasing power found its way into securities and real estate speculation. Public optimism stimulated confidence and nourished the fever until even the weakest securities representing the most marginal companies were in great demand. Between 1925 and 1928 stock prices advanced to higher and higher plateaus, with the *New York Times* industrial index increasing from 134 to 311. The assets of securities dealers and brokers grew from a total of $4 billion in 1922 to over $10 billion in 1929.[13] The number of investment trusts and holding companies grew from fewer than 40 in 1921 to over 750 in 1929; more than 450 were organized after 1927. Their assets had increased from less than $100 million to nearly $8 billion. By 1929 these investment companies were handling more than one-third of all new capital issues and were rapidly becoming the dominant force on the securities exchanges.[14]

The more traditional institutions of the money market were not immune to this speculative fever. During the twenties their investment policies shifted under the influence of the boom. The unprecedented capital gains were irresistible, and the rapidly expanding capital markets and rising interest rates attracted the investment funds of virtually every financial institution. Some institutions, of course, were cautious and discreet, but all too many joined the economic delirium. Life insurance companies, building and loan associations, and mutual savings banks increased their investments in real estate. Since federal borrowing had all but ceased during the decade and the yield on government bonds remained below 4 percent, these institutions liquidated many of their government securities and invested in more profitable private markets. And with the returns on mortgage and real estate investments consistently above 6 percent and on corporate bonds nearly 6 percent, most financial institutions naturally channeled their funds in those directions.

Between 1920 and 1930 the percentage of life insurance company assets secured by real estate and urban mortgages increased from 25 to 45 percent, while holdings of government securities declined from 18 to 2 percent. In 1929 railroad bonds constituted 25 percent of assets; corporate and utility bonds equaled 21 percent; and state, county, and municipal bonds totaled 6 percent. Most of the $6 billion in new assets held by building and loan associations consisted of real estate mortgages. Similarly, between 1920 and 1930 the total investments of mutual savings banks in real estate and mortgages increased from 44 to 55 percent, while their holdings of government bonds declined from 18 to 11 percent. In 1930, railroad bonds accounted for only 13 percent of their assets. Finally, the budding credit union movement had over 40 percent of its assets invested in real estate by 1929.[15]

Unfortunately, these portfolio decisions were tragically shortsighted and almost criminally imprudent. By 1929 thousands of financial institutions had become less liquid than ever before and less able to respond effectively to economic emergencies. Any decline in the home construction industry; any puncture of the real estate bubble; or any erosion in the value of railroad, corporate, or utility bonds would severely inhibit the ability of private money market institutions to meet demands by their clients for funds.

New developments in corporate finance also weakened commercial banks. Enormous profits during the twenties had liberated the largest corporations from their traditional dependency on bank credit as the source of equity and working capital. Ease in selling stocks and bonds prompted many corporations to acquire equity capital by issuing securities rather than accepting bank loans. As a result, the annual production of commercial paper declined from $2.5 billion in 1923 to approximately $1 billion in 1929.[16] Finding the demand for commercial loans insufficient to yield profits on all their resources, banks turned to the investment and real estate markets. While in 1923 commercial loans made up 71 percent of all bank loans, by 1929 they had declined to 53 percent.

Between 1923 and 1929 the real estate loans of commercial banks grew from $1.4 to $4.5 billion, from 5 to 13 percent of all bank loan assets. More conspicuous was the increase in call loans. Call loans had long been an important activity on the New York money market, but not until the 1920s did these loans assume overwhelming proportions. In 1927 bank loans to brokers reached over $2.5 billion, an increase of 100 percent since 1921. Two years later, banks granted over $8 billion in loans secured by stocks and bonds. Whereas in 1923 collateral loans had accounted for only 23 percent of all bank loans, in 1929 they rose to 33 percent.[17]

These shifts in loan policy weakened banks. When enormous pressures for liquidation of loans and securities developed after 1929, all the remaining liquidity disappeared from loans secured by real estate and securities. Borrowers were unable to repay their loans, and the loans were often unmarketable because the collateral banks had acquired to cover the defaulted loans had depreciated in value. And, to add to the problem, panic-stricken depositors were attempting to withdraw their cash.[18]

Commercial bank investors succumbed to the same temptations. During 1920-1930 their holdings of corporate and foreign bonds were increased by nearly $3 billion and local government bonds by $1 billion. Many of the bonds of real estate developments, holding companies, and investment trusts were of questionable value. Because the yield on these bonds was higher than the return on U.S. government securities, bank investors turned to them during the 1920s. After 1923 when government bonds were 35 percent of commercial bank investments, a significant liquidation occurred, and by 1929 only 28 percent of bank investments were in government securities. The banks had traded liquidity for yield.[19]

Although most banks did not realize it, they were in serious trouble by 1929 because their ability to withstand a liquidity crisis had been compromised. Whereas self-liquidating, short-term commercial paper had dominated bank portfolios before the decade, most assets in 1929 consisted of loans and investments whose liquidity depended on general capital values.[20] Under stable financial conditions, stocks and bonds were liquid assets because they could be sold readily at the exchanges. First mortgages were also highly marketable. But if economic conditions deteriorated and panic ensued, bank assets would quickly become frozen as large volumes of securities and loans were converted to cash. Under those circumstances many banks would be hard pressed to survive. In the late twenties such a development seemed only hypothetical, but after the stock market crash it became all too real.

The policies of the federal government failed to tighten the money market, restrain the investment mania, or prevent dangerous changes in investment policies; indeed, U.S. government fiscal policy actually contributed to financial instability during the 1920s. Under Andrew Mellon, the Treasury Department pursued relaxed monetary policies because they decreased the interest rate on the federal debt and facilitated the financing of new Treasury obligations. Earlier in the decade, Mellon had reduced taxes on corporate and personal incomes because of surpluses in goverment revenues. These reductions released new disposable income to the wealthy and intensified speculative pressures. Corporations reported higher profits, which yielded higher dividends and generated higher stock prices. Tax cuts on capital gains allowed investors to redirect their funds away from tax-free municipal and state bonds toward common stock, which also inflated securities prices. Finally, Mellon's policy of retiring the national debt eliminated one market for private funds, even though government bonds had already become less attractive investments. Since federal expenditures amounted to less than 4 percent of the gross national product, Treasury fiscal policy remained only a minor contributor to the speculative boom.[21] But considering the weaknesses that had developed throughout the money market, any new pressure was potentially dangerous.

Far more serious were the inadequacies of Federal Reserve Board policy during the 1920s. The board might have helped tighten money market conditions by selling government securities in the open market and increasing the rediscount rate. But two important problems, along with certain erroneous assumptions about monetary policy, confused Federal Reserve Board authorities and left them unable to take decisive action. Part of the problem involved the postwar shift of the world's financial capital from London to New York. Since 1914 the United States had gradually become the principal free gold market in the world; by 1924 the United States held over 40 percent of the world's monetary gold stock. In addition to increasing bank reserves in this country, the huge collection of gold made it more difficult for Great Britain and France to return to the gold standard. During the twenties economic leaders in the United States and Europe believed that international financial stability could not be permanently restored until all the major industrial nations returned to the gold standard, which required a credit rate differential between the New York and London money markets sufficient to stimulate American investment in foreign markets and restrict gold imports into the United States. Federal Reserve officials agreed with that assumption, but they were caught on the horns of a dilemma: to discourage the investment boom in the United States the board would have to raise interest rates, but such restrictive policies would only serve to attract foreign capital to America. Moreover, an easy money policy that lowered domestic interest rates, while pleasing to foreign leaders and conducive to the international resumption of the gold standard, would further stimulate the speculative mania in the United States. Either choice left board officials with an unacceptable economic problem.

The second problem facing the Federal Reserve Board in the twenties was the need to discourage securities speculation without simultaneously inhibiting legitimate business growth. The choice that frustrated and preoccupied them throughout the decade was whether to hurt business (and discourage speculation) by tightening interest rates or to stimulate business (and encourage speculation) by easing money market rates. No wonder the Federal Reserve officials were divided and bewildered; as a result the board followed an ambiguous and confusing set of policies until 1929 and a helpless policy of relative inaction thereafter.[22]

The board first became concerned about the unprecedented securities speculation in 1925. Refusing to tighten credit for fear of depressing commerce and industry, the board simply requested that bankers borrow from Federal Reserve banks only to meet nonspeculative needs. To discourage the importation of more gold and to stimulate a slightly stalled economy, the board lowered the discount rate to $3\frac{1}{2}$ percent in 1927, which eased credit conditions and naturally stimulated investment and speculation. But in 1928, worrying about how to stem the speculative tide, the board again embarked on a restrictive policy and returned rates to 4 percent. As securities prices and the volume of brokers' loans continued to increase, the board increased the discount rate to $4\frac{1}{2}$ percent and then to 5 percent.[23]

However, the fear that legitimate business might be injured by restrictive monetary policies generated a contradictory policy in which the Federal Reserve banks purchased banker acceptances while discount rates remained high. Federal Reserve officials believed that the funds banks received from the sale of acceptances would be used only for legitimate business needs and not for speculation. They assumed that the method of increasing the money supply determined the uses to which the funds would be put by the banks; they failed to understand that the purchase of acceptances increased the volume of excess reserves that could then be invested in the securities markets. The board actually hoped that its high discount rates would discourage speculation while its purchases of bankers' acceptances would stimulate a credit expansion and business growth. The assumption was erroneous.[24] With the fresh infusion of Federal Reserve funds, bankers increased their reserve balances and reduced their Federal Reserve bank indebtedness, negating the impact of the discount rate. Stock prices continued to rise until 1929, when the board concluded that the call loan rate, then running between 7 and 12 percent, was so high and speculation so intense that the manipulation of the discount rate was almost completely ineffective.[25]

Federal Reserve officials did not appreciate the impact that high discount rates had on open market rates: the board stimulated the call money rates and attracted nonbank lenders into the market. Many corporations, finding it more profitable to speculate with surplus funds than to reinvest them, diverted their surplus cash into the call loan market. These funds financed many of the 1928 and 1929 price increases on the exchanges. The Federal Reserve Board's range of vision was too narrow at that time to include control of nonbank lenders as a legitimate responsibility. Federal Reserve and bank credit were their only concerns, and they were astonishingly complacent about the enormous power of corporate lenders. The board did not consider itself responsible for controlling the flow and destination of nonbank investment funds. This neglect nullified much of the board's effectiveness over the money market in the last years of the decade and contributed substantially to the eventual collapse of the stock market.[26]

The stock market crash of 1929 and the onset of the Great Depression jeopardized the entire American money market. With the existence of thousands of marginal financial institutions and money market funds tied up in real estate and corporate securities, the response mechanism of the nation's credit apparatus weakened. The flexibility so necessary to successful monetary activities was lost; and the tremendous decline in commodity prices, land values, and securities threatened thousands of financial institutions with insolvency. Rural banks, with their assets secured primarily by agricultural mortgages, suffered from the decline in farm prices and the accompanying drop in land values. Bewildered depositors, frightened by economic stagnation and suspensions of neighboring banks, withdrew their savings and the banks found themselves with shortages of liquid capital and frozen mortgage assets. Unable to meet depositor demands for cash, thousands of rural banks closed, imposing severe difficulties on small depositors and stimulating even more fear and instability.[27]

These weaknesses in the rural credit structure inevitably had a chain-reaction effect on the larger urban banks. The larger banks that had made substantial loans to collapsing rural banks or maintained large correspondent networks sustained partial losses of funds.[28] The crash of the stock market in 1929-1930 had already hurt their assets; and when rural bank failures undermined depositor confidence, large banks began to liquefy their holdings through the sale of prime securities. This action severely weakened their investment portfolios, and with thousands of banks trying to convert securities into cash, the selling mania further deflated stock prices. It was a vicious circle.[29] Furthermore, the sluggish pace of business activity reduced loan repayments and increased defaults, intensifying the pressure on the money market.[30]

The depressed condition of American railroads produced another weakness in the money market. During the 1920s railroads faced increasing competition from automotive and airline carriers; freight rates and profits had begun to soften long before the decline in industrial activity occurred. After 1929, railroad freight volume and revenue fell sharply; a substantial number of important roads failed to meet their short- or even long-term obligations.[31] When Class A lines began to default on their dividends, railroad bonds depreciated in value. The decline in railroad revenues and the value of their bonds had a special impact on the financial community because for years railroad bonds had served as important investment markets for many commercial banks, savings banks, and life insurance companies. As bonds depreciated in the face of collapsing revenues, the assets of many financial institutions fell commensurately in value. Previously one of the most highly valued possessions of securities portfolios, railroad bonds became unmarketable assets, further weakening important institutions of the money market.[32]

During 1930 and 1931 the stability of the banking system and the money market in general steadily deteriorated. In 1929 there were only 641 commercial bank failures, an astonishing number by contemporary standards but not abnormal when compared with the 5,400 suspensions that had occurred during the twenties. And for the first ten months of 1930, bank failures increased only slightly to 750, a large but not alarming number. In October 1930 the true severity of the banking crisis was exposed following the collapse of the National Bank of Kentucky. A contagious chain reaction spread to several surrounding states, eventually resulting in more than one hundred bank failures in Missouri, Arkansas, Indiana, Iowa, and Illinois. Then, in December, the Bank of United States in New York City, with nearly $200 million in deposits, closed its doors. It was the worst bank failure in American history, and a brief nationwide panic ensued. During the last two months of the year, more than six hundred banks failed, bringing the total for 1930 to over 1,350, the worst year in U.S. history.[33]

Because of new instabilities in foreign money markets as well as domestic problems, financial conditions degenerated in 1931. In May Austria's largest private bank, the Kredit-Anstalt, suspended operations, and a ripple of fear spread throughout Europe. Several important banks in Germany closed in July, and the liquidity panic spread to France, Belgium, and the Netherlands in August. Battered by constant news and rumors of international banking difficulties, American depositors became more nervous and restless. Between January and September they withdrew nearly $3 billion in deposits, and at the same time nearly one thousand banks failed. Finally, the British decision on September 21, 1931, to abandon the gold standard intensified the crisis. The other nations of Western Europe, expecting the United States also to suspend its gold standard, immediately began to convert their dollar reserves, liquidate their investments, and withdraw their gold from the country. This action on the part of European central banks and private investors resulted in a $275 million decline in the United States gold supply during the last two weeks of September. The external drain on bank funds increased the difficulties of the private money market, and the news that even the prestigious Bank of England had been unable to survive the crisis unscathed made Americans all the more uneasy. In September alone another 450 commercial banks in the United States failed.[34]

These problems in the money market reverberated throughout the rest of the economy. In addition to the poor distribution of income, excessive business inventories, the jerry-built system of corporate holding companies, and the decline in exports, consumers were frightened about the apparent collapse of the banking system. They began to postpone major expenditures in anticipation of a serious economic collapse, and personal consumption outlays dropped from $77 billion in 1929 to $60 billion in 1931. Bankers, afraid of their own depositors, protected themselves by converting their assets into cash and contracting the credit supply. Businessmen, who were searching for working capital, could not find it; and most of them were confused and worried about the state of the economy and the decline in consumer purchasing power. They had lost confidence in the long-term prospects for economic growth; and as their current profits weakened they decided to postpone investment in plants, equipment, and inventories. Between 1929 and 1931, business investment dropped from approximately $16 billion to only $5.6 billion, reinforcing and accelerating declines in consumer spending.[35]

American financiers became rapidly demoralized because of the chaos within international banking circles, the frightening instability in the domestic money market, and the decline in industrial activity. Confronted by an economic crisis that defied all private attempts at amelioration, they shelved their laissez-faire philosophy and turned to the Hoover administration for assistance. Seeking a political and governmental solution for their problems, the banking community resurrected an old idea and demanded the rebirth of the War Finance Corporation.[36]

Congress had created the War Finance Corporation (WFC) in 1918 to strengthen the private capital investment markets and to make loans to industries engaged in wartime production. While stabilizing the money markets, the WFC also sustained the government's financial program by periodically purchasing federal bonds.[37] During World War I the WFC had lent funds to a wide variety of enterprises, including public utilities, electric power plants, mining and chemical concerns, railroads, and banks. In the postwar years the WFC underwent several important changes. During the depression of 1920-1922, Congress transformed the WFC into a peacetime, emergency finance corporation, authorizing it to lend money to exporters and to grant agricultural loans to individuals, banks, and local credit agencies. The Agricultural Credits Act of 1921 converted the WFC into an agricultural finance agency capable of providing farmers with intermediate credit to renew or to extend their existing obligations. By 1924 the WFC had loaned over $300 million for agricultural purposes. Congress considered its activities so successful that the Agricultural Credits Act of 1923 established the Federal Intermediate Credit bank system to assume many of the duties and responsibilities of the War Finance Corporation. The government began to liquidate the WFC in 1924, and five years later Congress officially dissolved it.[38] By the autumn of 1931 private bankers were clamoring for its reincarnation.

Never before had the country been threatened with the collapse of its entire credit apparatus, and never before in its peacetime history had the federal government been forced to consider drastic public remedies for such an emergency. The traditional fears of concentrated governmental power that businessmen had glibly articulated in years past became immediately anachronistic. As the value of real estate and securities declined in 1931, and as rising unemployment brought massive defaults on loans and depositor runs on the banks, political and economic leaders realized that formal public intervention was inevitable. The Great Depression, obliterating even the philosophical attractiveness of laissez-faire, completed the ideological work initiated by the Industrial Revolution. President Hoover and the Republican administration would shortly be forced to transcend not only the classical liberalism of the nineteenth century but even the urbane progressivism of the twentieth.

2

Hoover and
American Individualism

LATE in the summer of 1931 after months of grim concern about financial matters, President Hoover undertook to protect the economy from the dangers of public panic and forced liquidation. Only a series of bold and extraordinary measures on the part of the federal government, he had determined, could save the system from collapse. It was a disturbing and frustrating time for the President. Just two years earlier in his inaugural address he had confidently proclaimed that America was a

land rich in resources; stimulating in its glorious beauty; filled with millions of happy homes; blessed with comfort and opportunity. In no nation are the fruits of accomplishment more secure. In no nation is the government more worthy of respect. No country is more loved by its people. I have an abiding faith in their capacity, integrity and high purpose. I have no fears for the future of our country. It is bright with hope.[1]

By 1931 these remarks had become ludicrous. Hundreds of money market institutions teetered on the brink of annihilation while thousands of others were only marginally solvent. Millions of people were out of work and businesses were failing in unbelievable numbers. Furthermore, commercial banks, savings banks, building and loan associations, and insurance companies were reluctant to make commercial and mortgage loans to customers. While interest rates were declining and the pool of eligible borrowers was gradually evaporating, bankers were protecting themselves from certain losses by curtailing the volume of commercial credit. For Hoover it was the worst action they could have taken, because shrinking business credit aggravated the depression by stimulating cuts in production and employment. Individual bankers, struggling to save themselves, were collectively destroying the economy. So Hoover decided to intervene personally in the crisis to prevent financial weaknesses from further damaging the economy. The nature of his response was an extension of his political philosophy and successful bureaucratic career.[2]

Herbert Clark Hoover personified both classical liberalism and the great American dream. He enjoyed membership in a most exclusive club:

14

the relatively few Americans who truly embodied the Horatio Alger saga. Hoover was born on August 10, 1874, in the Quaker community of West Branch, Iowa—an agrarian village of only a few hundred people. The future president of the United States had an especially difficult, transient childhood. In 1880 his father died of heart failure, and four years later pneumonia complicated by typhus took his mother. During the next year he was shuttled back and forth among several sets of Quaker relatives in Iowa; in 1885 he went to live with his uncle, John Minthorn, in Newberg, Oregon. His uncle was the principal of Pacific Academy, and for three years Hoover worked part-time and went to school. In 1888 they moved to Salem, and his uncle set up the Oregon Land Company and began selling real estate. Hoover worked in the family business for two more years, took courses at a business college, and in 1891 entered the first class at Leland Stanford University. He had come from a lonely, economically simple background, and on entering college he was driven by more than an average share of ambition. Indeed, Herbert Hoover was determined never to return to the semifrontier poverty of his midwestern childhood. In 1895 he graduated from Stanford with a BA in geology.

The mid-1890s were inauspicious years for new college graduates. Because of the industrial depression of 1893, he was initially unable to find an outlet for his professional talents. After working as a common miner in Nevada, he joined the London mining firm of Bewick, Moreing and Company, where his success as businessman and engineer was rapid and spectacular. Between 1897 and 1911 he served the company as promoter, engineer, and troubleshooter and filled assignments in Australia, Burma, Ceylon, Egypt, France, Germany, India, Korea, Japan, New Zealand, Rhodesia, and Russia. In 1914, after nearly seventeen years abroad, Hoover was a multimillionaire enjoying annual earnings well in excess of $100,000.

With the outbreak of war in Europe, Hoover discovered an opportunity to balance his extraordinary economic success with a Quaker-inspired impulse to serve his fellows. Despite the importance to him of economic security and independence from relatives and friends, Hoover still nurtured the Quaker beliefs in peace, equality of opportunity, and neighborly kindness. He was living in London in 1914, and after the formal declaration of hostilities the U.S. consul-general asked him to assist American citizens in England who were unable to convert their assets into British currency. He also established the American Relief Committee to assist the thousands of Americans arriving from the Continent. In 1914 as chairman of the Commission for Relief in Belgium, Hoover took charge of feeding nearly ten million people in the face of almost insurmountable difficulties with belligerent governments. President Woodrow Wilson called Hoover home in 1917 and named him to head the new United States Food Administration, where he successfully sponsored voluntary programs of conservation and food rationing. After the war Hoover directed the American Relief Administration, distributing $3.5 billion worth of food and clothing to over thirty million people and averting economic collapse and social revolution in Europe. By the fall of 1919, Herbert Hoover had become an international symbol of hope and American benevolence. His public image blended that of the Great Engineer with that of the Great Humanitarian. In 1921, following the election of President Warren Harding, Hoover joined the Republican cabinet as secretary of commerce and by 1928 had further enhanced his personal reputation. The American public regarded him as a man of humane sympathies and a master bureaucrat—the one man most likely to perpetuate the Republican prosperity of the 1920s. His career reached a fitting climax in the election of 1928, and he entered the White House as a symbol of international power and prestige.[3]

It is little wonder that Hoover celebrated the United States with a genuine patriotism; he loved and respected America for giving him so much opportunity. He viewed the United States as a unique society that had transcended social and economic convulsions so common elsewhere. For President Hoover, the genius of America involved its fluid social structure, a condition which had eliminated the aristocratic and class divisions characteristic of virtually all other societies in all other times. The United States had achieved a unique synthesis of enlightened in-dividualism and equality of opportunity. Herbert Hoover constructed his personal philososphy on one foundation: the United States guaranteed to every member of the community uninhibited access to wealth, power, and prestige. The only obstacles to success acknowledged by Hoover's "American Individualism" were incompetence and indolence. Race, religion, and national origins were social and political irrelevancies.[4] American Individualism rewarded ability and ambition with success and fulfillment. The President considered himself living evidence of his philosophy.

Hoover also maintained a tempered faith in a closely related concept: Adam Smith's formulation of entrepreneurial self-interest. American Individualism enjoyed special distinction, the President maintained, because it had survived the Industrial Revolution and retained its vitality even in the presence of corporate power, technology, and urbanization. Like Adam Smith, Hoover believed that economic self-interest and social progress were compatible and even inevitably reinforcing. In the nineteenth century powerful individuals and groups had risen spon-taneously to aggrandize their own economic positions by rationalizing control of the national market and exerting pressure on political leaders. For the most part they had been concerned about themselves and not about society, but their activities had eliminated inefficiency and poor communication in the economy. By introducing technology and scientific management to the production process, they had spectacularly raised the American standard of living. For Hoover, economic strength was the foundation of political stability and social progress. In 1922 he had written that

high and increasing standards of living and comfort should be the first of con-siderations in the public mind and in the government. . . . We have long since realized that the basis of an advancing civilization must be a high and growing standard of living for all the people, not for a single class; that education, food, clothing, housing, and the spreading use of what we often term nonessentials, are the real fertilizers of the soil from which spring the finer flowers of life.[5]

Economic growth, while not redistributing wealth, had nevertheless improved the living standard of most Americans, eliminating the social and political tensions that always accompany extreme, chronic poverty. Economic self-interest and social progress were not contradictory, at least in terms of the American experience. Indeed, they were logical extensions of one another—intimately related characteristics of twentieth century U.S. history.

But if the President's political philosophy glorified the idea of self-interest and social progress, his historical consciousness prevented him from worshipping any god of inevitability; it was contradicted by too many instances of scandal, war, and depression. Hoover did not naively suppose that the system would always function perfectly, and because of this he reluctantly parted company with the laissez-faire assumptions of the classical economists. He was an engineer, a man of precision, who had been naturally attracted to the mechanistic simplicity of classical economics. The reason, order, and inherent justice of its self-regulating capacity were appealing concepts. But Hoover also realized that the organizational realities of the Industrial Revolution had upset the mechanism. The economy was no longer self-governing because the laws of competition and supply and demand had been superseded. Since the Civil War, business and industry had made enormous gains in production with more centralized administration. The President generally praised this development because these groups had raised the standard of living. But by controlling increasingly larger shares of the national market, some of these businesses had placed themselves beyond public control and beyond what classical economists once considered immutable economic laws. Some of these corporations had become almost an entrepreneurial aristocracy; they manipulated the economic system to augment their own wealth and remained irresponsibly oblivious to the impact of their activities on the country as a whole.[6]

For two hundred years American liberalism had attempted to eliminate all artificial impediments, be they racial, economic, or political, to individual opportunity. But in the nineteenth century the rise of the supercorporations had raised the specter of economic tyranny; some business and industrial giants were powerful enough to exploit the public and retard social progress. To check that power, the progressive movement had created the regulatory state, and the federal government had risen as a "countervailing power." Hoover understood and reluctantly condoned the transition American public policy had been forced to make between the laissez-faire liberalism of Andrew Jackson and Thomas Jefferson and the progressive liberalism of Theodore Roosevelt, Herbert Croly, Woodrow Wilson, and Louis Brandeis.[7]

In this sense Hoover was a progressive. Just after leaving the White House, he complained to a friend that the Brain Trust and their superiors are now announcing to the world that the social thesis of laissez-faire died on March 4. I wish they would add a professor of history to the Brain Trust. The 18th century thesis of laissez-faire passed in the United States half a century ago. The visible proof of it was the enactment of the Sherman Act for the regulation of all business, the transportation and public utility regulation, the Federal Reserve System, the Eighteenth Amendment, the establishment of the Farm Loan Banks, the Home Loan Banks, the Reconstruction Finance Corporation. All are but part of the items marking the total abandonment of that social thesis.[8]

The President believed strongly in the usefulness of government, and he realized the need to police the activities of powerful economic interest groups. Through such agencies as the Federal Trade Commission, the Department of Commerce, and the Department of Justice, the federal government could enforce the laws against tax evasion, fraud, and monopolies and guarantee that economic affairs operate within prescribed legal boundaries. President Hoover had no intention of letting interest groups function in a power vacuum.[9]

But his recognition of the need for some regulation did not leave him satisfied with the methods the federal government had used in the twentieth century. Hoover was always keenly aware of the threat government posed to American Individualism. Because of his experience with the Department of Commerce during the twenties, Hoover possessed a clear understanding of bureaucratic dynamics and worried that the regulatory state could not be contained within the boundaries set by American Individualism. Impulses to expand the authority of the federal government would be persistent and dangerous; once created, new government bureaucracies could be dismantled only with great difficulty because each program supported a constituency dedicated to its perpetuation. He knew that modern bureaucracies had insatiable desires for growth. As he feared the potential of certain private interest groups he also worried about the potential of bureaucratic tyranny. He retained this fear throughout his life.[10]

Other, more compelling reasons contributed to Hoover's general uneasiness about the responsibilities of the federal government. In particular he had come to the conclusion that the regulatory programs of the progressive movement, though necessary at the time, were actually quite primitive, transitional steps from the laissez-faire ideology of the nineteenth century to the more sophisticated, corporate, "associative" ideology of the twentieth. For Hoover, such agencies as the Interstate Commerce Commission (ICC) and the Antitrust Division of the Justice Department tended to be cumbersome, inefficient, and poorly managed. Instead of responding quickly and decisively, they were usually dilatory and demanded more information, called for new investigations, and postponed important decisions. The regulatory agencies were also too capricious for Hoover; they were too subservient to the political establishment or to the industries they were supposed to regulate, and they often made contradictory decisions in a vain and futile attempt to please

competing politicians and interest groups. To Hoover's precise, administrative mind, inconsistency was one of the worst sins of all. Perhaps most important, Hoover believed the progressive regulatory state lacked foresight and vision in treating problems rather than anticipating them. Like all police actions, the regulatory agencies enforced rather than proposed and reacted rather than predicted; instead of preventing problems, they tried later to control and solve them and usually failed to do even that. Hoover envisioned another, more positive approach to the economic affairs of the twentieth century—an approach that made big government unnecessary. He, like the classical liberals, wanted an essentially self-regulating political economy, but one that was relevant to modern, industrial realities. He wanted to resurrect the spirit, not the substance, of Adam Smith's philosophy in creating a rational, self-governing economic system.[11]

So Hoover's thought contained a certain tension—an intellectual dialectic—between private and governmental programs as well as between rural values and industrial technologies. From his Quaker childhood in Iowa and his adolescence in Oregon, Hoover had come to believe in the importance of family unity, brotherly love, ambition, hard work, and thrift as the building blocks of individual character and integrity. Unlike many of his contemporaries, Hoover did not automatically associate these values with preindustrial societies. Although he realized that rural cultures were usually more conducive to family harmony and social cohesion, he believed these virtues could be, indeed had to be, preserved in urban societies. In his view the worst fate for America would be for rural values and industrial technologies to become mutually exclusive. Hoover believed in the value of the Industrial Revolution because science and technology, with their stupendous increases in production and efficiency, had raised the standard of living for all Americans. Somehow, rural values and industrial realities would have to coexist, and the challenge of the twentieth century would be to preserve and strengthen both.[12]

As Hoover searched for some means of guaranteeing economic growth and preserving entrepreneurial individualism and rural values while avoiding both industrial dictatorship and bureaucratic tyranny, he concluded that the organizational revolution accompanying industrialization seemed to provide a workable solution. Between 1870 and 1920, virtually every section of American society, in trying to cope with the disrupting impact of the Industrial Revolution, began to look outward and form certain communities of interest. In less than fifty years American workers, for example, had formally organized and replaced the feeble Knights of Labor with the more formidable railroad brotherhoods, the United Mine Workers, and the American Federation of Labor. During the same half century a new middle class had emerged: doctors, lawyers, professors, teachers, and social workers—all organized into various professional associations. The American Bar Association, the American Medical Association, the American Historical Association, the National Education Association, the American Political Science Association, and the National Conference on Social Work each sought to represent the interests of their constituents. Finally, the new class of businessmen formed trade associations, chambers of commerce, and marketing cooperatives to enhance their position in the national economy. Eventually, such groups as the United States Chamber of Commerce, the National Association of Manufacturers, and the American Farm Bureau Federation became enormously powerful.13 An "associative" evolution had occurred in America, and Herbert Hoover looked on it as a convenient device for promoting economic prosperity, underwriting social justice, and safeguarding American Individualism.

In the rise of these private associations Hoover saw the formation of a new, more rational economic system that was a synthesis of individual entrepreneurship and corporate enterprise — of rural simplicity and the technocratic commonwealth. For several reasons he believed these private associations were perfectly suited to the challenge of reconciling nineteenth century values and twentieth century realities, that is, of preserving the best of the old and promoting the best of the new. In the first place, these associations transcended parochial points of view in favor of a national perspective; they realized that the structural dynamics of the modern economy required cooperative action among like-minded groups. In this sense these private organizations fostered the vision of a national community, a single people, cooperating to improve the quality of their lives. Equally significant, the private associations had risen spontaneously in response to industrialism; their activities were purely voluntary, independent of the federal government, and in the finest spirit of American Individualism. So despite the fact that an incredible amount of organizational activity was going on, the spirit of rural America, with its voluntary cooperation and community service, remained intact.

And just as the associations preserved the spirit of an older America, they promoted the techniques of modern industrialism. Their interest in scientific management and technology, precision, and order had vastly increased efficiency and productivity. The debilitating, sometimes destructive, competition of an earlier era had disappeared as had the inefficiencies so characteristic of preindustrial economies. In the process the gross national product had increased tenfold since 1860 while the population had only tripled. In Hoover's view virtually every member of American society was better off because of that phenomenal growth, and the social structure was quite stable. Not only was the United States enjoying cooperative individualism in an urban, industrial setting, but each citizen was more economically secure than ever before.

Finally, the network of associations held out the promise of a form of private government in which the economy was essentially self-regulating. In emphasizing professional standards, ethical codes of conduct, and rational problem solving, the private associations were self-disciplining and self-improving; and as they policed themselves internally they naturally contributed to social harmony. Even more important, the rise of the private associations had reoriented the American social structure just in time to avert absolutism. The Industrial Revolution and the growth of the supercorporations had threatened to arrange American society along vertical lines with power flowing down from a corporate dictatorship to the working masses. Such a system preserved stability in the short term but almost guaranteed violent class confrontation in the future. The progressive solution to this problem, in which the federal government intervened to control the corporations, offered no real change because it only replaced one form of vertical authority with another. But when the private associations developed, the social and economic structure in America assumed a horizontal dimension in which power flowed laterally, back and forth, among a large number of equally powerful interest groups. Here there was a natural separation of powers—an economic check and balance system—with the likelihood of tyranny by one group remote and the need for federal intervention unusual. In Hoover's opinion, the associative state would be able to preserve social justice, equality of opportunity, and political compromise.[14]

Hoover's ideal system, therefore, would have no need for an oppressive regulatory state. Instead the federal government would promote economic prosperity and supervise the exchanges of power between the functional interest groups. He believed that government, rather than ignore the ups and downs of the business cycle, must be responsible for maintaining stable prices and full employment. The federal government would pursue this objective in several ways. To overcome narrow competition and at the same time to effect some private but national economic planning, Hoover wanted the federal government to continue to encourage the creation of trade associations, farm cooperatives, labor unions, and professional societies. To improve productivity and increase wages the federal government should provide business with reliable economic statistics, encourage the use of "scientific management," and assist in research and development. The President intended to promote economic stability by inspiring voluntary cooperation among all the private associations. If the federal government could convince each that prosperity was good for all, then destructive price wars, strikes, boycotts, and legal confrontations could be avoided. The federal government was to be the coordinator of the associative state—promoting the interests of each group, negotiating their differences, and occasionally regulating their activities. Only then could the government simultaneously guarantee prosperity and ensure the survival of the noncoercive, individualistic, progressive society.[15]

Hoover's successful prepresidential career had confirmed in his own mind the validity of his personal philosophy and his opinions about the future of the American economic system. As a well-traveled mining engineer before World War I, he was able to compare the living standard of the United States with those of other nations and conclude that his native country was the richest and most benevolent nation in the world. As Food Administrator during the war, he marveled at the voluntary cooperation of Americans in accepting production quotas on agricultural commodities and at their patriotism in supporting the war effort. The incredible political and bureaucratic difficulties of finally liquidating the Food Administration after the war remained indelibly imprinted on his memory as an example of the dangers of governmental activism. While leading the American Relief Administration after the war he relied heavily on voluntary contributions and cooperation among charitable organizations, such as the Red Cross and the Friends Service Committee, to sustain his efforts to feed an impoverished Europe.[16]

As Secretary of Commerce between 1921 and 1928 Hoover had worked diligently to direct and inspire the associational activities in which he had so much confidence. The Bureau of Domestic and Foreign Commerce, in order to expand foreign trade, strengthened its ties with private associations and provided them with relevant economic and political information. The Bureau of Standards during the same period worked with trade associations to improve product quality and safety. The Census Bureau collected data on prices, production, inventories, and technology and published it in a government periodical. And Hoover sponsored a series of conferences on such far-ranging subjects as labor relations, productivity, public works and the business cycle, unemployment, child welfare, housing, emergency relief, and research and development. Under his direction the federal government coordinated the activities of the private associations and strengthened the economy without raising the specter of bureaucratic tyranny.[17]

After entering the White House, President Hoover continued to rely on the voluntary activities of the private sector to bring an end to the depression. Because of his philosophy and experience it was only natural that in responding to the financial crisis of 1931, Hoover would draw on his past and attempt to implement a voluntary program of cooperation among bankers to end the vicious cycle of forced liquidation. Once the bankers were relieved of their liquidity fears, they would expand commercial credit and increase industrial production and employment in the process. Under these favorable conditions a complete economic recovery would develop. President Hoover firmly and enthusiastically believed in the promise and potential of American Individualism. He wanted to preserve ''normalcy'' in an economy that was rapidly disintegrating and prove to the world and to his critics that American liberalism could overcome even the greatest crisis. He articulated these hopes when he said:

Time and time again the American people have demonstrated a spiritual quality, a capacity for unity of action, of generosity, a certainty of results in time of emergency that have made them great in the annals of the history of all nations. This is the time and this is the occasion when we must arouse that idealism, that spirit, that determination, that unity of action, from which there can be no failure in this primary obligation of every man to his neighbor and of a nation to its citizens, that none who deserves shall suffer.[18]

The President fully expected the bankers and businessmen to serve as the neighbors of the American public and to act rationally and benevolently in easing the impact of the Great Depression. It was a noble objective, inspired by Hoover's boundless faith in American society. His faith was soon to be tested by the very ideals in which he fervently believed; the voluntarism, the altruism, and the cooperation he expected and wanted would not be forthcoming. He was willing to use the federal government to deal with the crisis, but business intransigence, political controversy, and economic miscalculation would prevent his programs from successfully easing the depression. During a period of relative prosperity, Herbert Hoover would very likely have been one of America's great presidents; his sophisticated understanding of corporate, industrial, and bureaucratic realities would have permitted him to coordinate the economy and at the same time restrain the governmental bureaucracy. The Great Depression, however, upset his hopes, and turned his political philosophy into his greatest enemy.

3

National Credit Corporation

TO meet the rapidly growing financial crisis President Hoover summoned Eugene Meyer, chairman of the Federal Reserve Board, to the White House on September 8, 1931. He told Meyer that the crisis could be ended by voluntary, cooperative action on the part of private bankers—inspired but not controlled by the federal government. If the bankers would create a private credit corporation to assist troubled banks, the public would be calmed and no longer demand conversion of deposits into cash. The sense of relief would ease the deflationary pressures on the entire money market. Meyer promptly asked the chairmen of the twelve Federal Reserve banks to give Hoover's suggestion careful consideration.[1] At a meeting of the Federal Reserve Advisory Council on September 15, the President carried his plan a step further by calling on bankers to create a $500 million credit pool. The money loaned to weak banks would forestall suspensions and provide the banking system as a whole with the liquidity it so desperately needed.[2]

Meyer, among others, was skeptical of Hoover's proposal; he considered it inadequate to confront the financial problem. But he did not disagree with Hoover about the nature of the depression, and both men approached the financial debacle with inaccurate economic assumptions. They firmly believed that economic growth would not resume until commercial banks began making more loans to business and industry and considered the expansion of bank credit a prerequisite to economic recovery. Both were convinced that businessmen and consumers desperately needed and wanted commercial credit, placed the blame for the depression's severity on overcautious bankers, and maintained the depression would continue until bankers resumed commercial lending. Unfortunately, no individual of stature in the Hoover administration understood the reasons behind the decline in bank loans. In addition to the caution of the banking community, there was a decline in the demand for credit by frightened businessmen, a startling decline in the number of adequately secured borrowers, and the decisions of many large corporations in the twenties to finance expansion with surplus profits or new securities issues. All these factors caused commercial loans to decline. Ignorant of these other developments, the administration confidently assumed that bankers were in complete control of the situation and with courage and discipline they could increase their commercial loans. Hoover and Meyer were preoccupied almost exclusively with the supply dimension of the credit crisis and were oblivious to the problem of business and consumer demand for credit and manufactured goods. It would be several years before American political leaders understood the concept of the liquidity trap and the inability of orthodox monetary policy to stimulate the demand for money as well as the supply.[3]

Although Meyer agreed with Hoover's economic model, he did not share the President's faith in the financial community. Suspicious about the willingness of private interests to contribute the necessary $500 million, Meyer joined the bankers in urging Hoover to revive the War Finance Corporation. Meyer believed that the economy was too weak and unstable to expect private bankers to invest $500 million in a private credit agency that planned to make loans to admittedly weak banks. He had little faith in Hoover's American Individualism and believed that only the federal government could muster the discipline and funds necessary to strengthen the money market.[4]

Although President Hoover realized that a revival of the War Finance Corporation might soon be necessary, he temporarily rejected Meyer's advice, hoping that in the two months before the convening of the Seventy-second Congress bankers would establish an effective credit association. Hoover was reluctant to resurrect the WFC because to do so would require a special session of Congress, which might convince the already frightened public that the condition of the economy was truly precarious and cause more intense runs on the banks. The President preferred to wait until December at least, when the regular session of Congress would begin.[5]

The President also feared the potential consequences of direct intervention in the economy. The specter of the War Finance Corporation recalled the images of the World War I economy and the all-pervasive role the government had played. Although he could justify governmental activism when national survival was threatened, Hoover believed that large-scale federal intervention in a peacetime economy was dangerous and irresponsible. In a revitalized War Finance Corporation the federal government would be underwriting private banking and planting the seeds of an ominous relationship. A few months later the administration would see the peacetime depression as a serious enough threat to national survival to justify governmental activism. But in September 1931 Hoover still insisted on giving voluntarism and private initiative another chance. Only when the resources of the financial community were completely exhausted would he resort to federal planning and control.[6]

Finally, the President still believed in American Individualism. With proper supervision by the government, he believed that bankers would respond patriotically to the proposal, create a new credit association, and their enlightened efforts would quickly relieve tension in the financial community and bring the crisis to an end. His faith in the potential of the associative state was still strong.[7]

Hoover overestimated the willingness of bankers to cooperate. Their behavior revealed American Individualism's dependency on prosperity. Voluntarism and cooperation were useful public relations ideas during times of affluence; but when the object of economic activity was survival rather than profit, slogans were expendable. The conditions that created the need for the WFC during World War I and the severity of the 1931 crisis had undermined laissez-faire in most banking circles.[8] Only after three weeks of pleading and promising did Meyer finally persuade a group of New York bankers to meet with Hoover in Washington, D.C., to discuss his proposal for voluntary cooperation. Fully aware of Hoover's intentions, the bankers privately agreed during the trip from New York City not to provide money for any type of emergency credit agency unless the federal government provided an appropriation as well; they wanted the federal government to channel its vast resources directly into the private money market. It was a major departure in both policy and rhetoric for the financial community: bankers were admitting their own impotency and simultaneously recognizing the dominance of the federal government. Laissez-faire was no longer an accurate reflection of economic reality or a credible vision of the future.[9]

On October 4, 1931, in Secretary of the Treasury Andrew Mellon's Washington apartment, Hoover presented his proposals to the bankers. He urged them to create a privately controlled $500 million credit pool to rediscount the sound but frozen assets of banks. Unaware of the bankers' intense commitment to federal intervention, the President threatened them with the prospect of a federal credit agency unless they established a private association. In addition, to supplement the activities of the private agency, Hoover expressed hope that Congress would relax the eligibility requirements of the Federal Reserve system. Under existing law, Federal Reserve banks would rediscount only self-liquidating assets, such as the tax anticipation certificates of state and local governments, U.S. government bonds, and ninety-day commercial paper. By allowing Federal Reserve banks also to discount sound but slow assets, such as high-class corporate bonds, Hoover intended to liquefy the portfolios of many banks and enable them to cope with the emergency and eventually increase their commercial lending.[10]

The bankers at the meeting, realizing that financial conditions exceeded their power to end the crisis, praised Hoover's intention to relax the eligibility regulations but rejected his proposal for a private agency. They unanimously demanded the reestablishment of the War Finance Corporation. In a historic irony, it was necessary for the President, who had just threatened them with federal intervention, to promise that should the private agency fail to stabilize the economy he would ask Congress to revive the WFC. With this promise the bankers reluctantly agreed to organize the credit association.[11]

On October 6, Hoover presented the plan for the association to a bipartisan meeting of leading congressmen. Senator Carter Glass of Virginia opposed changing the Federal Reserve eligibility requirements and Speaker of the House John Nance Garner wanted a special session of Congress, but most members present supported Hoover's proposals. On October 7, when news of the program reached the public, the financial community responded favorably. The American Bankers' Association publicly endorsed the idea, and congratulatory messages from all over the country poured into the White House. Hoover was delighted.[12]

Initial response was deceptive. Most state and local bankers, caught up in economic forces over which they had little control, welcomed the proposals since they thought their more liquid and healthy urban associates might assist them. But more powerful bankers doubted that Hoover's plan would work. Over and over again the President received their public praise, but privately these bankers expressed serious misgivings. Skeptical about their economic discipline, they were anxious to accept the government alternative. As far as they were concerned, the President's promise to recreate the War Finance Corporation, made public on October 7, was far more significant than his desire to establish a private credit association. These bankers emphasized this belief in public statements. Almost immediately after meeting with Hoover on October 4 they transformed his tentative promise of government assistance into a guarantee of federal help, and this doomed the private agency to failure even before its formal inception.[13]

Nevertheless, the banking community dutifully went through the motions of cooperating. George Harrison, governor of the Federal Reserve bank of New York, promptly organized a committee of leading New York bankers to formulate plans for the credit corporation. The committee members, politically conservative and representing some of the most prestigious banks in the country, consisted of Mortimer Buckner, chairman of the New York Trust Company; Charles S. McCain of the Chase National Bank; Harry E. Ward, president of the Irving Trust Company; George Davison, president of the Central Hanover Bank and Trust Company; and Gordon Rentschier, president of the National City Bank. Under the leadership of Buckner the committee began work and soon received a pledge of $150 million from the member banks of the New York Clearing House Association.[14] The committee was capable of marshaling enormous resources for the bank rescue program, but unfortunately, they were unwilling to use all the funds they would receive.

On October 13, Buckner announced the formal organization of the National Credit Corporation (NCC). Its by-laws authorized it to issue up to $1 billion in debentures and indicated that the nation's private banks would subscribe to at least $500 million of that total.[15] Under the terms of its incorporation, the NCC offered membership to any bank subscribing 2 percent of its net time and demand deposits to the association. The NCC organizing committee elected officers in mid-October. Mortimer Buckner was named president and George M. Reynolds, chairman of the Continental Illinois Bank and Trust Company, was named chairman of the board. Daniel Wing, president of the First National Bank of Boston, and Walter Smith of the First National Bank of St. Louis served as vice-presidents. The newly elected officers immediately divided the National Credit Corporation into a series of local associations and local loan committees in each Federal Reserve district. On subscribing to the gold notes of the corporation, any member bank could apply to its local association for a loan; if the loan was approved, the national office of the NCC would forward the money after an appropriate review of the application.16

President Hoover envisioned complete economic recovery as the result of the National Credit Corporation loans. For solvent but temporarily embarrassed banks, he believed the NCC would liquefy assets ineligible for rediscount at the Federal Reserve banks, relieving the deflationary pressures on the securities markets and halting the deterioration of bank assets. Banks would then be more willing, Hoover assumed, to increase their commercial loans, which he hoped would restore public confidence and stimulate an economic recovery.17

The National Credit Corporation represented the ultimate embodiment of Hoover's personal philosophy. Far from adhering to laissez-faire, the federal government had stimulated private initiative. At the same time the government had acted with restraint by not offering direct assistance to the banks. In calling on leading bankers to organize the credit pool, Hoover illustrated his faith in the voluntary cooperation of private associations — even though his own support for the plan often bordered on coercion. The NCC willingness to vest local branches with complete control over the granting of loans coincided with his belief in decentralized administration. For Hoover the National Credit Corporation was the "American way to assist business. . . ."18 He predicated his ideas on the willingness of bankers to cooperate; cooperation would prove to be the elusive element in the President's plan to revive the economy.

Hoover's suspicions about the enthusiasm of the NCC officers were aroused shortly after its formal organization. He was especially upset about delays in making loans. During the last week of October and the first week of November, Hoover and Undersecretary of the Treasury Ogden Mills sent telegrams to the leaders of the National Credit Corporation, criticizing them for procrastination.19 Buckner and the other officers apologized for the delays and claimed that organization of the local committees was taking more time than originally anticipated.20 Finally, on November 7 the directors announced that the National Credit Corporation had formally opened for business.21

Despite his displeasure with early delays, Hoover was satisfied with the initial impact of the NCC on the economy. Bank failures in October dropped weekly after the announcement of the plan, and suspensions for the first half of November were among the lowest of the year.22 Late in October the prices of common and preferred stocks and corporate bonds rallied.23 At this stage the President had every reason to believe that the National Credit Corporation would be a complete success — the ultimate vindication of his personal philosophy and proof that the revival of the War Finance Corporation was unnecessary.

But the economic upturn brought further delays. Hoping that the financial recovery sparked by the announcement of the plan would be permanent, the NCC officers decided in the first week of November to suspend making loans. Privately they hoped that the agency could be dissolved without making any loans.24 To protect themselves if some loans became necessary, they established severe collateral requirements. The National Credit Corporation accepted U.S. government securities at only 75 percent of their market value, appraised securities at depressed market values, and advanced loans at only 40 percent of the market value of the collateral. And the NCC would not accept real estate and agricultural paper as collateral at all.25 Nevertheless, Hoover still remained confident that the National Credit Corporation would be successful and that a revival of the WFC would be unnecessary.

Events quickly shattered everyone's hopes. Whether the October rally represented a seasonal fluctuation or a temporary rejuvenation of public confidence, it was short-lived and collapsed late in November. Bank failures, which had seemed to be leveling off, increased alarmingly.26 Securities prices entered another period of decline.27 In the last week of November 1931, Herbert Hoover realized that American Individualism, in this instance at least, had failed: ultraconservative businessmen, in whom he had placed such great faith, were unwilling to engage in a sincere attempt to ease the crisis. Hoover asked Meyer to go ahead with plans to revive the War Finance Corporation. Meyer worked closely with Walter Wyatt, a staff assistant at the Federal Reserve Board, and they jointly drafted the legislation to create a Reconstruction Finance Corporation.28

Although disappointed with the failure of private initiative, Hoover accepted the alternative of federal intervention. American Individualism never paralyzed Hoover; it only made him cautious, deliberate, and in this case convinced him to wait two months before creating the new federal agency. When the need for the RFC became obvious, he went ahead enthusiastically. He had no intention of allowing the new corporation to become a permanent addition to the federal bureaucracy; it would be a temporary, emergency government agency. With this attitude Hoover submitted the bill to Congress on December 7, 1931, asking them to pass it as quickly as possible.29

After Hoover's proposal to revive the WFC, the officers of the National Credit Corporation decided to liquidate the few loans they had made.30 However, several developments delayed their closing, and ironically, the NCC functioned effectively only after Hoover had abandoned it. During the hearings on the RFC bill in mid-December, many congressmen openly criticized the National Credit Corporation and expressed misgivings about assisting people unwilling to help themselves.31 To disarm these critics, the NCC officers began vigorously making loans late in December. Also, Senator Glass modified his resistance to Federal Reserve reform; the bankers realized that the frozen assets the NCC acquired from weak financial institutions would be eligible for rediscount by Federal Reserve banks. The NCC assets would automatically be more liquid. This too convinced them to make more loans. Finally, the passage of the RFC bill appeared imminent despite scattered congressional criticism. If it passed, bankers would then be able to replace their NCC advances with Reconstruction Finance Corporation funds because the RFC loans would probably carry lower interest rates. With assurance of the liquidity of their new collateral and the rapid repayment of their loans, the officers of the National Credit Corporation pursued a comparatively enthusiastic credit policy during January and February of 1932.[32]

Despite later criticisms of the National Credit Corporation,[33] it performed a valuable service during the two-month interval between Hoover's call for the RFC and congressional enactment of the measure. In those two months the NCC loaned over $143 million and in several instances prevented the failure of important banks. Late in December, for example, a serious financial situation developed throughout the South, and NCC loans to banks in North Carolina, Mississippi, Georgia, and Louisiana ended the regional crisis. Additional loans to banks in Iowa and Illinois postponed disasters there.[34] Although the National Credit Corporation failed to end the banking crisis, it did provide temporary assistance during the months when Congress was debating the RFC bill. Still, as a symbol of American Individualism, the National Credit Corporation left Hoover disappointed and somewhat embittered. He had committed himself and the presidency to a proposal that in the long run did little to relieve the suffering of millions of Americans.[35]

For many reasons, the National Credit Corporation was an inappropriate means of ending the crisis. The NCC was not authorized to deal with the continuing deterioration of the railroad bond market. Immediately following the organization of the NCC, George Harrison, of the Federal Reserve Bank of New York, wrote to Hoover informing him that the NCC would eventually fail to save the banks because it could not make loans to railroads.[36] Hoover was aware of the problem and had already made tentative plans for the formation of a federal committee to study the situation. In mid-October, encouraged by the initial success of the NCC, Hoover asked railroad executives to form a voluntary Railroad Credit Corporation.[37] But railroad officials were even more unwilling than bankers to part with their funds voluntarily. Earnings for October 1931 were $120 million less than a year before, and in November the bottom fell out of railroad bond prices.[38] In 1931 alone, nineteen railroads failed and went into receivership. Government loans permitting railroads to meet the obligations of maturing bank loans, bond issues, and equipment trust certificates now became imperative. Any further decline in the value of railroad bonds would threaten the solvency of savings banks, life insurance companies, and some large commercial banks. By the end of November Hoover began to consider means of providing special government assistance to railroads, and the revival of the War Finance Corporation seemed to be the best approach.

Structural weaknesses also prevented the NCC from operating effectively. Its regulations excluded many weak banks from its assistance.

Banks verging on failure and most in need of help were often unable to contribute the 2 percent subscription for membership; and since only member banks could receive loans, many small, weak banks could not participate.[39] Late in November 1931 frequent pleas from small banks throughout the country, demanding replacement of the National Credit Corporation with a government agency, reached the President.[40] Their criticisms doomed the NCC. These small bankers, who initially provided Hoover with his greatest support, now joined more prominent bankers in questioning the ability of the private money market to solve its own problems.[41]

Another weakness was that the National Credit Corporation did not provide new credit or improve the liquidity of the banking system as a whole. At best it only redistributed available funds by creating a central credit institution that facilitated the loaning of existing money. The NCC infused no additional funds into the system. The crisis threatened many banks with not merely a lack of liquidity, but with insolvency. The collapse of real estate values, the agricultural depression, and the catastrophic decline in securities had seriously impaired the value of bank assets. Too many banks needed new capital, not just new loans. The banking crisis did not end until 1934-1935 after the stock market had partially recovered and the RFC had granted loans and made preferred stock purchases totaling more than $3 billion. The $500 million of the National Credit Corporation, even had it ultimately been distributed liberally, was inadequate to solve the problem.[42]

Moreover, the entire money market was in desperate circumstances. Life insurance companies, credit unions, savings banks, industrial banks, building and loan associations, and a variety of other financial intermediaries suffered from frozen assets. The NCC could make loans only to commercial banks and was powerless to assist the other institutions of the money market. Only a comprehensive program of financial aid could ease the crisis.

Finally, the caution of private bankers inhibited the National Credit Corporation. As originally proposed, the NCC was part of a financial program that included relaxing Federal Reserve eligibility requirements. Bankers hoped that the frozen collateral the National Credit Corporation acquired from its loans might be eligible for rediscount by Federal Reserve banks. But when the measure to relax the eligibility regulations encountered stiff congressional resistance in November 1931, it became evident that bankers probably would not be able to take advantage of rediscounting.[43] By loaning their pooled assets to threatened banks, solvent members of the NCC would be indirectly accepting slow and frozen assets into their portfolios, a development that they studiously avoided. By December 1931 the National Credit Corporation had made only a paltry $10 million in loans.[44] Only first-class banks in relatively good condition received loans because of strict collateral requirements.[45] Even then, the conservatism of the NCC officers led them to make only short-term loans for sixty days. This procedure did not provide bankers a real solution for their fundamental problems but only a postponement of their difficulties.[46]

President Hoover had no choice but to give up on the bankers, abandon the National Credit Corporation, and revive and rename the War Finance Corporation. For the remainder of his life he criticized the bankers for their behavior during the crisis of 1931. Besides openly requesting the intervention of the federal government, they had been reluctant, over-cautious, and self-serving in their administration of the NCC. Ultimately, in Hoover's view, American Individualism had not really failed; instead, it had been purposely scuttled by the very group it had attempted to serve.[47] However, in this case it had failed since its central premise was that private businessmen would cooperate to extricate themselves and the country from the crisis. The President was keenly disappointed. Now, in proposing the Reconstruction Finance Corporation he was temporarily suspending his personal philosophy. Herbert Hoover, the most famous spokesman for voluntarism and limited government, was about to adopt a program of governmental activism that would lead directly to the New Deal.

4

Reconstruction Finance Corporation

ON December 7, 1931, President Hoover asked Congress to enact a comprehensive legislative program aimed at stimulating economic recovery. One part of that program called for creating the Reconstruction Finance Corporation (RFC), which would offer government credit to a wide variety of financial institutions in an attempt to liquefy their assets. Hoover also asked for $125 million to strengthen the Federal Land banks to enable them to make loans to farmers and to rural banks, thereby relieving credit conditions throughout the countryside. He also called for the establishment of a new system of federal home loan discount banks to grant loans to building and loan associations, thus encouraging mortgage lenders to increase loans and stimulate the construction industry. Sensitive to the needs of frightened bank depositors and believing that the release of those funds would stimulate purchasing power, Hoover also asked Congress to develop a plan for the early distribution of savings deposits tied up in closed banks. Finally, the President again urged Congress to relax the eligibility regulations for Federal Reserve banks. He had put this proposal to congressional leaders in October, but because of Senator Glass's opposition the Banking and Currency Committee had not even considered it. [1]

Although these proposals appear mild when compared with the vast changes in the responsibilities of the federal government since 1932, Hoover had taken an important step forward in the history of American public policy. The RFC proposal made obsolete the ceremony of Wall Street financiers organizing to end a panic or rescue the federal government from bankruptcy, and it coincided perfectly with Hoover's interpretation of the Great Depression. For Hoover, only a crisis of confidence threatened the economy, and the RFC was designed to restore that confidence. Hoping to ease the crisis, the Federal Reserve Board had already manipulated interest rates without effect. Many banks were still insolvent. Similarly, the Open Market Committee of the Federal Reserve Board had actively acquired government securities during the latter part of 1931, but the purchases had had little impact on the volume of commercial loans — excess reserves continued to accumulate in New York among liquidity-conscious bankers. The money market needed fresh capital, especially for its weaker institutions, and the administration believed the RFC would be able to supply those funds. Hoover also hoped the RFC would alleviate the all-pervasive fear afflicting so many bankers and assured himself that the RFC would quickly be dismantled after the crisis. [2]

The administration firmly believed that bankers, refusing to grant new loans, were unnecessarily restricting credit operations and making it impossible for businessmen to finance expansion. Ogden Mills remarked,

Aside from the affirmative assistance which this corporation would render, I visualize it as constituting a solid wall under the protection of which men and institutions can carry on their normal operations without fear of sudden and devastating interruption. I know of no instrument better designed to lift the psychology of fear, which should play no part in American economic life. [3]

The RFC, by ending bank suspensions and preventing the collapse of the railroad bond market, would relieve liquidity fears and reopen normal credit channels. [4] Businessmen would then be able to acquire fresh working capital and increase their investment in equipment, inventories, and payrolls. Unemployment would quickly decline and the new consumer purchasing power would bring a recovery. [5]

In this approach, the President and his associates expressed the prevailing orthodoxy of the monetary economists, who considered the availability of bank credit the most important ingredient for complete recovery. [6] Hoover, Meyer, new Secretary of the Treasury Ogden Mills, and Undersecretary of the Treasury Arthur Ballantine all agreed with this assumption. Their entire approach to the depression, embodied in Hoover's message to Congress on December 7, contemplated nothing less than the revitalization of the private money market. Such a program would stimulate the entire economy, and RFC funds poured into the largest financial institutions would eventually "trickle down" to businessmen and consumers. The Great Depression would rapidly become only a memory. Eugene Meyer later remarked,

As to the statement made in comparing the Hoover and Roosevelt administrations that Hoover wanted to pour money in from the top in the hopes of stimulating big business, which would help the small men, while Roosevelt poured it in directly at the bottom to help the small man without waiting for it to seep through, that's just a lot of bunk. If I loan through 4,375 country banks and about a hundred livestock loan companies in the critical areas enough money to take care of major troubles, and that was reflected in the buying power and the easing of the money market and the restoration of labor to activity and production and exchange of goods, that is a practical approach. . . . You don't have to deal with every individual direct to reach every individual in the country. [7]

With such confidence, the President sent the RFC bill to Congress on December 8, under the legislative management of Senator Frederic Walcott of Connecticut and Representative James Strong of Kansas. The President's own sense of urgency was more acute after he learned that the important Bank of America chain in California was on the verge of collapse. Only massive assistance from the Reconstruction Finance Corporation could prevent its suspension and the national panic that would undoubtedly follow. Hoover asked Congress to act quickly on the measure. [8]

The Democratic Congress, however, jealous of its own prerogatives, antagonistic toward the administration, and interested in getting home before Christmas, delayed. The measure was not ready for Hoover's signature until January 22, 1932. [9] Debate over the bill raised several important questions that postponed enactment but never threatened passage. The response of businessmen to the bill was so overwhelmingly positive that progressive and liberal congressmen were immediately suspicious. Representatives of commercial banks, railroads, savings banks, building and loan associations, and life insurance companies all praised the bill in glowing terms, claiming that it was essential to the survival of the money market. They all believed that the Reconstruction Finance Corporation would liquefy their assets and stimulate a resumption of commercial credit and investment; their commitment to the bill was absolute. [10]

Already reluctant to sanction the philosophy behind the Reconstruction Finance Corporation, progressive Republicans and liberal Democrats were upset about the enthusiasm businessmen expressed for the President's proposal. Representative Fiorello La Guardia of New York City was incensed, calling the bill a

millionaire's dole and you can not get away from it. It is a subsidy for broken bankers—a subsidy for bankrupt railroads—a reward for speculation and unscrupulous bond pluggers.[11]

Representative Louis McFadden of Pennsylvania was even more vitriolic, claiming that the bill was simply a vicious scheme by financial "criminals" for

gouging $500,000,000 out of the Treasury of the United States. It is a scheme for taking $500,000,000 of the people's money produced by labor at a cost of toil and suffering and giving it to a supercorporation for the sinister purpose of helping a gang of financial looters to cover up their tracks. It is a scheme for giving those financial looters a chance to dispose of evidence, which, if brought into the light of day, would cause the doors of our Federal penitentiary to close upon them for a long term of years.[12]

Senators Smith Brookhart of Iowa and John Blaine of Wisconsin demanded to know why the taxpayers of the United States should be expected to pay for the folly and dishonesty of the great financiers; while Senator Robert Bulkeley of Ohio, along with many other congressmen, criticized the lackluster performance of the National Credit Corporation. Although these sentiments were not representative of the whole Congress,

Hoover was disturbed by their implications. He would hear the progressive refrain frequently in future months. [13]

In the long run, the visibility of the crisis provided Hoover with his greatest weapon in convincing recalcitrant congressmen. Most politicians realized that the public was both frightened and enraged about bank closings and frustrated by excuses and calls for patience. The public expected drastic action to save the economy. Senator Robert Wagner of New York was a case in point. The very idea of the RFC irritated him, particularly in view of his consistent support for expanded federal unemployment relief and public works programs. In a speech to a group of his constituents on January 15, 1932, he said of the RFC:

We replied that we would lend them the aid of the Federal Government; that we would lend them the money out of the United States Treasury. . . . We did not preach to them rugged individualism. We did not sanctimoniously roll out sentences rich with synonyms of self-reliance. We were not carried away with apprehension over what would happen to their independence if we extended them a helping hand. . . . But when millions of Americans . . . cry out in despair "Give us work," we suddenly are overwhelmed with devotion for the preservation of self-reliance. We plug our ears to the cry of the multitude while the prophets burn incense upon the altar of rugged individualism. [14]

Regardless of his frustration with Hoover's apparent insensitivity to the suffering of the unemployed, Wagner received hundreds of telegrams from businessmen in New York urging him to support the RFC bill; the alternative, they argued, was an economic disaster far worse than anything the nation had yet experienced. [15] The Reconstruction Finance Corporation bill, though conceptually distasteful to many congressmen, appeared to be a viable approach to the problems of financial institutions. Wagner repeatedly assured New York financial leaders that he would support the bill despite his objections to its line of approach. In January 1932 Wagner and his colleagues in Congress could offer no alternative means of halting the economic decline. [16]

Hoover still faced important opposition from Senator Carter Glass, a self-appointed protector of the Federal Reserve system. By 1932 the seventy-four-year-old senator from Virginia was one of the senior Democrats on Capital Hill and a bipartisan leader of conservatives from both parties. Born in Lynchburg, Virginia, Glass had entered the House of Representatives in 1902 and later secured a seat on the House Finance Committee. In 1913 he helped draft the Federal Reserve bill and shepherded it through the House as floor manager. President Woodrow Wilson appointed him secretary of the treasury in 1918, and in 1920 Glass was elected to the Senate. By 1931, he ruled the Senate Committee on Banking and Currency with an iron hand, treating the Federal Reserve system in particular and financial issues in general as his personal domain. Hoover had no choice but to court Glass's favor.

The Senator objected to a clause in the RFC bill permitting the

Federal Reserve banks to discount the debentures and financial obligations of the RFC. The administration hoped that this eligibility clause would render RFC securities more marketable in the investment community and decrease the interest rates the RFC would eventually have to pay for its funds. Senator Glass, however, was deeply concerned that this would not only stimulate "bank mismanagement and the spirit of speculation that pervades the whole nation" but would directly weaken the Federal Reserve System. Senator Bulkeley shared Glass's fear. Both men believed that eventually the RFC debentures might be secured by the bank assets it accepted as collateral for its loans. The Federal Reserve system, by discounting the RFC securities, would indirectly be incorporating into its own portfolio eroded and deteriorated assets. Cognizant of the jealousy with which Glass "guarded" the Federal Reserve system, President Hoover decided not to contest the senator's claims. He eliminated the clause from the RFC bill and instead authorized the United States Treasury to purchase the corporation's securities. [17]

Glass was still not satisfied with Hoover's bill. In its original version, the President intended to have five directors for the RFC. Two would be appointments while the other three would serve as ex officio officers: the chairman of the Federal Reserve Board, the secretary of the treasury, and the federal farm loan commissioner. But these three men were Republicans, and Senator Glass, believing that Republicans loyal to the administration might dominate the Board of Directors, insisted that the Reconstruction Finance Corporation Board of Directors be expanded from five to seven members with no more than four coming from the same party. This would probably mean that the President would appoint one more Republican and three Democrats to the board. Realizing that compromise with Glass on this issue would not substantively alter the effectiveness of the RFC, Hoover accepted the amendment. [18]

Finally, both Senator Glass and Senator Robert La Follette of Wisconsin opposed a clause in the RFC bill permitting the RFC to make certain business loans to "bona fide institutions." They thought that such a provision was too vague and might permit loans to businesses that could not get credit from more traditional sources. That of course was precisely what the administration had in mind. Hoover wanted the RFC to make loans to industries that already had production contracts but could not fill them because of a lack of credit; with a limited number of industrial and commodity loans from the RFC, businesses would be able to maintain or even increase production, expand employment and purchasing power, and stop the cutting of prices. Glass and La Follette would have none of it. They argued that the clause provided the RFC with too much discretionary power, and they preferred to limit its lending powers to a specific list of private financial organizations. They also wanted to ensure that the RFC would not assist the National Credit Corporation; they preferred to let the bankers liquidate it. Realizing that neither Glass nor La Follette would compromise the President again relented, this time with some bitterness, for he believed they were obstructing the ability of the RFC to bring recovery. Nevertheless, because their amendment did not hurt the RFC's power to assist financial institutions, Hoover agreed to drop the industrial loan clause from the bill. [19]

Once Glass was satisfied, it became likely that the RFC bill would move quickly through Congress. Hoover succeeded in acquiring the loyalty of other leading southern Democrats through a series of important compromises. He immediately agreed to Arkansas Senator Joseph Robinson's amendment to grant loans to livestock and agricultural credit corporations, to Federal Land banks, and to joint stock land banks.[20] Hoover then consented to an amendment offered by Senator Ellison ("Cotton Ed") Smith of South Carolina authorizing the RFC to grant $50 million to the secretary of agriculture for small crop loans to farmers.[21] Finally, Hoover asked Senate majority leader Robinson and Speaker of the House Garner each to select a member of the RFC Board of Directors.[22] With the support of Glass, Robinson, and Garner, and with the manifest urgency of the crisis, passage of the RFC bill appeared certain.

The President still faced one serious threat to the bill from northern, urban Democrats. Senator Royal Copeland of New York, at the request of Mayor Jimmie Walker of New York City, suggested that the RFC be permitted to make relief loans to cities. Hoover would not support this, since he feared the amendment would dilute RFC funds and delay the ability of banks to resume commercial lending. The kind of loans Copeland suggested did not coincide with the administration's recovery plans. Pouring funds into the bottom of the economic system would only be postponing the revitalization of major banks and corporations. The Copeland amendment, the administration believed, was counterproductive. The President was by no means a doctrinaire opponent of direct federal relief and public works programs, but he believed they would be superfluous once the credit machinery of the country had been strengthened. Although Hoover would in a matter of months propose a major federal relief program, he was not ready to do this in January 1932. Public support for the Copeland amendment was substantial, but a coalition of regular Republicans and southern Democrats defeated it in the Senate 45 to 28. [23]

The RFC bill then moved quickly through Congress. Despite the misgivings of most progressives and liberals, the majority of congressmen, Democrats and Republicans, were convinced that without the RFC the financial system would collapse. So with only token resistance from midwestern progressives, some urban Democrats, and several recalcitrant southern Democrats, the bill passed the House 335 to 55 and the Senate 63 to 8. Party lines were largely obliterated on the RFC vote. In the Senate, 34 Republicans and 29 Democrats favored the measure, while only 3 Republicans and 5 Democrats opposed it. In the House, 154 Democrats and 181 Republicans voted for it, while only 43 Democrats and 12 Republicans opposed it. On January 22, 1932, President Hoover signed the bill, duly praising the "patriotism of the men in both houses of Congress who have given proof of their devotion to the welfare of their country, irrespective of political affiliation." [24]

The Reconstruction Finance Corporation Act provided for massive and direct governmental assistance to the entire U. S. money market. The federal government, despite several generations of public suspicion of banks and bankers, was about to underwrite the financial establishment. The RFC could make loans to commercial banks, savings banks, insurance companies, trust companies, building and loan associations, mortgage loan companies, credit unions, Federal Land banks, joint stock land banks, Federal Intermediate Credit banks, agricultural credit corporations, livestock credit companies, receivers of closed banks, and railroads. The federal government subscribed the initial capital of $500 million, and the RFC could issue bonds, debentures, and notes to obtain an additional $1.5 billion. The RFC act also allotted $200 million of the total RFC endowment to the Department of Agriculture for crop loans. Finally, it required that without the express written permission of the President the RFC would have to liquidate its operations on January 1, 1933; at that time, after a presidential executive order, it could continue without further congressional authorization until January 1, 1934. The administration hoped that the RFC would revive the financial system without becoming a permanent fixture in the federal bureaucracy and restore prosperity while preserving the spiritual quality of American life. At the same time Hoover looked to the new agency as a means of restoring his own reputation. [25]

The mere passage of the Reconstruction Finance Corporation Act did not guarantee success. Immediately following congressional approval, the President formally turned to the task of nominating the RFC Board of Directors. It was a delicate political challenge, since Hoover desperately wanted to avoid a controversy over personnel. The men he eventually selected were prominent bankers, businessmen, and public servants. By selecting capable men and by allowing Democrats in Congress to participate in the appointments, Hoover guaranteed a positive reception for the RFC and averted a long congressional evaluation of its prospective leaders.

For chairman of the RFC board, Hoover nominated ex officio director Eugene Meyer, loyal Republican and fifty-seven-year-old native of California who had accumulated a personal fortune through banking and investments. Meyer had served on the War Industries Board in 1917 and later was named by President Wilson to the Board of Directors of the War Finance Corporation. In 1927 Coolidge appointed him director of the Farm Loan Board, and in 1930, after gaining the attention of President Hoover, he became chairman of the Federal Reserve Board. Meyer was regarded in the financial world as a cautious banker and political conservative closely linked, socially and philosophically, with the New York banking and investment community. [26]

Ogden Mills was also an ex officio member of the RFC Board of Directors by virtue of his position as the new secretary of the treasury. Hoover for some time had wanted to replace the conservative Andrew Mellon with Ogden Mills. Early in January the President named Mellon ambassador to Great Britain and moved Mills to the cabinet post. Mills, born in 1884 into a rich and socially prominent New York family, had

attended Harvard and later practiced law in New York City. After Mills
had served four terms in the House of Representatives, President
Coolidge named him undersecretary of the treasury. During the next four
years, Mills impressed Hoover through personal loyalty and superior
ability, and by 1932 they had become close friends. Secretary Mills, like
Meyer, was close to the eastern financial community and almost perfectly
reflected Hoover's political philosophy. [27]

H. Paul Bestor served as the other ex officio member of the RFC
board, simultaneously presiding over the Federal Farm Loan Board.
Raised in Iowa and Missouri, Bestor taught Latin-American history at Yale
before joining the St. Louis Federal Land Bank in 1922. He was known in
Washington as a protégé of Eugene Meyer and had served with Meyer on
the Farm Loan Board. Specializing in agricultural finance, Bestor relied
heavily on the opinions of Meyer and Mills in other economic areas.
Bestor, Meyer, and Mills would soon form a triumvirate on the RFC
reflecting the financial concerns of eastern bankers. [28] The three men also
worked closely with Hoover, and during the first few months of the corporation's existence, the President agreed with their collective view of the
crisis.

As president of the RFC and the fourth Republican director, former
Vice-President of the United States Charles G. Dawes brought to the
agency valuable financial experience and international prestige. Once
comptroller of the currency, Dawes later served as ambassador to Great
Britain and as architect of the Dawes Plan for German reparations, and he
shared with Sir Austen Chamberlain the Nobel Peace Prize in 1925. The
sixty-six-year-old Dawes reflected the interests of the Midwest and
sometimes had to subdue his hostility toward the major eastern and Wall
Street banking houses. Wall Street in turn came to look on Dawes with
skepticism. Nevertheless, he tended to balance the board, and with his
appointment the RFC gained the prestige that accompanied an in-
ternationally prominent man. [29]

The appointments of Meyer, Mills, Bestor, and Dawes completed the
legally eligible number of Republican directors. In naming the three
members from the other party, President Hoover sought Democrats
concerned enough about the financial crisis to ignore political par-
tisanship. He also hoped to achieve a regional balance of power on the
RFC board. To repay Senator Joseph Robinson's support of the RFC act,
the President decided to accept Robinson's recommendation of Harvey C.
Couch. A native of Pine Bluff, Arkansas, Couch was a southern Democrat
who had transcended the poverty of his youth by constructing railroads
and public utilities throughout the South. By 1932 he had become a
prominent economic and social leader in the Southeast and was serving on
the boards of several banks and railroads. He brought to the RFC a
cautious but compassionate political philosophy that President Hoover saw
firsthand when Couch headed the administration's relief committees in
Arkansas. In Harvey Couch the President found a kindred spirit, a man
who exemplified the ideals of American Individualism. [30]

In the same spirit that he accepted Robinson's suggestion, the President approved Speaker Garner's recommendation of Jesse H. Jones of Texas. Jones had accumulated a fortune through various banking, newspaper, construction, and real estate enterprises in Houston. He actively supported Democratic candidates, possessed a strain of conservatism and a sympathy for banking and business, and was ideal for the RFC board. Jones was an energetic booster of the emerging urban-industrial economy of the Southwest, and with Couch he rounded out the southern representation on the RFC. [31]

For his final Democratic appointment, the President wanted a westerner. Mills, Bestor, and Meyer were associated with the East. Jones and Couch were from the South and Southwest. Dawes, a prominent Chicago banker, reflected the views of the Midwest. So to provide a regional balance Hoover nominated Wilson McCarthy, a conservative banker-lawyer from Salt Lake City. Born in American Fork, Utah, McCarthy was a graduate of the University of Utah and the Columbia University Law School. In 1922 he joined the Pacific Coast Joint Stock Land Bank and shortly after became its manager. McCarthy considered himself an expert in agricultural finance and a spokesman for the small rural bankers. [32] With McCarthy, the RFC conformed with the provision of the RFC act requiring four Republicans and three Democrats — a bipartisan arrangement providing Hoover with a political majority. Because of the regional balance on the board, the support of both Robinson and Garner, and the eminent qualifications of all seven nominees, the Senate acted quickly and confirmed them by the first week of February. [33]

The administration's next problems, involving housing, equipping, and formally organizing the RFC, consumed less than a week. The Department of Commerce gave the RFC space in its old office building at the corner of Pennsylvania Avenue and Nineteenth Street in Washington, D.C., in the same office Hoover had worked during the twenties as secretary of commerce.[34] Meyer furnished the building with desks and typewriters borrowed from the Federal Reserve Board offices.[35] The Interstate Commerce Commission took over the duty of examining the loan applications from railroads and the Federal Reserve banks agreed to act as the fiscal agents and collateral depositories for the RFC. [36] Finally, the Department of the Treasury promised to purchase on demand all future bond or debenture issues of the RFC and assured the corporation of its full capitalization. [37]

Hoover and Meyer then considered the staffing and organization of the agency. The War Finance Corporation provided the administration with an invaluable precedent. In philosophy, personnel, and organization the two institutions were remarkably similar. The WFC and the RFC were specifically designed to serve only as temporary, emergency institutions, having no rationale under normal economic conditions. In concept both agencies' most important objective was to be the rejuvenation of the private money market through massive government loans. Men in both agencies initially hoped that a revival of public confidence would make large expenditures of government funds unnecessary. They saw their respective problems as crises of confidence rather than structural weaknesses in the economy. Both groups of men believed that as financial tensions eased throughout the country, credit would resume its flow in normal channels; and with the increase of employment and production, the federal government's credit agencies would gradually retire from the money market and leave private institutions in complete control once again. [38]

In addition to these philosophical similarities, the War Finance Corporation and the Reconstruction Finance Corporation were linked by key personnel. Many individuals who once worked with the WFC found themselves as employees of the RFC. Meyer, an early supporter of the RFC and its new chairman, had served as chairman of the War Finance Corporation during its formative years. To ensure efficient operation of the RFC, Meyer recruited experienced WFC personnel. George Cooksey, a former advisor and director of the WFC and a member of its liquidating committee from 1929 to 1932, became the first secretary of the RFC.[39] Meyer chose Morton G. Bogue, formerly special legal counsel to the WFC, as RFC general counsel and head of the Legal Division.[40] For the all-important Examining Division, Meyer selected three well-qualified officials: Leo Paulger, George C. Holmberg, and George M. Brennan, all of whom had been examiners with the War Finance Corporation and had had much private experience in evaluating the financial condition of banks and trust companies.[41] With these men on hand, the initial pressures in creating the RFC were relieved. They provided the RFC with a sense of continuity as well as a sense of the past.

Finally, RFC leaders adopted an organizational framework that nearly duplicated the structure of the War Finance Corporation. Like the WFC, the RFC had eight separate divisions: auditing, legal, treasury, secretarial, agency, examining, statistical, and railroad.[42] Also like the WFC, Meyer established thirty-three local RFC offices to receive and screen loan applications. Loan agencies were established in Atlanta, Birmingham, Boston, Charlotte, Chicago, Cleveland, Dallas, Denver, Detroit, El Paso, Helena, Houston, Jacksonville, Kansas City, Little Rock, Los Angeles, Louisville, Memphis, Minneapolis, Nashville, New Orleans, New York, Oklahoma City, Omaha, Philadelphia, Portland, Richmond, St. Louis, Salt Lake City, San Antonio, San Francisco, Seattle, and Spokane. When Leo Paulger began to organize the RFC local examining committees, he drew up a list of bankers who had assisted him with the WFC during the twenties and recruited as many of those men as possible to staff the committees. [43]

Thanks to the experience of the War Finance Corporation, the assistance of the executive branch in Washington, and the general approval greeting Hoover's RFC appointments, the RFC was successfully making over one hundred loans per day within two weeks after the President had signed the act into law. By the end of February, Meyer had hired over six hundred people to staff the RFC central office in

Washington and its thirty-three local agency offices throughout the nation. It was an auspicious beginning. [44]

In its final administrative form, the Reconstruction Finance Corporation violated the tenets of American Individualism. The very premise of RFC authority—subsidizing the private money market through government loans—was antithetical to Hoover's personal philosophy. In addition, the RFC organizational framework and bureaucratic independence further emphasized its departure from American Individualism. Like no other powerful governmental agency, the RFC was able to maintain a jealous independence from both the Congress and the director of the budget. It could sell its notes and obligations to the public, and repayments on earlier loans provided it with a revolving fund to finance daily and future transactions. The power of the purse, which Congress traditionally exercised over the executive branch, was partially nullified in the case of the RFC. If managed properly, the RFC could operate indefinitely on the original allocation Congress had appropriated in 1932. Although the corporation had to issue monthly and quarterly reports to Congress, it was not required to reveal either the names of borrowers or the amounts of individual loans. The RFC consistently enjoyed an unusual degree of insulation from probing congressional investigations. [45]

An even greater contradiction of American Individualism involved the RFC local loan agencies, its most important internal institution. Each of the thirty-three local agencies established an advisory committee composed of the area's leading bankers and a credit department to review loan applications and scrutinize collateral. All applications for loans from the RFC had first to be processed and approved by the local agency serving the Federal Reserve district in which the applicant was located—the same procedure used by the WFC during the agricultural crisis of the twenties. The formation of the local agencies was a further movement away from the President's philosophy, for at the local level the federal government and the private economy became one and the same—because the local committees consisted of local bankers, the RFC was delegating political power to men who also possessed great economic power. American Individualism recognized the potential danger of such relationships; the President acquiesced in this arrangement because it was an inexpensive means of acquiring talented assistance, and because he believed that the whole operation would be temporary. [46]

The establishment of the RFC was indeed a startling departure from traditional American public policies. Never before had peacetime government become so intimately involved in private economic affairs. The gravity of the decision was not overlooked by perceptive observers. Senator George Norris of Nebraska maintained that even in his wildest dreams he had never envisioned "putting the government into business as far as this bill would put it." [47] Hoover also understood the implications of his decision; in fact he was somewhat anxious about the RFC. Technically, he was committed to governmental intervention in the economy as the only means of stimulating a general recovery. But a technical commitment did not necessarily imply a concomitant psychological commitment. The administration, although standing on the threshold of the New Deal, was reluctant to create a federal agency capable of exerting controls over the economy. To ease their fears Hoover and his associates sought a psychological rationale—a justification for their unprecedented public policies. Ready to activate an enormously powerful federal agency, they needed a historical frame of reference. They sought a precedent for their actions in World War I, a time in American history when similarly extraordinary measures had been warranted. [48]

For Hoover, the Great War and the Great Depression were related phenomena. In the President's view, the depression was simply the last phase of World War I. In 1931 he said that

. . . I believe you will all agree with me that the destruction of life and property, the great tax burdens, and the social and political instability which resulted from the Great War have had large responsibility in its [the depression's] origins. Over three quarters of the commercially important population of the world has been in a state of social and political upheaval at some time during the past three years. . . . These political and social disturbances necessarily undermine that confidence on which economic life, both domestic and international, must thrive.[49]

In seeing the depression as an outgrowth of the war and both as a threat to national survival, Hoover could easily compare the magnitude of the two great crises. Both had brought drains on national resources, and both had become in their own time the country's most important priority. During the debate over the RFC bill, for example, Hoover said that

combating a depression is, indeed, like a great war, in that it is not a battle on a single front but upon many fronts. These measures all are a necessary addition to the efficient and courageous efforts of our citizens throughout the nation. [50]

Early in February 1932, the President went on to say,

The forces with which we are contending are . . . invisible forces, yet potent in their powers of destruction. We are engaged in a fight upon a hundred fronts just as positive, just as definite and requiring just as greatly the moral courage, the organized action, the unity of strength, and the sense of devotion in every community as in war. [51]

Other officials of the Hoover administration shared his view of the crisis and repeated his constant allusions to the war. Ogden Mills remarked that the

great war against depression is being fought on many fronts in many parts of the world. One of the most stupendous activities of this great front has been the long battle . . . to carry our financial structure safely through the worldwide collapse. [52]

Eugene Meyer drew on military vocabulary to describe the banking situation in 1931 and 1932 as a "retreating action, conducting a retreat and counterattacking whenever we had opportunities." [53] Such words as "tactics," "enemy," "fronts," "machine," "attack," and "campaign" recur frequently in the speeches of administration officials during 1931-1933, suggesting a powerful psychological tension in their policies. [54]

Military rhetoric and wartime images helped justify the momentous changes the administration was making in public policy. The proposal for the Reconstruction Finance Corporation carried serious psychological consequences, particularly for men whose careers had been devoted to controlling the exercise of governmental power. Suddenly to be forced by the pressure of impersonal economic forces to contradict years of traditional attitudes would naturally tend to be traumatic. The analogy between depression and war was a convenient rhetorical and psychological device that justified the administration's actions and soothed its misgivings about the stunning expansion of federal authority represented by the RFC. The analogue-of-war idea put history at Hoover's disposal. He had maintained throughout his career that wartime threats to national security often required a suspension of American Individualism and a creation of powerful agencies to defend the nation. By comparing the depression to the war Hoover could justify his own economic measures. In a 1932 radio address, he said:

As I have stated before, in the shifting battle against depression, we shall need to adopt new measures and new tactics as the battle moves on. The essential thing is that we should build soundly and solidly for the future.[55]

When he called for the creation of the RFC, Hoover institutionalized the analogue-of-war concept: the RFC was little more than the reincarnation of the WFC, which had its origins in the American past—it had served two presidents of two parties, Wilson and Harding; and it had dealt effectively with financial difficulties in the war and postwar years. Therefore Hoover patterned the RFC after its World War I predecessor, looking on the RFC as the reapplication of an emergency economic measure.

Bankers and industrialists employed the same tool to justify their support for the Reconstruction Finance Corporation. They too needed to rationalize their abandonment of laissez-faire, and the analogue-of-war concept provided them with a plausible argument. In a news summary of the congressional debate over the RFC bill the *Magazine of Wall Street* said that big business,

always complaining of public intervention in economic matters, is, ironically enough, as insistent now for governmental relief as the farmers have been and are.

In fact, the Reconstruction Finance Corporation is regarded as primarily for the relief from the top down, through the banks and railroads. It is earnestly advocated and supported by the great bankers, railroad presidents, and industrialists.

The answer made by representatives of business to the charge of socialism is that in all great emergencies, war for example, governments have always thrown themselves into the breach, because only they can organize and mobilize the whole strength of the nation. In war every country becomes practically a dictatorship and every man's resources are at its command; the country is now in an equally great emergency.[56]

With the creation of the RFC, old assumptions of a natural antipathy between business and government severely weakened; both government and business realized that during times of crisis—particularly wars or depressions—cooperation was essential to the national well-being. It was only one step further to argue that it was also essential for the continuation of prosperity. Along with President Hoover, the business community had come to accept the need for the federal government to underwrite prosperity by assisting the private sector and to plan for future growth and development. In the years that followed, businessmen would not contest the principle of government assistance, however critical they were of the methods. Ironically on January 22, 1932, when Hoover signed the Reconstruction Finance Corporation Act, he helped pave the way for the New Deal.

Hoover's personal ordeal revolved around the relationship between the federal government and the private economy. The severity of the financial crisis and the complexity of the modern, industrial economy demanded federal intervention, but because of shortcomings in Hoover's economic thought, the RFC ultimately failed to ease the depression. Hoover's confidence that he would be able to dismantle the RFC rested on these same economic assumptions; and as the depression and the financial crisis worsened, he lost control of the very bureaucratic apparatus he had created. Far from dismantling the RFC, Hoover was forced over the next fourteen months to strengthen it through new responsibilities and more funds. He never imagined that the RFC would survive for twenty years, would loan more than $50 billion to tens of thousands of businesses, and would become one of the most powerful government agencies in the history of the United States. The Reconstruction Finance Corporation became a bureaucratic giant not because of any internal dynamic of its own, but because the huge dimensions of the depression and the economic miscalculations of the Hoover administration forced it to assume new responsibilities. Hoover had ceased to be a slave of American Individualism, but his new freedom shortly succumbed to the limitations inherent in his economic thought. In the end, Herbert Hoover not only sacrificed his political philosophy, but he sacrificed it to a losing cause.

5

Failure of Consensus

BY the first week of February, the Reconstruction Finance Corporation was a beehive of activity, granting dozens of loans each day and evaluating hundreds of applications. In view of the huge volume of applications, the Board of Directors divided their responsibilities to increase efficiency. Charles Dawes, Eugene Meyer, and Ogden Mills handled all loans to banks, trust companies, and other urban financial institutions; Jesse Jones and Harvey Couch generally supervised the RFC Railroad Division; and Paul Bestor and Wilson McCarthy looked after the agricultural loans and assistance to rural financial institutions.[1]

Because of Hoover's philosophy and the backgrounds of the RFC directors, the corporation moved cautiously. Its directors were businessmen with a wealth of experience in banking, railroad finance, agriculture, and public utilities; all the directors hoped to end the financial crisis without too much expense for the federal government. They insisted that all RFC loans be repaid promptly and that all collateral fully secure the corporation's investment. To ensure the safety of the funds, the RFC established strict collateral requirements, most of which compared in severity to those imposed by the National Credit Corporation. They accepted as collateral only 80 percent of the market value of the highest grade securities and were unwilling to accept more than 50 percent of the market value of other assets. A bank accepting an RFC loan had to deposit its most liquid assets, at only a fraction of their previous value, as collateral. The corporation also reserved the authority to demand increased collateral deposits in face of future declines in securities and asset values. Combined with the six-month maturation date for most of the initial RFC loans, these regulations would prevent the corporation from significantly easing the liquidity problems of many banks.[2]

The RFC directors also shared Hoover's fears that making loans to a variety of financial institutions might hurt usual lenders or drive them out of the market. To prevent unfair competition with private institutions, the directors purposely set RFC interest rates far above prevailing money market levels. By making loans to banks and railroads at 6 percent, the RFC could rest assured that it was not undermining the private sector of the economy. This assurance made RFC loans very expensive[3] and eventually limited the corporation's effectiveness. So, although the RFC was structurally prepared for bold action, its operating spirit was deliberately cautious because of fear of competing with legitimate business. Administration leaders, compelled by their own fears to limit the RFC, began their bank reconstruction program too carefully.[4]

Cautious policies were exactly what the economy did not need. Because of the frightened mood of bank depositors across the country, the RFC faced a particularly dangerous financial crisis. The failure of a large urban bank could easily set off a chain reaction of runs on other banks in the area. When a banker was unable to liquefy enough of his assets to meet the cash demand, he had to suspend operations and go into receivership. Hoover realized that confidence was an important element in any economic situation — if depositors had had strong faith in the banking system, bankers could have remained in business without federal assistance. Hoover and the RFC directors believed the corporation could assure the public that the federal government was prepared to make loans only to banks whose assets were essentially sound; that commitment would reassure frightened depositors and enable banks to deal with deflated securities markets and their capital problems in an atmosphere of relative calm. But if Hoover understood the importance of public confidence, he underestimated the forces of public fear and skepticism. The RFC was not able to restore optimism; bank failures had become an endemic problem in the United States, and the public was especially fearful.[5]

The administration also erred in assuming that lack of public confidence was the only weakness in the financial structure. Genuine structural weaknesses were also present. Commercial banks, suffering from frozen loans and depreciated securities prices, desperately needed long-term loans — three to five years — that would permit them to liquidate their assets without further eroding general market values. They also needed new capital. As the value of bank assets depreciated, bankers found their deposit liabilities exceeding the value of their assets. But under RFC provisions the corporation could only make loans, not provide new capital, to the troubled banks. Progressives in Congress had insisted that the language of the RFC act specifically state that loans be "fully secured" to prohibit any federal giveaway program for private business. The administration gladly accepted the provision, for Hoover too was reluctant about underwriting private business. But as long as asset values remained depreciated and defaults on commercial loans persisted, government loans would not provide a permanent solution. By law, the Reconstruction Finance Corporation could not supply the banks with fresh capital, and by design it would not provide them with long-term loans. As a solution to the financial crisis, the RFC was a disappointing failure.[6]

Without question the creation of the RFC brought a temporary sense of confidence to the American economy. Another piece of legislation — to relax Federal Reserve eligibility requirements — helped reinforce RFC activities by shoring up the confidence of commercial bankers. As early as July 1931 Senator Arthur Vandenberg of Michigan asked Hoover to permit

Federal Reserve banks to discount sound but slower assets, such as high-class corporate bonds. Hoover included the proposal in his October and December messages to Congress, but Senator Glass remained adamantly opposed to the idea. As bank failures continued to increase in January 1932 and the flow of gold abroad assumed serious proportions, the administration warned that without the legislation it might become necessary to abandon the gold standard. After a meeting on February 8 with President Hoover, Charles Dawes, George Harrison, and Eugene Meyer, who all vigorously reemphasized the need for relaxing the eligibility regulations, Senator Glass finally relented and agreed to sponsor the legislation. On February 27, 1932, Congress liberalized the eligibility requirements for Federal Reserve banks. The act permitted member banks to discount their commercial paper as well as their self-liquidating assets and greatly increased their potential liquidity. The member banks enthusiastically welcomed the measure.[7]

Along with his decisions to establish the Reconstruction Finance Corporation and reform the eligibility requirements of the Federal Reserve banks, President Hoover returned to the traditional formula of voluntary action to ease the pressures on the financial system. Since early in 1930 the amount of currency in circulation had grown by more than $1 billion as depositors turned their bank deposits into cash. This action had intensified the liquidity problems bankers were facing by compounding the already serious declines in asset values. So early in February 1932 Hoover created the Citizens' Reconstruction Organization, a voluntary association to sponsor an antihoarding campaign. Hoover obtained Frank Knox, owner of the *Chicago Daily News,* to direct the organization, and Hoover and Knox sponsored a national conference at the White House of more than forty private associations to discuss and promote the campaign. Throughout the country local Citizens' Reconstruction Organization groups were established to support the publicity campaign. The President placed great faith in the organization and hoped that it would complement the RFC and the new Federal Reserve rules in reviving public confidence in the banking system.[8]

The first month of operation of the RFC was perhaps the high point of the Hoover presidency. Despite the stringent RFC regulations, applications of thousands of desperate banks were received. During February the corporation resolved several disquieting situations and public confidence seemed to revive. The RFC loaned $15 million to the Transamerica Corporation in San Francisco to save the Bank of America, one of the nation's largest banking chains.[9] A $7 million loan two weeks later saved the East Tennessee National Bank in Knoxville and relieved depositors throughout the border states. The RFC authorized loans totaling more than $45 million to banks and trust companies during February. Another $25 million went to several of the nation's largest railroads.[10] In addition Secretary of Agriculture Arthur Hyde actively dispensed RFC funds that had been set aside for crop loans. The maximum loan consisted of $400; by the end of March Hyde had loaned nearly $40 million to over 200,000 farmers, permitting them to hold their crops until profitable marketing conditions developed.[11]

By April the RFC seemed to be saving the financial system by preventing bank suspensions and railroad receiverships. Bank closings dropped sharply. From a high of 66 suspensions in the first week of February, closings during the following weeks declined from 32 to 27 to 8.[12] The administration interpreted this development favorably, believing that it confirmed RFC effectiveness. During February and March, the corporation authorized 974 separate loans totaling over $238 million, of which approximately $160 million went to banks and $60 million to railroads. They distributed the remaining $18 million to building and loan associations, savings banks, life insurance companies, and mortgage loan companies. Clearly the RFC intended to concentrate its resources on assisting commercial banks and railroads, hoping that most remaining financial institutions would be able to survive in the more relaxed financial atmosphere. Only 45 banks failed in March, compared to 334 in January and 125 in February. The financial situation finally seemed to be under control.[13]

Administration leaders were particularly pleased about the modest decline during March in the volume of currency in circulation—proof, they believed, that the efforts of the RFC and the Citizens' Reconstruction Organization were reviving public confidence. Bank capital remained impaired, but the availability of RFC loans seemed to have calmed bankers. The scenario of economic recovery that Hoover, Mills, and Meyer had originally envisioned appeared to be on the verge of fulfillment. Morale among RFC directors and in the White House would never be higher; they had undertaken an extraordinary responsibility and seemed to be getting extraordinary results. The administration confidently anticipated an increase in commercial lending and a revival of industrial production and employment.[14]

Unfortunately, this world of confidence and hope was temporary. Late in March the corporation became the object of bitter criticism from progressive Republicans and liberal Democrats. For them the apparent success of the RFC in dealing with the banking crisis was irrelevant; they still disapproved of the philosophy behind the corporation's activities and deplored the fact that no governmental assistance had gone to the poor and the unemployed. President Hoover was assaulted from the political left, and he realized that the RFC was about to become a pawn in the presidential election that was drawing near. The general consensus of January 1932 had begun to fall apart.

In mid-March the first sign of trouble appeared. On March 19 Hoover convened a special meeting of the Association of Railway Executives, the Interstate Commerce Commission (ICC), and the RFC Board of Directors in an attempt to iron out a controversy over RFC railroad loans. One of the main RFC objectives for 1932 was to end the wave of railroad receiverships that had developed the previous year. The administration realized that in 1932 alone $250 million of railroad securities would mature, along with over $150 million of short-term paper. The railroads would need large RFC loans to make payments and prevent widespread financial delinquency. The loan payments and securities redemptions would shore up the value of railroad bonds and strengthen the asset position of commercial banks, savings banks, and life insurance companies. The administration and the RFC were strongly committed to that goal as the only way of preventing further erosions in the portfolios of thousands of private financial institutions.[15]

Early in March the RFC agreed to lend the Missouri-Pacific Railroad a total of $12,800,000. The Interstate Commerce Commission was reluctant to approve the loan because $5,850,000 of the total was to be turned over to J. P. Morgan and Company; Kuhn, Loeb and Company; and the Guaranty Trust Company of New York City as payment on earlier loans. The ICC insisted that both commercial and investment bankers extend or refinance railroad obligations before the Reconstruction Finance Corporation made loans to the roads. Joseph B. Eastman, head of the ICC, thought that the RFC loans, unless given under these conditions, would assist Wall Street more than they would help the railroads. But assisting the banking houses was exactly what the Hoover administration intended to do. The RFC railroad loan program was not intended to be an end in itself; it was designed to stabilize the value of railroad bonds and in the process underwrite the value of commercial bank and money market assets. Meyer resented the ICC demand; he believed that instead of liquefying financial assets it would burden banks, savings banks, and insurance companies with heavier debts. Although the ICC commissioners eventually approved the Missouri-Pacific loan, their grumblings stimulated new criticisms of the RFC.[16]

As news of the Missouri-Pacific loan controversy became public knowledge, progressive Republicans, especially Senators James Couzens of Michigan, Robert La Follette, and William Borah of Idaho, picked up the politically explosive issue. Even before the loan Hoover was facing political defections from the left wing of the Republican party. Throughout the 1920s the party had been divided between such Old Guard senators as Reed Smoot of Utah, George Moses of New Hampshire, and Simon Fess of Ohio and such left-wing progressives as La Follette and Borah. By 1932 the progressive group had grown to include (in addition to Couzens, La Follette, and Borah) James Blaine of Wisconsin, Bronson Cutting of New Mexico, George Norris of Nebraska, Peter Norbeck of South Dakota, Smith Brookhart of Iowa, Hiram Johnson of California, Gerald Nye and Lynn Frazier of North Dakota, and Henrik Shipstead of Minnesota. Most of these progressives had serious reservations about the reelection of Hoover and had already deserted him during the 71st Congress over the nomination of John J. Parker to the Supreme Court, the Muscle Shoals issue, and the veterans' bonus bill. Several of them, such as George Norris, were already committed to Franklin Roosevelt as the next president of the United States. (In fact, Norris organized the National Progressive League in September 1932 to garner Republican support for

Roosevelt.) Most progressive Republicans, genuinely frustrated with Hoover (and some facing reelection in 1932), were anxious to disassociate themselves from Hoover. The Missouri-Pacific loan controversy provided an excellent opportunity. Couzens charged that during the congressional hearings in December and January, the administration had promoted RFC railroad loans to assist the roads in meeting long-term obligations which could not be refinanced because of poor money market conditions; the administration did not contemplate or even intimate to Congress the wholesale assumption of current bank loans by the RFC.[17] Senator William Borah added that no

good reason has been shown for approving a government loan to enable the applicant to make a 50 percent payment on the bank loans maturing April 1. I would have no difficulty in joining in such approval if there were any evidence that the loan is needed in the public interest. But no one has made or attempted to make such a showing.[18]

For progressives, the RFC railroad loans were only one more example of the federal government assisting the rich while ignoring the poor.

The administration leaders were upset by the criticism, since they believed the reasons for the loan were self-evident. If the Missouri-Pacific Railroad defaulted, the value of its bonds would fall commensurately and hurt every bank that had invested in the road.[19] The RFC directors supported the philosophy behind the corporation's loans. President Charles Dawes, in testimony before the House Ways and Means Committee in April, strongly defended the RFC:

The reason why Congress authorized loans by the RFC to railroads, as disclosed by the discussions in Congress, was not only for the protection of railroad corporations as the backbone of our transportation system and as employers of hundreds of thousands of men, but for the protection as well of the trustee institutions of this country, including insurance companies and savings banks, owning the securities of railroads, in which institutions and their normal functioning the great public has a direct interest.[20]

Progressive Republicans were not convinced by the administration's argument that improved railroad bond values would strengthen the entire money market.[21] They were convinced that the RFC injected the federal government too deeply into ordinary finance, lining Wall Street pockets at the expense of the taxpayer. Consequently, they sponsored a bill early in April to suspend all RFC loans and ignited a legislative controversy that would plague the corporation until the inauguration of Franklin D. Roosevelt in 1933.[22] Liberal Democrats echoed the criticisms of the progressive Republicans.

Ironically, the Missouri-Pacific controversy developed simultaneously with the issue of bonus payments to American veterans. While publicly defending the philosophy behind the Missouri-Pacific loan, Dawes, Meyer, and Mills all condemned the idea of early bonus payments to the country's unemployed workers.[23] This attitude reinforced the fears of critics that the Hoover administration was oblivious to the needs of the poor and cared only for the rich and the powerful. For liberal Democrats the administration's description of the "trickle-down" effect of RFC loans was only a deceptive means of subduing the popular reaction to economic discrimination. [24]

The very premise on which the RFC was founded, that of federal aid to the nation's largest and most powerful economic units, offended many liberals. The "trickle-down" theory provided them with a devastating campaign theme in 1932. [25] In April, just after the Missouri-Pacific controversy surfaced, Franklin Roosevelt inaugurated the theme he employed throughout the election campaign: Hoover, the Republicans, and the RFC were concerned only with rescuing bankers and wealthy businessmen. In his famous "Forgotten Man" speech of April 8, Roosevelt said:

The present administration . . . has either forgotten or it does not want to remember the infantry of our economic army. These unhappy times call for the building of plans that rest upon the forgotten, the unorganized but the indispensable units of economic power, for plans like those of 1917 that build from the bottom up and not from the top down, that put their faith once more in the forgotten man at the bottom of the pyramid. . . . The two billion dollar fund which President Hoover and the Congress have put at the disposal of big banks, the railroads, and the corporations of the nation is not for him. [26]

Other Democrats repeated Roosevelt's sentiments and touched a responsive chord with the frightened public. Many people had been stirred to righteous indignation by early policies of the RFC. That the corporation appeared to be successful in stabilizing the crisis was of no consequence; liberals criticized the RFC not for what it accomplished, but for what it failed to do.

The criticisms of progressives and liberals widened existing differences on the RFC board. As long as an external consensus prevailed about corporation activities, internal political divisions on the board remained dormant; but when the corporation began to be criticized from outside, board members naturally aligned themselves with certain positions. In the Missouri-Pacific controversy Meyer, Mills, and Bestor favored a policy of bailing out banks from their high-risk loans, since this was the only way to revive the bond market and restore solvency to certain financial assets. Although Charles Dawes agreed with RFC railroad philosophy, he resented the effect of raising bond levels because RFC funds would find their way into Wall Street banking houses; he sided with the ICC in demanding that the RFC actively seek to renegotiate and refinance at least part of the railroad debt. Jesse Jones, Harvey Couch, and Wilson McCarthy supported Dawes and argued that before the RFC approved railroad loans, banks and insurance companies would have to show good faith and a cooperative spirit by agreeing to extend railroad obligations. [27] This is not to say that they agreed with the progressive senators; to some extent all the RFC directors, both Democrats and Republicans, accepted the "trickle-down" idea of recovery. It was just that Dawes, Jones, Couch, and McCarthy were more reluctant than

Meyer, Mills, and Bestor to underwrite completely the bank debts that railroads had accumulated with eastern financial concerns.

Hoover, at least in this stage of RFC development, maintained great confidence in Eugene Meyer and Ogden Mills. He communicated with them by telephone daily and met with them several times each week. The President had intentionally permitted the RFC to become a bipartisan agency to ease its passage through Congress and to shield it from external political criticism, but in doing so he guaranteed a certain amount of political conflict among the directors. The division of opinion was also along philosophical and personal lines. The Democrats (Couch, McCarthy, and Jones) aligned themselves against the Republicans (Mills, Meyer, and Bestor). Only Dawes was politically independent, often mediating between the two groups. But their most significant differences were personal and philosophical rather than political. Dawes joined McCarthy, Jones, and Couch in resenting Meyer's domination of the board and his close working relationship with the President. They felt that Meyer was dictatorial in making decisions; even though he was often in the minority, he was able to prevail because of the support he received from Hoover. The Missouri-Pacific loan was a case in point. Meyer had succeeded even though Dawes, Jones, Couch, and McCarthy essentially agreed with the ICC.

At the same time, Jones, Dawes, McCarthy, and Couch thought that the triumvirate of Mills, Meyer, and Bestor was too closely associated with the problems of the eastern banking community and not concerned enough with farmers and rural banks. They felt that Meyer was too willing to assist the largest institutions even when they really did not need assistance. That Meyer also had the confidence of the President only intensified their dilemma.[28] These differences became more exaggerated in the upcoming months, and the personal relationships on the board seriously deteriorated.

President Hoover had expected such internal controversies. Complete unanimity on the RFC board was impossible, especially in an election year. What he did not anticipate was criticism from the banking community. As RFC procedural guidelines became established and more widely understood, many bankers began to express mild displeasure with the corporation. While liberal Democrats and progressive Republicans attacked Hoover and the RFC for giving too much assistance to big business, conservative bankers attacked them for being too cautious and restrictive, for not loaning enough money, or for loaning it with interest and collateral requirements that were far too severe. Although most bankers, like the administration, hoped that the corporation would not have to spend its entire appropriation, they nevertheless expected the RFC to spend whatever proved necessary to remedy the situation. For financial leaders the end of the depression, not the safety of the government's funds, was the primary objective of the Reconstruction Finance Corporation. An editorial in the *Wall Street Journal* on February 3, 1932, expressed that expectation:

. . . it is not to be supposed that the R.F.C. will tell the banks to sell-out the collateral before seeking a loan, if the collateral appears to promise recovery of marketable value once the general pressure for liquidity has been lifted. It is just to provide liquidity without enforced selling out of assets or pledged collateral that the Corporation was established.

What needs to be remembered is that Congress has decided that federal funds and taxing power to a possible maximum of $2,000,000,000 shall be staked upon the prospects of industrial recovery enhanced as those prospects are assumed to be by this very advance of additional capital through the banks. In the nature of the case, the Reconstruction Finance Corporation cannot hold out for the assurance of safety in every specific loan. [29]

But as far as financial leaders were concerned, the RFC was not fulfilling their expectations in the first months of 1932. Many bankers believed that the corporation's primary objective was not to rescue troubled banks but to prevent a loss of government funds because of its high interest rates and severe collateral regulations. The corporation's loans in 1932 often compounded the problem of frozen assets, since bankers often were forced to use their most liquid assets as security for RFC advances. If withdrawal pressures continued or intensified, they claimed the banks would have to sell their less marketable assets, often at greatly deflated prices, to obtain the cash necessary to meet depositor demands. This action would further erode their capital and leave them ineligible for future RFC loans because the value of their collateral would no longer cover the loans they needed. In April 1932, for example, the RFC loaned the Reno National Bank of Nevada over $1.1 million but in the process took as collateral over $3 million of the bank's best assets, leaving it ill-prepared for further pressures from depositors. [30]

The Reconstruction Finance Corporation also insisted that all loans carry short-term maturity dates, forcing many banks to repay loans long before their fundamental solvency had been restored and imposing additional pressures on them. For many banks receiving RFC assistance, survival became a month-to-month affair. The Henderson Banking Company of Reno, Nevada, for example, received an initial RFC loan of $150,000 on May 17, 1932; on June 28 it had to request another $55,000 and in July it had to apply for another $200,000. Many bankers were frustrated; the RFC, ostensibly designed to attack vigorously the nation's economic problems, had instead become a cautious, conservative government bank that was more concerned with the safety of its own funds than with the condition of the financial system.[31] Hoover and the RFC directors could not simultaneously satisfy liberal Democrats, progressive Republicans, and the business community; the Reconstruction Finance Corporation was becoming a distinct political liability despite its apparent initial success in easing the pressures on the money market. [32]

Finally, a host of Federal Reserve officials joined the banking community in criticizing the RFC. From the beginning several prominent Federal Reserve officials expressed fear that the powerful RFC might eclipse the Federal Reserve system as the dominant public institution in the money market. In December 1931, George Seay, governor of the Federal Reserve Bank of Richmond, worried that the RFC might become a "permanent burden upon the Federal Reserve System." [33] Other leaders on the Federal Reserve Board, especially Charles Hamlin, resented the appointment of their own governor, Eugene Meyer, to head the RFC, feeling that he gave the corporation priority and neglected the needs of the Federal Reserve system. [34] These internecine jealousies strained the relationship between the RFC and the Federal Reserve system, creating a resentment that grew under the political pressures exerted by the Great Depression.

Consequently, such prominent Federal Reserve officials as E. A. Goldenweisar, Charles Hamlin, and Adolph Miller in Washington and George Harrison and Owen D. Young in New York worked out a recovery program that gave economic supremacy to the Federal Reserve system but responsibility for stabilizing the financial crisis to the Reconstruction Finance Corporation. The main duty of the RFC, they felt, was to prevent both bank failures and railroad receiverships, relieving bankers of liquidity fears and calming the public mind. Once the bankers felt confident about their solvency, the Federal Reserve Board would revive commercial lending by manipulating discount rates and reserve requirements, purchasing government securities, and educating the public. Banks would then be more willing to loan money and have the excess reserves to do so. In this broad program of economic recovery, the RFC would play an important but clearly secondary role. [35]

Although the views of the Federal Reserve Board and the administration were not mutually exclusive, both proved to be economically naive. Hoover and his associates on the RFC board could tolerate criticism when they were convinced that their own theoretical position was correct. But during the spring of 1932 they gradually realized that their economic theories were not working. To be sure, a financial recovery appeared to be in the making, but hope that an industrial recovery would automatically follow was slim. Although bank failures had declined and bank deposits had begun to increase, industrial recovery had not begun; there was no expansion in the volume of commercial loans to finance production and employment. In fact, the liquidation of commercial loans continued unabated. Bankers, it appeared, were choosing to maintain their liquidity rather than expand their lending. The banks were accumulating excess reserves and their investment policies were undergoing drastic change; they were now doing exactly what they had failed to do during the 1920s: concentrating heavily on investment in government securities. [36] Without active commercial lending by stable commercial banks, the administration felt that its recovery program was doomed. The morale and convictions of the administration deteriorated when industrial production failed to revive in the wake of improved financial conditions.

No one in the administration or in the Federal Reserve system really understood the phenomenon of excess reserves; that is, why bankers would refuse to relieve themselves of that financial burden by increasing their commercial loans and investments after the Federal Reserve banks had fulfilled their obligation to create the excess reserves. During the spring of 1932 over $500 million in government securities were purchased, raising the excess reserves of member banks to $280 million by mid-May.[37] Yet commercial loans remained depressed; bankers preferred to maintain nonearning assets as a safety valve in case the liquidity crisis resumed. Rather than accept any responsibility for the persistence of the industrial depression and the liquidation of commercial credit, Federal Reserve officials sought an explanation, or scapegoat, for the lack of response in the banking community. The RFC became their target.

It was easy to blame the RFC for the failure of bankers to shift their excess reserves into profitable loans and investments. Federal Reserve authorities maintained the RFC obviously had not relieved bankers of their liquidity fears; and the RFC, not the Federal Reserve system, must bear the responsibility for the continuation of the depression. Federal Reserve officials joined bankers in criticizing RFC credit policies. They urged Meyer and Hoover to relax RFC interest and collateral requirements and to concentrate more on improving the general banking situation than on protecting the government's funds. The RFC, they argued, must be prepared to accept certain losses in order to liquefy bank assets. Until the corporation liberalized its procedures and overcame its fears of losing money, the Federal Reserve Board could not be expected to bring about any significant expansion of bank lending. The burden of responsibility for the continuing depression, according to men like E. A. Goldenweisar, George Harrison, Owen D. Young, Charles Hamlin, and George Seay, rested solely on the Reconstruction Finance Corporation. Hoover generally agreed with the assumption that bankers did not yet feel secure enough about the future to employ their excess reserves; but the administration resented the patronizingly critical attitude of Reserve officials.[38]

By late spring, morale within the administration was rapidly deteriorating. Liberal Democrats, progressive Republicans, and bankers were all critical of RFC policies and the fact that the RFC had not been able to stimulate an industrial recovery. The President was angry. He felt that descriptions of RFC parsimony were unjustified since it had loaned more than $500 million by the end of May. And the critical bankers who had received that money were not passing on those funds in the form of new loans. Hoover sincerely believed that a genuine recovery depended completely on bankers restoring loans to their predepression levels. Under these circumstances, Hoover's relationship with Meyer began to show strain. For months Meyer had promised Hoover that bankers would respond to RFC loans by increasing their business loans, but no such expansion had occurred. In view of Hoover's growing frustration with the banking community and the criticisms of Meyer's leadership of the RFC, it was no wonder that their personal relationship wore thin. Hoover realized that a change of policy and even of leadership might be necessary for the corporation. [39]

The President began to search for a method to force bankers to increase their commercial loans. By this time he was quite upset with them. At first they criticized the RFC for being too cautious and conservative; and then when they had received government funds, they refused to convert them into credit and instead chose to liquefy their own financial positions at the expense of the economy as a whole. Once again the older idea of beneficent self-interest seemed to conflict with the goal of social progress. But Hoover still insisted that significant demand for credit by legitimate businessmen existed throughout the country, and banker selfishness and parochialism were prolonging the duration and impact of the depression.[40]

Hoover supported a financial project undertaken by the Federal Reserve Bank of New York in May. Secretary of the Treasury Ogden Mills had consulted closely with the directors of the bank, who had created a banking and industrial committee in the New York Federal Reserve District. Owen D. Young was chairman of the committee, whose function was to coordinate private credit supplies with business demands. The President was impressed with the idea, particularly because of its voluntaristic overtones, and he urged the establishment of similar committees in each of the twelve Federal Reserve districts. He recognized that in its ultimate objective the Reconstruction Finance Corporation had not yet succeeded.[41]

But the President had not given up his hopes for the RFC. Although it had not yet stimulated a general economic revival, Hoover believed that it had at least stabilized the financial system. In April and the first two weeks of May, bank failures continued to decline, bank deposits increased, and national confidence appeared to be growing stronger. Although administration leaders were troubled by the criticisms of the RFC and frustrated with the continuing erosion of bank credit, they still believed that bank credit would eventually revive as a result of RFC loans. But now they wondered whether the revival would occur soon enough to be a political asset.[42]

The administration's limited sense of economic security was short-lived. Financial institutions still suffered from badly depressed assets and impaired capital structures. The banking community's apparent stability rested on a shaky foundation. Although public confidence was stronger than it had been in years, any breach in that confidence, especially in a major financial market, could trigger nationwide panic and bank suspensions. The President's modified sense of accomplishment evaporated in early June as word spread of a new financial crisis in Chicago.[43] On June 6 Charles Dawes, because of difficulties with Meyer and problems involving his Central Republic Bank and Trust Company in Chicago, resigned as president of the RFC. His resignation increased the administration's fears. Despite $500 million in RFC loans since January, the possibility of a national banking disaster was still present.[44]

A series of failures among small banks in northern Illinois during late May and early June undermined depositor confidence in the Midwest, and runs began on some of Chicago's largest financial institutions. Even before the June panic the Central Republic Bank and Trust Company was suffering from deflated assets and the collapse of the Insull utilities empire. By late June, runs on the bank were so serious that Dawes tentatively decided to suspend operation. Jesse Jones and Wilson McCarthy were in Chicago attending the Democratic National Convention, and Dawes got in touch with them. They analyzed the situation and decided that only massive assistance from the RFC could save the bank. Melvin Traylor, head of the First National Bank of Chicago and a dark horse candidate for the Democratic presidential nomination, called Hoover and told him that if the Central Republic Bank closed, every other bank in Chicago would also be forced to close; and if the Chicago money market collapsed, the nation could expect an immediate national banking panic and the suspension of every bank in the country. Traylor's predictions alarmed Hoover. Bank failures for June had climbed to 151, the highest monthly total since January,[45] and deposits of member banks of the Federal Reserve system declined in June by over $400 million.[46] The President agreed with Traylor. Hoover faced a manifestly simple choice: either save the Central Republic Bank or preside over the destruction of the United States banking system. On June 27, the RFC authorized a loan of $90 million and took as collateral every asset of the Central Republic Bank and Trust Company.[47]

The unprecedented loan postponed the national banking disaster. Although the Central Republic Bank was unable to survive, it underwent liquidation two months later without public fanfare or panic.[48] Dawes had immediately publicized the RFC loan to reassure his depositors. As a result of this loan and the additional $130 million that the RFC loaned to banks and trust companies during June, the crisis in the Midwest eased. In July bank failures dropped to 131.[49] In August bank deposits increased again, and bank suspensions dropped to only 85.[50] The administration took heart, hoping that the summer crisis was the last economic problem they would have to face. They hoped bank failures would continue to drop in future months, bank credit would begin to increase, industrial production would revive, and unemployment would decline — bringing the Great Depression to an end.

Though financially justifiable within the context of economic conditions and thought in 1932, the loan to the Central Republic Bank was a political disaster for it strongly reinforced liberal and progressive criticisms of the RFC. Like the Missouri-Pacific loan, the Central Republic loan became a disastrous irony for the Hoover administration. Early in June the municipal leaders of Chicago sent a delegation headed by Mayor Anton J. Cermak to the RFC offices in Washington to appeal for aid to the city. Their request probably would have been acceptable under the amendment that Senator Royal Copeland had offered to the RFC act in January. Specifically, Cermak asked for a loan of $70 million secured by city tax warrants to enable the city to pay its teachers and municipal employees. The RFC lacked legal authority to make loans to municipalities.[51] Although the denial was unavoidable it attracted bitter political abuse, for almost simultaneously with the denial came the news of the loan to the Central Republic Bank. The Hoover administration, it was charged, withheld $70 million to pay the salaries of thousands of impoverished workers in Chicago but gave $90 million to a single Chicago bank. Hoover attempted to counter criticism by arguing that millions of people benefited from the bank loan—had the Central Republic failed, every citizen with savings in a bank would have been hurt by the chain reaction of failures that would have ensued. But all the statistics could not offset the fact that $90 million had gone to one bank while thousands of poor Chicagoans received nothing. The whole affair haunted the President through the election in November. [52]

The loan to the Central Republic Bank also brought renewed criticism from small bankers who contended that the RFC channeled its resources to the largest and wealthiest financial institutions and ignored the needs of thousands of small banks. The RFC, they argued, was only repeating the National Credit Corporation's neglect of small banks. In rebuttal, the directors of the RFC assembled a statistical file demonstrating that over 70 percent of all RFC loans had gone to banks located in towns with populations of less than 5,000, and that only 2 percent of the loans had gone to banks in cities of one million or more.[53] That did not quiet the critics, however, who were not interested in *where* the money went but in *how much* went to the large banks. The same statistics provided the critics with the information that over 40 percent of RFC funds had gone to banks located in cities containing more than 200,000 people.

The critics of the Dawes loan failed to realize that considering the nature of the financial community in 1932, this was a normal development. In 1932 approximately 22,000 banking units operated in the country; only two hundred of these banks, however, less than 1 percent of the total, possessed over 40 percent of all the nation's bank deposits. The entire banking system was weak in 1932—large banks as well as small suffered from frozen and depressed assets and frightened depositors. Both small and large banks appealed to the RFC for assistance in 1932. Banks with massive deposits were often burdened with massive amounts of frozen assets; if they had to come to the RFC for help, it was likely that they required a large loan. The critics were right: the RFC did grant substantial loans to large banks. In 1932, the RFC authorized approximately $950 million in loans to banks and trust companies, of which $330 million went to twenty-six of the nation's two hundred largest banks. But this was certainly not inconsistent in a financial system where 1 percent of the banks controlled 40 percent of the deposits. When all the banks were in trouble and a small number of banks possessed a large portion of the total assets, it was natural that a small number of loans would account for a large segment of the total authorization made by the RFC.[54]

By July 1932 the RFC had authorized 5,084 loans totaling $1,054,184,486 to 4,196 institutions. Of that total, $642,789,313 had been earmarked for 3,600 banks and trust companies and $213,882,724 for 38 railroads. The RFC distributed the remaining $200 million to building and loan associations, credit unions, insurance companies, mortgage loan companies, and various agricultural credit organizations. Despite these unprecedented federal measures, the Hoover administration could find no real economic improvement. Not only were banks still refusing to increase their commercial loans despite huge volumes of excess reserves; the RFC, because of the crisis in Chicago, could no longer be sure that its policies were really strengthening the banking system. Indeed, Hoover and his associates realized that the stability they had counted on in the summer of 1932 was tenuous and depended on the fragile state of public confidence.[55] Their hopes for an immediate industrial recovery dimmed. Also, the political consensus characterizing the final congressional vote on the RFC had turned into a bitter three-way controversy involving the administration, the banking community, and the progressives and liberals in Congress. Hoover had no choice but to initiate new programs to ease the depression.

For several reasons, the President committed himself to major changes in RFC policies and leadership. He realized that the increase in commercial loans would not develop as soon as he had earlier hoped; some form of federal unemployment relief was necessary. Hoover had previously opposed federal relief programs because he believed that the RFC would quickly stimulate a general recovery. Demands for such a program were becoming more and more insistent. Also, the President was ready to revive his original proposal for RFC loans to businesses unable to secure credit from private sources until banks were willing to live up to their credit responsibilities. Finally, Hoover was convinced that Eugene Meyer must be replaced as chairman of the RFC. With innumerable complaints about the corporation his leadership had become a liability; Meyer also opposed expansions of RFC authority into welfare, relief, and public works, and he did not want the RFC to make direct loans to business. The crisis in Chicago sealed Meyer's fate on the RFC board; Hoover was ready to move to the left within his own administration and this meant that Meyer must go.[56]

President Hoover had again found it necessary to depart from the institutional arrangements of American Individualism. Already he had abandoned voluntarism with the demise of the National Credit Corporation; he had established an enormously powerful federal agency to bolster the private money market; and he had permitted the RFC to develop into an administrative unit nearly independent from the Congress with economic control and bureaucratic authority combined. Now, because of the persistence of the banking crisis and the depression, Hoover took the step he had fervently wanted to avoid: he called for a major expansion in power and responsibility for the Reconstruction Finance Corporation.

6

Emergency Relief
and Construction Act

THE Great Depression had taken Americans by surprise. The glitter and gaiety of the later twenties—with the worship of prosperity, frequent neglect of social problems, and nostalgia for an older, simpler America—gave way after 1929 to a pervasive pessimism. Deflation, unemployment, and financial instability transformed euphoria into despondency, confidence into doubt, and security into fear. Americans suffered from confusion, anger, anxiety, and frustration. No one was immune. Between 1929 and 1932 President Hoover witnessed the near collapse of the United States economy; his optimism and his appetite for challenge gradually declined under severe economic and political pressures. The presidency, which had begun with great promise, became a personal and political ordeal.

Nevertheless, Hoover maintained an enduring concern for the nation's economic ills and for its suffering citizens. By the spring of 1932 the President realized that drastic action was necessary; the federal government would have to initiate changes in economic and relief policy. The national mood was too gloomy and resources too depleted to expect any new, aggressive antidepression activities by private business or local communities. As Hoover considered new programs for combating the depression, he turned to the Reconstruction Finance Corporation as the proper administrative vehicle. The RFC had become his most important ''weapon'' in fighting the depression and the only tool at his disposal with even the potential for restoring prosperity. In mid-May, he approached Congress with a request for a massive expansion of RFC responsibilities. His proposals, incorporated into the Emergency Relief and Construction Act, foreshadowed many parts of Franklin D. Roosevelt's early New Deal.

The President's momentous decision to expand the scope of the RFC was an outgrowth of political pressures, of RFC failure to stimulate a sustained recovery, of infighting among the RFC's Board of Directors, and of the President's own political philosophy. In the first place, increasingly hostile criticisms of the RFC pushed the President toward an expansion of its authority. The Interstate Commerce Commission believed that the RFC was too lenient with the railroads and with the bankers who owned railroad debt obligations in allowing them unfettered access to the U.S. Treasury. Progressive Republicans shuddered at the sight of massive governmental assistance to the nation's most powerful financial and transportation institutions. Liberal Democrats wondered when, if ever, the Hoover administration would provide comparable assistance to the poor. The Federal Reserve Board, in what could only be considered a camouflage of its own failure to restore prosperity, held the RFC responsible for the periodic rash of bank failures and for the unwillingness of the financial community to provide adequate credit to eligible businessmen. The bankers felt cheated by the RFC: it had been too stingy, its interest rates were excessive, and its loan periods were too brief. These criticisms were not lost on the President; he was conscious of and affected by them. Changes in RFC policy were necessary to satisfy these diverse but uniformly displeased groups, especially in view of the presidential election in the fall. To remain politically alive, the President had to restore the corporation's public reputation.

Internal RFC politics also strained the administration's effectiveness. Fundamentally the Republicans and the Democrats on the board disagreed over the nature of policy decisions and particularly over the liberality in making loans. The Democrats were usually more concerned with making funds available to smaller banks and limiting the flow of government credit to the eastern financial houses; the Republicans believed that the safety and stability of the largest banks were more important to the economy than the health of smaller institutions. Also, the differences between board members Meyer, Mills, and Bestor on the one hand and Dawes, Couch, Jones, and McCarthy on the other gradually became more pronounced. Resentment of Meyer's domination of the board increased. Hoover was looking for a replacement. Meyer had not been able to use the RFC effectively enough to ease the depression, and he also opposed Hoover's wish to expand the RFC into relief and public works. Hoover realized that only startling changes in RFC policy and personnel could temper the public's hostility. The removal of Meyer might reunify the Board of Directors, blunt public criticism, and make the shift into relief work more tenable.

Surprisingly, the President's own political philosophy also contributed substantially to his commitment to broaden RFC authority. Throughout his career, a powerful strain of progressive idealism existed in Hoover's approach to social and economic problems. American Individualism in its purest form was to him an affirmation of the American past and an idealistic vision of its future. The problem with American Individualism, as with progressive and idealistic philosophies in general, was its dependence on progress and economic growth.[1] Any indications of chronic imperfection or inherent corruption in the economic or political system would destroy an idealistic world view. In the case of American Individualism especially, prosperity was the Achilles' heel. As long as the economy continued to expand and the standard of living and prospects for security improved for most Americans, the public would tolerate and even revere American Individualism's faith in the benign, voluntaristic politics of the private sector. President Hoover was aware of this dimension of his philosophy. In 1922, in *American Individualism,* he wrote that economic security was the foundation for political stability and cultural enrichment — "the real fertilizer of the soil from which spring the finer flowers of life." [2]

Ever since World War I, Hoover had realized that the social and economic foundations of philosophical idealism were fragile and tenuous; concepts of freedom, democracy, and social progress were all based on economic prosperity and its accompanying political stability. Consequently, economic growth must be the objective of the federal government; only then could American Individualism be preserved. In a 1931 speech Hoover remarked that the

economic system is but an instrument of the social advancement of the American people. It is an instrument by which we add to the security and richness of life of every individual. It by no means comprises the whole purpose of life, but it is the foundation upon which can be built the finer things of the spirit. Increase in enrichment must be the objective of the Nation, not decrease. [3]

The President believed that once economic stagnation set in, the foundations of social stability and political consensus would begin to decay and idealism would dissolve into bitterness and violence under the impact of revolution and economic depression.

During World War I Hoover personally witnessed the consequences of economic stagnation and political chaos. Rigid class structures combined with the physical and economic destructiveness of war to create an ideal seedbed for the growth of revolutionary violence. [4] Out of that experience, Hoover had come to believe that

anarchy or Communism . . . was the pit into which all governments were in danger of falling when frantic peoples were driven by the Horsemen of Famine and Pestilence. [5]

In describing the European nations of 1918-1919, Hoover wrote that the

specters of impoverishment, unemployment, and debt haunted them. The emotions of hatred and vengeance . . . were at a fever pitch among their people. [6] . . . I have the feeling that revolution in Europe is by no means over. The social wrongs in these countries are far from solution and the tempest must blow itself out, probably with enormous violence. [7]

As a result of his experience in Europe, Hoover had dedicated himself to economic growth and social stability in the United States. Later in life, during a 1940 campaign speech for Wendell Wilkie, he remarked that

. . . another liability to liberty from this industrial revolution comes from a variety of instabilities that have arisen in this economic system itself. These are the periods of booms and their consequent depressions, with their widespread unemployment and farm losses. There is the possible loss of the job at any time. There are the accidents of family or personal disaster. There is the insecurity of old age. These insecurities all stifle the freedom of the individual spirit and haunt it with fear. The full blossom of liberty requires a reasonable confidence by the individual in his economic security. [8]

But in 1929 the development unthinkable to most Americans occurred: the U.S. economy entered the worst depression in its history. The ordeal of Herbert Hoover revolved around the economic erosion of American Individualism's philosophical rationale. In *Memoirs*, he wrote

There is no economic failure so terrible in its import as that of a country possessing a surplus of every necessity of life in which numbers, willing and anxious to work, are deprived of these necessities. It simply cannot be if our moral and economic system is to survive. . . . [9]

The survival of America's moral and spiritual system was the President's objective. His obligation was clear: he either had to restore prosperity or immediately ensure adequate relief to the growing numbers of unemployed.

Until 1932 the President and his associates took solace in the social stability that characterized the United States despite the severity of the depression. Since the stock market crash in 1929, the President's advisers had maintained a weekly log of significant international events, such as wars, revolutions, and changes in governments.[10] By late 1931, the list was long. But Hoover observed that in the United States

. . . we can say with satisfaction that we have had fewer strikes and lockouts than in normal times; that we have had no mob-violence worth noting to trouble the police or the militia; we have not summoned a single Federal soldier to arms. The first duty of the Government—that is, to secure social tranquility and to maintain confidence in our institutions—has been performed. That has been accomplished by the good will and cooperation in the community and not by either force or legislation.[11]

As long as the social fabric had remained intact, the President had felt confident that he could continue his antidepression policies without fear of violence or revolution and that soon the RFC would stimulate an economic revival and obviate the need for any federal relief legislation. American Individualism would be saved for the future.

But events in the winter of 1931/32 destroyed this complacency. The increasingly militant members of the Unemployed Councils of the United States organized 1,670 men into National Hunger Marchers and descended on Washington in the last weeks of 1931, demanding cash payments and unemployment insurance. One month later, Father James R. Cox, a Roman Catholic priest from Pittsburgh, led 15,000 men in another march on Washington. Between December 28, 1931, and January 9, 1932, Senator Robert La Follette's Subcommittee on Manufactures held hearings on the relief crisis. A parade of social workers and local politicians presented eyewitness accounts of staggering poverty and destitution in the United States. The hearings provided unquestionable evidence that immediate federal relief efforts were imperative. [12]

During early spring, still more evidence of unrest and frustration accumulated, particularly after the Workers' Ex-Servicemen League organized bonus protests in New York, Chicago, Cleveland, and Toledo. In April a prominent journal of social analysis, *Survey,* published a study revealing the desperation existing in most urban communities.[13] Even the President's Organization on Unemployment Relief presented a frightening analysis of nationwide suffering.[14] In May the National Conference of Social Workers demanded federal relief programs for the unemployed, and the Bonus Marchers began their descent on Washington. In the farm belt during the same month the National Farm Holiday Association was organized with talk of nationwide food strikes and moratoriums on food distribution.[15] The President knew such concrete evidence of instability was a threat to the United States, and he concluded in May that a federal relief program would have to be created.[16]

The President was also motivated by the political pressures of a presidential election. Several leading Democrats had already introduced relief legislation. In December 1931 Senators Edward Costigan of Colorado and Robert La Follette had jointly submitted a measure to Congress that called for the distribution of $375 million in the form of grants to various states for unemployment relief. The Hoover administration had opposed the bill for two reasons: it would drain the Treasury and make a balanced federal budget impossible. Also, the RFC had not yet been given a fair chance of bringing recovery. In February a coalition of administration Republicans and conservative Democrats defeated the La Follette-Costigan bill.[17]

Even conservative Democrats believed that some type of limited relief legislation was necessary. The same February Hugo Black of Alabama, Thomas Walsh of Montana, and Robert J. Bulkeley of Ohio introduced a relief measure similar to the La Follette-Costigan bill except for one important detail: the $375 million would be loaned, not granted, to the states. The congressmen believed this provision would make the bill acceptable to the administration, and liberal Democrats would at least feel it was a step in the right direction. Nevertheless, Hoover and his followers, still unconvinced that massive relief legislation was necessary, defeated the measure.[18]

On the following day, Senator Robert Wagner of New York continued his quest for federal relief legislation by introducing a bill authorizing $375 million for relief purposes to the states with the money to be advanced against post-1936 federal highway allotments.[19] In March, Wagner submitted another bill calling for a $1.1 billion public works program to be financed through a bond issue by the federal government. In May Senator Costigan submitted a bill permitting an outright grant of $500 million to the states, also to be financed through a bond issue. Finally, Senator Royal Copeland of New York resurrected his initial amendment to the RFC act permitting the corporation to make direct relief loans to cities as well as to states.[20] The welfare and relief picture on Capitol Hill was becoming complicated, and the President felt that he should offer an administration measure to preempt the relief bills of the liberals; otherwise, Hoover's prospects in the election would be dim indeed.

The President was in a dilemma. His commitment to a balanced budget to restore business confidence forced him to oppose all the relief bills. On the other hand, the growing relief crisis, the failure of the RFC, his fears of social cataclysm, and the political aggressiveness of Senate liberals pushed him inexorably toward a federal relief program. Just as important was his realization that the "trickle-down" theory of recovery was not working. By May 1932 Hoover felt that recovery would be gradual and it was necessary for the government to expand the scope of the RFC until employment increased. [21] The real problem he faced was to find an approach to relief that would adequately meet the public need, satisfy the liberals, and still permit a balanced budget.

Ironically, a group of conservative Democrats provided Hoover with the solution. Many Democrats, such as Newton Baker, Bernard Baruch, Hugh Johnson, and Senator Joseph Robinson, shared Hoover's commitment ot a balanced budget. Yet they too realized that some form of federal relief was absolutely necessary. During the spring, Baruch and Robinson worked out a public works proposal that called for the construction of self-liquidating projects, such as toll bridges and highways, hydroelectric plants, public housing, and water works and sewage systems, that would become profitable immediately on completion. To stimulate their construction, the RFC would loan funds to the state and local governments sponsoring the projects; on completion, the RFC would be repaid out of operating revenues. Such a plan would provide new employment without violating the administration's principle against grants. The program would eliminate the need to draw on current Treasury revenue and would not threaten a balanced budget. On May 11, 1932, Senator Robinson sent Hoover a memorandum outlining these proposals and simultaneously issued a public statement. [22]

The Baruch-Robinson plan offered an escape for the President from an increasingly difficult political problem. He agreed to the basic concept of the plan and invited Senator Robinson and Senator James Watson of Indiana and the RFC directors to the White House for consultation. During the next few days the administration, after searching through all the relief bills of the previous months, created a proposal for an omnibus relief and recovery bill that would not only ease the nationwide unemployment but also stimulate the economy. To ease the relief crisis without affecting the budget, Hoover adopted the principle of the Black-Walsh-Bulkeley bill, which he had previously opposed, and called for $300 million in relief loans to the states. To assist the cities, Senator Copeland's plan to permit RFC loans to municipalities was adopted. [23] To avoid a bond issue for public works, the administration accepted the Baruch-Robinson proposal calling for RFC financing of self-liquidating public works. [24] Finally, to compensate for the failure of commercial banks to grant adequate business loans, the President suggested RFC loans to businesses unable to secure credit from traditional sources. To be eligible these businesses would have to have guaranteed orders for their products, and these loans would also be self-liquidating. Just as in December 1931, Hoover proposed an unprecedented program that was an outgrowth of social reality, economic failure, and political philosophy.[25] Again the President reverted to the analogue of war. On May 14, 1932, he remarked,

The battle to set our economic machine in motion in this emergency takes new forms and new tactics from time to time. We used such emergency powers to win the war; we can use them to fight the depression, the misery and suffering from which are equally great.[26]

The President believed the amendments to the RFC act would relieve suffering throughout the country, lessen political criticism in an election year, and lessen the possiblity of social revolution. Also, direct RFC loans to businesses could stimulate a widespread increase in production and employment.[27]

After the President released his version of the Emergency Relief and Construction bill, Senate Democrats organized a subcommittee to draw up a compromise relief bill. Senator Robert Wagner headed the subcommittee, which included Robert Bulkeley of Ohio, Joseph Robinson of Arkansas, Thomas J. Walsh of Montana, and Key Pittman of Nevada. They all realized that a milestone had been passed in American history. Only two months before, the debate over relief had centered on its legitimacy; the debate was now concerned only with its form. A consensus had developed among Republicans and Democrats: local relief and public works sponsored by the federal government were absolutely necessary, and the Reconstruction Finance Corporation should direct the program.[28]

Putting the legislation into final form proved to be difficult. A major complication developed late in May when John Nance Garner submitted a relief measure to Congress. Immediately it was apparent that the relief struggle was not just between Democrats and administration Republicans; the Democrats, because of Garner's position, were divided among themselves. With the Democratic National Convention only a month away, Garner was seriously considering a try for the presidential nomination. His bill called for a public works bond issue of $1.2 billion; an appropriation of $1 billion for RFC loans to any state, city, business, or individual needing funds for employment-producing projects; and an appropriation of $100 million to be used by the President for relief loans.[29]

President Hoover believed the Garner bill grossly irresponsible. The clause outlining the public works bond issue would eventually imbalance the federal budget far more than the Wagner proposal of $500 million, which Hoover had already denounced. Even more serious was the provision for unlimited and unsecured loans to businesses and individuals that would quickly dissipate RFC funds in projects not bringing recovery. That provision, moreover, threatened the President's more limited desire to permit RFC loans to self-liquidating industrial enterprises. In the Senate, even Democrats were upset with the bill and considered it a grandstand play aimed more at getting support of the Democratic National

Convention than at solving the national relief crisis. They feared Garner's bill would destroy the entire relief effort in Congress by alienating President Hoover. But Garner was as adamant as he was powerful, and the House began to consider the proposal late in May. [30]

Hoover trusted the Democratic subcommittee in the Senate to offer a reasonable version of the administration's relief proposals. On May 20 subcommittee members publicized the bill they had written. Senator Wagner insisted on keeping the provision for a $500 million public works bond issue, knowing the President would object. The bill called for a total of $300 million in RFC relief loans to the states, with $200 million allotted on the basis of population and $100 million on the basis of need; and the bill included a clause permitting $1.5 billion in RFC loans for self-liquidating construction projects, an institutionalization of the Baruch-Robinson plan. Unfortunately, the bill did not include provision for RFC loans to businesses unable to secure adequate credit elsewhere. Hoover considered such a recovery provision necessary in a bill that otherwise exclusively concerned relief. Hoover thought the Senate bill, though far more responsible than the Garner bill, was still inadequate. In comparing his approach with that of Congress, Hoover wrote,

These proposals of huge expansions of "public works" have a vital relation to balancing the Federal budget and to the stabilizing of national credit. The financing of "income-producing works" by the Reconstruction Corporation is an investment operation, requires no Congressional appropriation, does not unbalance the budget, is not a drain on the Treasury, does not involve the direct issue of Government bonds, does not involve added burdens upon the taxpayer either now or in the future. It is an emergency operation which will liquidate itself with the return of the investor to the money markets. [31]

On May 30-31, the President held a series of White House conferences with leading congressmen from both parties and outlined his objections to both the Wagner and the Garner bills. On the evening of May 31, Hoover presented his own ideas to Congress. He denounced the individual loan feature of the Garner bill as wantonly irresponsible. As for the Wagner bill, Hoover argued against the $500 million public works bond issue as too expensive for the government. He also objected to the clause forcing him to distribute $200 million of the $300 million on the basis of population rather than need; Hoover suspected that such a clause would permit states with lighter relief loads to shirk their reponsibility to raise local funds. Finally, Hoover wanted a business loan feature in the relief bill. He went on to praise the parts of the bill calling for direct relief loans and self-liquidating construction loans. [32] The President decided to introduce a relief bill of his own.

On the weekend of June 5-6, Hoover met with the RFC board at his retreat in Rapidan, Maryland. Mills wrote the final version of the bill, and the board selected Senator Warren Barbour of New Jersey as floor leader. In its final form the bill eliminated the portions of the Garner and Wagner bills that Hoover opposed. The administration bill permitted the RFC to increase its issue of securities to a maximum of $3 billion to enable it to purchase the bonds of political subdivisions for the construction of self-liquidating public works. Included in the provision for public works loans was RFC authority to make industrial loans to private corporations that already possessed sufficient production contracts to guarantee payment if these businesses could prove their inability to secure credit elsewhere. Also, $300 million was provided for direct relief loans to the states, the entire amount to be allotted on the basis of need. Finally, the administration bill went beyond other relief bills in promising RFC loans for domestic and foreign marketing of farm surpluses.[33] On June 7, 1932, Senator Barbour introduced this Emergency Relief and Construction bill to Congress.

The battle lines were drawn. On the same day that Barbour submitted the administration bill the House approved the Garner legislation 216 to 182. On June 8, by a vote of 9 to 6, liberals and progressives on the Senate Banking and Currency Committee defeated the Barbour bill, blocking its passage to the Senate floor. As expected, businessmen supported the bill, hoping that it would provide new credit. On June 10 the Senate passed the Wagner relief bill 72 to 8, permitting $300 million in RFC relief loans to the states. On June 23, by voice vote, the Senate ratified the Wagner bill for a bond issue of $500 million to finance public works.[34] In Congress Hoover had suffered a setback, and he prepared for negotiations with the conference committee.

The work of the conference committee was particularly difficult, since it took place simultaneously with the Democratic National Convention in Chicago. Congressmen were functioning in a highly charged political atmosphere and were anxious to get back home and prepare for the election. The administration was concerned about a relief bill, the Democratic convention, and the Central Republic Bank in Chicago. The responsibility of finding a bill acceptable to the House, the Senate, and the administration fell on Senator Wagner. Both Wagner and Hoover desperately wanted some relief legislation passed before Congress recessed, and Wagner, knowing the President opposed some parts of his bill, was willing to compromise. Late in June, wishing for more time, Wagner fought off amendments from both sides. Senator La Follette tried to expand public works funding, but on June 22 the Senate defeated the amendment 56 to 12. On the same day, the Senate turned away an amendment from George Moses of New Hampshire that called for eliminating the $500 million bond issue. Garner, in the House, was unwilling to compromise. He insisted that the conference committee report include his provision for unlimited RFC loans to businesses and individuals. House Democrats on the conference committee supported Garner and amended the self-liquidating clause to permit RFC loans to small businesses and to individuals on an unsecured basis. Senate Democrats were irritated by Garner's intransigence, realizing that it would destroy the relief bill by guaranteeing Hoover's veto.[35]

As the work of the conference committee continued into July, Hoover began to realize that the Emergency Relief and Construction bill might actually be passed with the Garner clause. On July 6, Hoover made his position clear to the conference committee:

The fatal difficulty is the Speaker's insistence upon provision that loans should also be made to individuals, private corporations, partnerships, States and municipalities on any conceivable security and for every purpose. Such an undertaking by the United States Government makes the Reconstruction Corporation the most gigantic banking and pawnbroking business in all history.

There are forty-eight States and 16,000 municipalities who could under its terms dump their responsibilities upon the Federal Government. The purpose to take care of unemployment distress in such centers is provided for in the proposals of employment and loans to the States.

The Speaker's proposal in no sense contributes to relieve such distress. It would compel the Reconstruction Corporation to attempt to deal with millions of people in terms of hundreds of thousands of small and large loans. It would result in dumping a vast amount of doubtful private and corporation debts on the Federal Treasury to no national purpose of relieving unemployment. [36]

Hoover's opposition to the bill was as strong as Garner's support for it. Compromise was impossible.

For Senator Wagner the controversy was damaging. In the second week of July the conference committee issued its final report. The Emergency Relief and Construction bill provided for a total of $1.5 billion in RFC loans to public agencies for self-liquidating construction projects and to private companies and individuals needing credit. The bill permitted the corporation to make $200 million in direct relief loans to the states on the basis of population and $100 million on the basis of need. Wagner had compromised by eliminating the bond issue and by decreasing the emergency public works provision from $500 million to $300 million, but the Garner clause had been included despite Hoover's fierce opposition. The conference committee report went to the House on July 7, where it passed 202 to 157. On July 9, it cleared the Senate 43 to 31. In both houses liberal Democrats and progressive Republicans outvoted administration supporters. On July 11, 1932, Hoover vetoed the bill.

It is important to remember that the President did not veto the Wagner-Garner bill because of its relief and employment provisions. In the hearings before the Senate Committee on Banking and Currency, Ogden Mills spelled out the administration position, which opposed only two phases of the pending relief legislation: the population ratio and bond issue proposals included in the Wagner-Garner loan clause. The President objected not to the federalization of relief but to the granting of unlimited and unsecured RFC loans to individuals. [37]

The President had the Democrats over a barrel, despite their control of Congress. They did not have the votes to override the veto, and they knew the Garner clause would have to be eliminated and a new bill submitted. To meet Hoover's demands while preserving Garner's public image appeared to be an impossible assignment. Neither man was ready to compromise.

Ultimately, Wagner supported the President; he agreed to the distribution of all $300 million of the relief allocation on the basis of need and to allow the RFC to make loans for the marketing of farm products. Garner finally conceded because he realized that further obstinancy would be politically dangerous; he did not want to appear to be the major obstacle to a relief bill. Garner gave up his demand for RFC loans to individuals on the condition that the President transfer the industrial loan provision of $1.5 billion for self-liquidating public works from the RFC to the Federal Reserve banks. Such a move would permit the Speaker to claim that he had only compromised, not conceded. Hoover was reluctant about giving this power to the Federal Reserve banks because he realized that he would not be able to exert much control over them. If the authority were placed with the RFC he would be able to administer the program directly. Nevertheless, to satisfy Garner and secure a relief bill, Hoover compromised. [38]

But the Speaker still had some unpleasant surprises for the President. Garner successfully inserted into the bill a clause requiring that all RFC loans be made public. Since its establishment the corporation had used elaborate secret codes to transmit messages to its loan agencies and individual banks.[39] The board feared that publicizing an RFC loan would undermine depositor confidence in the bank and stimulate a run on deposits. Yet pressure for public knowledge of RFC transactions had been accumulating ever since the facts of the Dawes loan had been revealed. The corporation directors, Democrats and Republicans, unanimously opposed the Garner amendment, but to no avail.[40]

In addition, the Garner forces amended the Emergency Relief and Construction bill to prohibit loans to any financial institutions whose officers or directors had been associated with the RFC during the previous twelve months.[41] The President realized that the public outcry over the Dawes loan had made the publicity and loan prohibition clauses popular, but he still considered vetoing the bill again. Senator Robinson assured Hoover that RFC reports would not be released to the press while Congress was in recess. Since the second session would not begin until after the election, Hoover decided he would have time to negotiate with Congress over publication. After that assurance he decided to sign the bill. On July 14 the House adopted the Emergency Relief and Construction bill 296 to 46, and on July 16 the Senate ratified it by voice vote.[42] A broad consensus had emerged in the United States over the relief crisis. On July 17, Hoover said,

While there are some secondary features of the measure to which I have objections, they are not so great as to warrant refusal to approve the measure in the face of the great service that the major provisions will be to the Nation. It is a strong step toward recovery.[43]

On July 21, 1932, President Hoover signed the Emergency Relief and Construction Act into law.[44]

The Emergency Relief and Construction Act marked another milestone in the development of federal responsibility for the social and economic welfare of the nation. It extended RFC authority deep into state and local relief, public works construction, slum clearance, low-income housing, reforestation, agricultural marketing, and agricultural finance. Title I provided for a total of $300 million in loans to states for direct relief, not more than 15 percent of which could be made available to a single state. Title II directed the RFC to make up to $1.5 billion available for public construction of income-producing projects. The act authorized the RFC to establish a regional agricultural credit corporation with $3 million in capital in each Federal Land Bank district. To stabilize farm prices, the corporation could make loans to financial institutions or marketing organizations to finance the sale of farm products in foreign and domestic markets. The act prohibited RFC loans to banks whose officers had within one year been associated with the corporation and compelled the RFC to make a monthly report to Congress of the names of borrowers and the amounts of loans. Finally, the act permitted the Federal Reserve banks to make direct business loans to industries needing credit.[45] It was an extraordinary piece of legislation.

With the passage of the Emergency Relief and Construction Act, President Hoover turned his attention to the personnel changes he felt the RFC needed. On the day he had vetoed the first version of the Emergency Relief and Construction Act, he had asked Congress to replace Eugene Meyer and Paul Bestor. To justify the removals, Hoover publicly claimed that the two men were becoming exhausted by trying to serve in their respective bureaucratic positions and as ex officio members of the RFC board.[46] Privately, Hoover wanted to give the RFC some fresh leadership to match its new responsibilities.[47] Congress complied with his wishes, and the final version of the Emergency Relief and Construction Act eliminated the requirement that the chairman of the Federal Reserve Board and the Federal Farm Loan Commissioner serve as ex officio directors of the Reconstruction Finance Corporation.

In late July Hoover had to replace Charles Dawes, Eugene Meyer, and Paul Bestor on the RFC board. The President felt the only way to deflect liberal criticisms was to appoint a Democrat as chairman. Hoover approached Newton D. Baker with the offer; Baker's economic opinions were conservative while his credentials as a Democrat were impeccable. Baker turned down the offer because he hoped to become the next Democratic presidential nominee.[48] Hoover then turned to Atlee Pomerene. Born in 1863 in Berlin, Ohio, Pomerene had graduated from Princeton and the Cincinnati Law School. Between 1911 and 1923 he had served in the U.S. Senate and built a reputation as a confirmed progressive. Before his Senate career he had gained some financial experience with the Commercial & Savings Bank in Canton, Ohio, and later he was legal counsel to the RFC in the fourth Federal Reserve district. The appointment of Pomerene was ideal for Hoover; he hoped he had found an individual who could please the Democrats and carry out the administration's recovery plans.[49]

Hoover filled the other vacancies with Republicans. To replace

Charles Dawes as president of the RFC, Hoover selected Charles A. Miller of Utica, New York. Born in Utica in 1867, Miller had attended Harvard and began practicing law in 1892. From 1907 to 1932 he served as president of the Savings Bank of Utica and was named president of the New York State Savings Bank Association in 1909. In 1910 he served as vice-president of the New York State Bar Association. In February 1932 Meyer asked him to manage the New York Loan Agency of the RFC. Miller appealed to the President because for years he had been active on local relief committees in New York, which Hoover believed prepared him for the new responsibilities the RFC was assuming. Also, as manager of the New York Loan Agency, Miller had been an outspoken critic of private bankers and particularly of their unwillingness to increase the volume of commercial loans. Since Hoover was considering new efforts to increase commercial credit, he saw Miller as an ideal choice to lead the program.[50]

To fill the last vacancy Hoover picked Gardner Cowles of Iowa. Cowles was born in 1861 in Oskaloosa, Iowa, and graduated from Iowa Wesleyan College in 1885. After serving two terms in the Iowa House of Representatives, he went into the newspaper business and became publisher of the *Des Moines Register* and the *Des Moines Tribune.* Cowles was a staunch Republican and longtime friend of the President. In 1929 Hoover had named him to the Commission on Conservation and Administration of the Public Domain. Like Miller, Cowles was philosophically comfortable with American Individualism, and he would be able to replace Dawes as the RFC Midwest representative.[51]

President Hoover was pleased with the new RFC board. The Democrats now controlled it four votes to three: Pomerene, McCarthy, Jones, and Couch as opposed to Mills, Miller, and Cowles. The President hoped that the removal of Meyer and Bestor would erase the image of the RFC as a tool of Wall Street. Mills and Miller were from the East, but Miller could hardly be considered a spokesman for eastern banks. Not only did he carry the savings banker's competitive antipathy toward commercial bankers, but he was especially critical of the liquidity fears of eastern bankers.[52] Pomerene and Cowles represented the Midwest, Jones and Couch the South, and McCarthy the West. Hoover naively hoped that the RFC would now be free from the criticisms it had been receiving since March.

One month after signing the Emergency Relief and Construction Act and installing the new RFC directors, the President summarized the achievements of his administration and added a warning:

The great war against depression is being fought on many fronts in many parts of the world. One of the most stupendous actions of this great front has been the long battle of the last eighteen months to carry our financial structure safely through the worldwide collapse. That battle may be likened to the great battle of Chateau Thierry. That attack on our line has been stopped. But I warn you that the war is not over, we must now re-form our forces for the battle of Soissons.[53]

Again Hoover employed the familiar and comforting metaphor of war to justify his policies. The creation of the RFC had been a unique governmental intrusion into banking, and just six months later the President had broadened federal responsibilities by allowing the RFC to engage in local relief programs. Hoover had wanted to avoid such expansions, but his hopes had dimmed in face of the stark reality of the crisis and he had stepped into the modern era of federal responsibility for local relief and welfare.

It was an ominous challenge, for by rejecting the bills the Democrats had offered, Hoover assumed the burden of easing the crisis. The Democrats and progressive Republicans were aware of his vulnerability. On July 17, 1932, after realizing that Hoover's Emergency Relief and Construction bill would become law, Fiorello La Guardia said,

We submit to the American public that to date the Reconstruction Finance Corporation has loaned or committed to loan the staggering amount of $1,954,814,486 and no visible or tangible benefit to unemployment or agriculture has been produced. To the contrary, the loans have been directed to sources that in part are responsible for the financial chaos and have been used to entrench their wicked position. [54]

House majority leader Henry Rainey of Illinois then set the stage for the political struggle of the next four months:

The President will get exactly what he wants and if he does not bring back prosperity by November, God help him politically. [55]

7

Toward the New Deal

THE tranquility Hoover enjoyed after signing the Emergency Relief and Construction Act was short-lived. He still had to implement the legislation. As Democratic Congressman Henry Rainey had warned, its implementation would be a major test of Hoover's political career.

In January Hoover had confronted a similar dilemma. He had hoped that the RFC would restore prosperity, but it had failed and became an object of bitter political debate. Now in August 1932, Hoover again intended to use the powers of the federal government on an unprecedented scale, this time in an effort to ease the suffering of the poor. The dilemma of January still existed: how to "combat" the depression without sacrificing the spiritual dynamic of American Individualism. More than once he had proven his ability to create useful antidepression agencies, but in each instance political circumstances, economic miscalculation, and the rhetoric of his personal philosophy limited his effectiveness. The Emergency Relief and Construction Act proved to be no different.

Implementing the Emergency Relief and Construction Act required administrative changes in the RFC. The Board of Directors organized a Self-Liquidating Division under the leadership of Harvey Couch to administer the new public works program.[1] Gardner Cowles was asked to establish a new Emergency Relief Division; after conferring with Walter S. Gifford of the President's Organization on Unemployment Relief, Cowles obtained the permanent services of Fred G. Croxton, assistant director of the organization. Croxton immediately became assistant to the RFC board, with special responsibilities for the Emergency Relief Division. He staffed the division with former employees of the President's Organization on Unemployment Relief.[2] Finally, the board appointed Wilson McCarthy to create a new Agricultural Credit Division, and McCarthy asked Ford Hovey, president of the Stockmen's National Bank of Omaha, to direct the program.[3] With these changes, the RFC was prepared to initiate the federal relief program.

Harvey Couch, of the Self-Liquidating Division, believed that unemployed workers would be eager to work if jobs were available. President Hoover and the other RFC directors, sharing this conviction, did not blame the poor and unemployed for their plight.[4] They appointed a special advisory committee composed of distinguished architects and engineers to study applications and recommend construction projects to the board. The federal government was not only willing, as in 1921-1922, but also financially prepared to assume the responsibility of providing jobs for the unemployed. [5]

From the outset the Self-Liquidating Division experienced severe problems. The administration promised that the $1.5 billion that had been earmarked for the program would provide tens of thousands of jobs during the winter of 1932/33. But time-consuming delays were inherent in the self-liquidating concept. Construction projects capable of producing a revenue involved complex planning. Bridges, toll roads, hydroelectric plants, electric power distribution lines, slum clearance and low-income housing, and urban sewer systems could not be initiated overnight. They required detailed engineering studies as well as political preparation before actual construction could begin. Although the administration hoped that new jobs could be created quickly, the program did not get into full swing until 1933. [6] With a national election approaching in November, the RFC could not escape Democratic charges of procrastination.

Instead of interpreting its assignment liberally, the administration chose to construct literally the language of the Emergency Relief and Construction Act. Fearing defaults and long-standing public debts, they insisted that all projects be self-liquidating. Eventual income would have to be sufficient to meet all operating and maintenance costs, interest assessments, and amortization payments. The RFC would make loans only to those projects capable of repaying the federal government in full. Minimum interest rates on the loans were set at 5½ percent, and all mortgages had to be repaid in a maximum of ten years.

These terms were too strict to stimulate an early, active employment program. Both Democrats and Republicans on the RFC board were cautious in their approach to the Self-Liquidating Division, and although caution was consistent with the language of the act, it was politically disastrous. In fact, the Self-Liquidating Division denied the vast majority of loan applications. Early in September 1932, for example, the city of Mexia, Texas, applied for an RFC loan to construct a new National Guard Armory. Without question, the project would have created some badly needed employment in the area, but the corporation rejected the application, explaining that the armory would not produce any income itself and therefore would not be able to repay the government. [7]

Late in September Jesse Jones complained that hundreds of applications from all over the country were denied because they were not self-liquidating. The ability of the federal government to recover its investment outweighed the need to provide jobs. Harvey Couch perfectly summarized the administration's position when he said,

It is anticipated that every penny loaned by the Corporation shall be repaid. It is further contemplated that the borrower shall receive a lasting economic benefit and not an economic burden from the construction thus financed. All projects must pay for themselves. There is to be no aftermath of public or private debt or default. [8]

As far as the administration was concerned the RFC was administering a self-liquidating public works program, not a general public works program. It was an important distinction.

The board purposely set the interest rates for self-liquidating loans above prevailing money market rates to guarantee that the government would not be competing with private financial institutions. Unfortunately, the 5½ percent rate was counterproductive. In November, for example, negotiations were underway with former Governor Al Smith and Senator Robert Wagner to finance slum clearance and low-income housing in New York City, but the RFC refused to decrease its interest rate. The board did not want to compete with private lenders even though Smith and Wagner insisted that private lenders were unwilling to invest in the project because of their inflated liquidity preferences. Still, the RFC refused; American Individualism had always warned against the dangers of governmental competition with private business. Negotiations broke down, much to the chagrin of the administration and the consternation of the New York Democrats. [9]

It was only a matter of time before Henry Rainey's July promise that the act would be a political test for Hoover would be redeemed. As the November elections approached, the attacks on the Self-Liquidating Division became more intense. On October 12, 1932, the *New Republic* carried the following criticism:

> The administering of these funds was put into the hands of the Reconstruction Finance Corporation. Probably the average citizen has assumed that in the two and a half months since the measure became law, a good part of this money must have been loaned out, and must now be helping to relieve unemployment and start the wheels of prosperity revolving once again.
>
> Any such supposition, however, is grossly in error. Although 243 applications have been made to the RFC for loans totaling $800,000,000 of this $1,500,000,000, up to the moment of writing only three of those applications have been accepted. . . . No matter what it may now do, it will afford no relief to unemployment, no aid to prosperity, until next February. As it is now proceeding, it will be precious little then. . . . . R.F.C. lawyers will proceed to stick all the pins they can through every project submitted. And if, in the meantime, a lot of people are mean enough to go and starve to death — that is no concern of theirs. [10]

Similar criticisms haunted the RFC during the final weeks before the election. Senator Wagner described the approach taken by the corporation as

> mile upon mile of red tape. The failure of the Government and the Reconstruction Finance Corporation to rush the construction authorized by Congress, and the delay by the Reconstruction Finance Corporation in lending every possible aid to hasten the launching of self-liquidating undertakings is depriving unemployed workers of jobs and is cruel and dangerous. [11]

The Self-Liquidating Division of the RFC was fast becoming a political disaster.

Responding to criticisms on the eve of the election, the RFC attempted to stimulate the program. In October, the board authorized a loan of $108 million for three gigantic projects in California: the bay bridge from Oakland to San Francisco, the waterworks system in Pasadena, and the Metropolitan Aqueduct to carry water from the Colorado River to Los Angeles. Both Couch and Hoover pursued these three projects, hoping they would create new employment in the West. The RFC relaxed its rates, setting 5½ percent as the maximum, not minimum, interest rate, with 5 percent loans becoming the most common. The board also extended the repayment period from ten to twenty-five years.[12]

But even these changes could not dispel growing public disillusionment with the corporation. Democrats interpreted the loans to California as politically inspired; what better proof did they have that the RFC was trying to "Buy California for Hoover" than three huge loans on the eve of the election?[13] Also, the amount of money actually disbursed for the projects was insignificant; by December 1932 only $360,000 had been loaned for self-liquidating public works. Most projects were too large and too complex and required months and even years before they actually created new jobs for the unemployed.[14]

By October 1932 the administration was desperate. Publicly they began to request applications for small-scale projects that did not require detailed planning, such as local roads and bridges and rural water systems. Projects that could be designed and initiated in relatively short periods of time were the only way of salvaging the program. Political criticisms and their own realization that major construction projects would not relieve short-run unemployment problems pushed them into a more active strategy.[15]

But by October it was already too late to begin enough small projects. As late as March 1933, the RFC had approved only ninety-two applications totaling $197 million. Of that amount, only $20 million had actually been distributed.[16] The hopes of all Americans for an employment program of $1.5 billion had been smashed by the early emphasis on large-scale projects and by administration fears that the RFC might compete with private enterprise. The program, designed to be bold and flexible, succumbed to poor planning and to economic misconceptions.

Still, the agency had brought a measure of relief to scattered communities throughout the country and initiated several projects that were completed during the New Deal. The most famous was the San Francisco–Oakland Bay Bridge. A favorite project of Hoover's for years, it was one of the earliest to receive RFC approval. In October, the corporation had approved a loan of $62 million for the bridge.[17] The RFC also provided loans for the construction of the Metropolitan Aqueduct to Los Angeles; the New Orleans Belt Railway Bridge; the massive electric transmission line from the Hoover Dam in Nevada to Los Angeles; sewage systems in Blackstone, Virginia, Bowling Green, Kentucky, and Tyler, Texas; waterworks systems for Ogden, Utah, Sandusky, Ohio, and Watseka, Illinois; and irrigation developments throughout the South, Midwest, and West.[18] The Self-Liquidating Division also established a precedent for federal slum clearance and low-income housing projects. Thousands of people benefited from the $20 million that the RFC actually spent in the winter of 1932/33 for these projects.

But it was only a drop in the bucket. Although the administration leaders did not originate the Self-Liquidating Division as a means of stimulating aggregate demand through federal spending, they had hoped it would provide widespread relief until the RFC financial reconstruction program brought a permanent recovery. Even the goal of temporary relief was a dismal failure that many considered further proof of the apathy, arrogance, and even cruelty of Herbert Hoover.

The Emergency Relief Division of the RFC experienced similar difficulties: good intentions and precedent-breaking legislation were undermined by the spirit of American Individualism and by the very dimensions of the relief crisis. Title I of the Emergency Relief and Construction Act authorized the RFC to lend up to $300 million to the states for relief. From the very outset, beleaguered state governors flooded the RFC with applications for their share of funds. It was immediately apparent that the $300 million would be inadequate; the relief situation was far more desperate than the administration had realized. The governors of Illinois, Ohio, Pennsylvania, Oregon, and New York each submitted requests exceeding $25 million. By the first of August thirteen states had applied for over $200 million of the $300 million.[19] It seemed obvious to the administration that the money would not go around and some requests would have to be reduced. And again President Hoover and the Reconstruction Finance Corporation appeared cold, apathetic, and stingy—protectors not of the people but of the vested interests of the country.

To guard the limited supply of funds, the board devised an elaborate list of rules and preconditions to be met before a state could receive funds. Each state had to make out separate applications for every political subdivision needing relief money. The governor had to list the funds at his disposal from state, local, and private sources. He had to list his state's relief expenditures for each month of 1931 and 1932 and in detail explain the reasons for any increases or proposed increases for 1932. And he had to outline the steps the state would take to increase the revenue available for relief.[20]

In an address to the Welfare and Relief Mobilization Conference in September in Washington, D.C., Atlee Pomerene outlined the philosophy behind RFC procedural guidelines:

Federal funds should be used only when the resources of the state or territory are inadequate for relief. This means that Federal funds may be used only when all monies then available or those which can be made available, are not sufficient. This means that private contributions must be resorted to. If and when all these sources of revenue are found to be insufficient, then the government of the United States places three hundred million dollars at the disposal of the R.F.C. to be distributed in accordance with its good judgement. . . . Every state and political subdivision thereof, and every religious and charitable institution, and every man and woman capable of so doing must continue his or its efforts for relief as heretofore, and that appeal to the Federal government must be made only when these and all other resources are inadequate. To take any other position would be to destroy the fine sentiment of brotherly love which is prevalent in every section of our country. [21]

The RFC was cautious for several reasons. The intense demand by state governors for funds forced the administration to plan so that funds would be available through the winter. The administration wanted the states to do everything possible to increase their own relief revenues; whether it involved philanthropic campaigns or increased taxes, the administration insisted that state and local governments do more than previously. Finally, the administration was deeply concerned about the future of American society; it feared that massive federal assistance would eclipse local groups and governments and permanently institutionalize the power of the Washington bureaucracy. The administration insisted that the states turn to the federal government only as a last resort. Preservation of initiative, voluntarism, and philanthropy was the first concern.

On receiving a loan application, the Emergency Relief Division carefully scrutinized the state's eligibility. Each state underwent complete evaluation of its tax base, its need, and its administrative ability to distribute the money. Three conditions determined the outcome of the RFC decision: (1) the corporation insisted that each state extend its tax base to the limit—no federal funds would be granted if more state money was available or the state maintained the potential to raise new revenues; (2) the RFC demanded that all states receiving aid must establish state, county, and municipal relief boards to administer the loans; and (3) the corporation would allot funds only for very short periods—applications for loans of longer than one month were denied. Pomerene believed that

if aid were to be extended for a long period of time, there would be a greater temptation to depend upon the Federal government rather than upon the state or local government or private charities. [22]

These restrictions created serious political problems for the administration even though the corporation was pleased with its early record. The RFC immediately granted some loans because several states had already met the eligibility requirements. Illinois, for example, had established the Illinois Emergency Relief Commission to administer all state relief funds and had recently floated a relief bond issue of $18,750,000. The Emergency Relief Division decided that the state's administrative machinery was in order, the state really was at the end of its financial resources, and its relief situation was truly desperate. By September, Cook County's welfare funds would be completely exhausted, and the state could offer no assistance. On July 27, 1932, the RFC granted Illinois a loan of $3 million, remarking that its application for $25 million was clearly extravagant. [23] Ohio also received several early relief loans. On July 27 Governor George White informed the RFC that the state had established the Ohio Relief Commission, had authorized counties and cities to divert to relief programs all revenue from gasoline and motor

vehicle taxes, had levied a special relief tax on eleven public utilities, and
had permitted the counties to issue bonds in anticipation of the tax. Early
in August Ohio received a loan of $850,000.[24] By the end of August the
Emergency Relief Division had loaned $17,321,669 to nine states. Illinois
because of extraordinary need received $9 million of the total. In Sep-
tember another $18,143,502 was distributed to twenty-one states. At this
point the administration was pleased: funds were being released prior to
the election while local resources were being stimulated.[25]

But political disaster engulfed the administration because of a bitter
controversy with Governor Gifford Pinchot of Pennsylvania. Since his
victory over William S. Vare and the Philadelphia machine in 1930,
Pinchot had vainly struggled to modernize Pennsylvania's relief
programs. He was seriously handicapped by conservatives in his own
party and by the provision in the state constitution prohibiting debt-
financing of relief appropriations. In the spring of 1932 Pinchot confronted
a social catastrophe: Pennsylvania had nearly 1,500,000 unemployed
workers, and state, local, and private resources for welfare appeared
exhausted.[26] His only alternative was federal relief, which he had been
advocating for over a year. By 1932 Pinchot was one of the nation's most
articulate spokesmen for federal relief. He was a member of the
Republican party, which meant he could not be charged with partisan
hostility for President Hoover. He was also a veteran politician and
reformer with a nationwide reputation and influence.[27]

On July 18, before the Emergency Relief and Construction Act had
become law, Pinchot had appealed to the RFC for a loan of $45 million,
calling it a "conservative estimate of Pennsylvania's urgent relief needs."
He then created the State Emergency Relief Board to handle relief
funds.[28] The Board of Directors of the RFC unanimously delayed action on
application because of its size—the $45 million that he had asked for was
15 percent of the total relief appropriation. In view of requests of other
state governors, the $300 million to be distributed by the RFC appeared
insufficient. The money had to be distributed equitably and had to last
throughout the winter. So the RFC board delayed Pennsylvania's early
application until their surveys could provide them with a reasonably accurate national picture.[29]

Governor Pinchot was disappointed. He realized that relief funds in
sufficient amounts from the RFC would be difficult to obtain. At the same
time the RFC was trying to conserve its relief funds, more than 300,000
people in Philadelphia were out of work; and needy families applying for
relief were being rejected because the city's funds were nearing
exhaustion. Conditions in the counties surrounding Pittsburgh were
similar. Pinchot was desperate and growing increasingly angry over the
apparent insensitivity of the Hoover administration.[30] The stage was set
for a confrontation.

On August 3, the board unanimously agreed that Pennsylvania had
not done enough to meet its relief needs. Both Democrats and Republicans
on the board felt that the state could raise more money of its own, and

Hoover was upset about the state's constitutional limitations on relief appropriations. Two days later, Pinchot and a delegation of state officials met with the RFC board to appeal the initial decision and to impress them with the magnitude of the state's crisis. The board remained adamant; Pomerene announced that the application had to be rejected. He informed Pinchot that Illinois had recently provided an extra $20 million for relief and Ohio had come up with $25 million, but Pennsylvania had raised only $10 million. The board unanimously agreed that this was not enough. Not until the state legislature raised more money would federal assistance be forthcoming. [31]

Still willing to cooperate, Pinchot decided to work through channels for the time being; he did not make public the extent of his disenchantment with the RFC. He simply objected to postponement of the loan, claiming that the people of Pennsylvania were already overtaxed and that relief services were all but nonexistent.[32] At about this time the Illinois legislature further undermined Pinchot's arguments by voting to double its property tax, which it hoped would bring in another $25 million for relief. The RFC responded with a loan of $6 million to Illinois.[33]

On August 19, Pinchot told Pomerene that a $12 million bill for unemployment relief had been passed by the Pennsylvania General Assembly. It would be financed through the 1 percent sales tax that the assembly had recently approved. The assembly had also passed a bill authorizing political subdivisions within the state to borrow against delinquent taxes for relief purposes, and Pinchot had submitted a constitutional amendment providing for state reimbursement of each subdivision. He then repeated his request for a loan of $45 million.[34]

Again the board rejected the request and urged him to raise another $20 million through a 2 percent gasoline tax, a diversion of highway funds, and an occupational tax.[35] It was too much for the governor. In September he decided that political discretion was fruitless, and he made public the deep bitterness he felt toward the RFC. He appealed to Senator Robert Wagner for support in the controversy over the intention of the Emergency Relief and Construction Act. Wagner responded by saying that

our first and undeviating objective in the making of the relief and construction act was the extension of aid to the hungry and destitute. In the practical administration of the act that purpose must be the final arbiter of every question. No administrative policy, the result of which is that the hungry and needy are denied adequate assistance, conforms to the intent of Congress in writing this humanitarian legislation.[36]

Throughout September Pinchot continued his attack. Earlier he had termed the RFC a dole to the wealthy,[37] and he was ready to repeat the charges unless the corporation surrendered on this issue. The RFC had no intention of surrendering. In an address to the Welfare and Relief Mobilization Conference, Pomerene had already made the administration's position clear, saying that the unemployment relief program of the RFC would not become a pork barrel for states that were unwilling to sustain themselves. Only when the state's entire capacity for relief, both public and private, was exhausted would the federal government intervene. As far as the RFC board was concerned, Pennsylvania was not yet in that condition.[38]

For Governor Pinchot, Pomerene's statement was the last straw. People in Pennsylvania were starving, and the RFC was preaching voluntarism, charity, and brotherly love. On September 17 he made a personal appeal to Hoover, asking him to cut the red tape and grant the loan. Pinchot was angry over what looked like RFC insensitivity to the relief crisis. On September 21, the RFC finally granted a loan of $2.5 million.[39] Pinchot considered it totally inadequate. Three days later, he leveled the ultimate criticism at the President, charging him with possessing a sympathy only for the rich. In a well-publicized letter to Pomerene, he charged:

in giving help to the great banks, great railroads, and great corporations you have shown no such niggardly spirit . . . our people have little patience with giving everything possible to the big fellow and as little as possible to the little fellow.[40]

From a member of the Republican party just six weeks before the election, Pinchot's attack was politically devastating.

The Pennsylvania governor would not be satisfied with anything less than $45 million from the RFC, and throughout the winter he engaged in a running battle with corporation officials over the size of their loans. In the middle of October he demanded that the RFC make relief funds available to Pennsylvania through April 1, 1933. Otherwise it would be too difficult to plan the relief program. On October 22 Fred Croxton informed him that RFC policy would not permit long-term relief grants.[41] Pinchot was extremely upset, and one week later he led a protest delegation of state officials to Washington to confront the RFC board. Pinchot bitterly complained that Illinois, with fewer unemployed workers than Pennsylvania, had received $20 million in RFC loans; while Pennsylvania, including a tentative grant made to cover relief needs in November, had received only $5 million. He asked the corporation to recognize that Pennsylvania now had a relief commission capable of administering the program in every locality and the state's industrial areas were in desperate condition. When Jesse Jones urged patience and Pomerene asked Pinchot what more the state legislature could do for relief, the governor refused to answer and abruptly terminated the meeting.[42]

Pinchot's tactics paid off again: on November 3 the Emergency Relief Division granted Pennsylvania another loan of $5,462,265, accompanied as usual with a stern warning from Pomerene. The entire RFC board was upset about Pinchot's last application. In his outline of projected relief needs for the month, he had indicated that $9.5 million was needed—$1.5 million was to come from state funds and another $1 million from private sources. He therefore requested a $7 million loan from the RFC. This meant that the board was being asked to carry 70 percent of Pennsylvania's relief burden, which it was not willing to do. As Pomerene argued, "The figures above clearly indicate that the state and some of its local political subdivisions are not doing their duty to the people of the state in meeting distress." [43]

Pinchot brought his campaign to a symbolic climax by making a public appeal to Senator Edward P. Costigan of Colorado. Pinchot charged that red tape, one-month grants, and restricted funds seriously handicapped the state's relief program. He accused the RFC and Hoover of granting assistance to Pennsylvania only because of the national election. Without that, he argued, Pennsylvania would have received little or no relief. He asked Congress to investigate the RFC and formulate plans for an expanded relief program. [44]

Despite the controversy with Pinchot, the Emergency Relief Division did establish an important precedent for the country. By March 1933 the RFC had made loans to every state in the union except Wyoming, New Jersey, Vermont, Nebraska, Maryland, Massachusetts, Connecticut, and Delaware—a total of $210,461,760. Of that total, $122,889,000 went to only six states: [45]

Illinois	$44,738,000
Pennsylvania	26,705,000
Michigan	13,809,000
New York	13,200,000
Ohio	12,525,000
Wisconsin	11,912,000

Never before in the United States had the federal government undertaken such an extensive public relief program. But because of the controversy with Pinchot in the fall of 1932, these loans only reinforced liberal and progressive criticisms of the Hoover administration.

The Emergency Relief Division failed to redeem the reputation of the RFC for several reasons. (1) The administration believed from the beginning that it would be difficult to make the $300 million last through the winter; if the board responded immediately to all the initial applications, the funds would be inequitably distributed and quickly exhausted. (2) Members of the RFC board, both Republicans and Democrats, desperately wanted to stimulate local resources by forcing the states to increase taxes or float bond issues for relief. By making RFC loans contingent on increased local taxes, the board assumed it would be able to increase substantially the total amount of relief funds throughout the country. (3) Philosophical caution inhibited the program. To preserve "local initiative and brotherhood" the Emergency Relief Division only granted small loans for monthly periods. Ohio for example received its loans in thirty-seven separate installments.[46] The board believed that only complete exhaustion of local resources and constant uncertainty among local officials over the source of their funds could preserve "the charitable disposition of the people generally." Nothing would be worse, it assumed, than for the federal government to usurp the responsibilities of local governments [47] Liberals and progressives exploited this policy as further evidence of Hoover's callous disregard for the suffering of the unemployed. It was a terrible irony: Herbert Hoover, once the greatest relief administrator in history, now appeared insensitive to the needs of the poor. Although the Emergency Relief Division had been far more active than the Self-Liquidating Division, the political consequences were the same: the RFC, so generous with the banks but so cautious with the unemployed, appeared to be an instrument of big business and completely oblivious to the real disaster engulfing the nation.

The Emergency Relief and Construction Act had also authorized the RFC to expand its agricultural loans—under the original RFC act the corporation had already provided over $130 million to the secretary of agriculture for crop loans to farmers. [48] The Emergency Relief and Construction Act called on the RFC to establish a system of twelve regional agricultural credit corporations to help farmers refinance outstanding obligations and sustain their agricultural activities. On August 19, with Wilson McCarthy and Ford Hovey directing the new Agricultural Credit Division, the RFC established one Regional Agricultural Credit Corporation (RACC) in each Federal Land bank district. The RFC then loaned each of these twelve corporations $3 million to begin work. [49] The RFC reserved the right to appoint all directors of the credit corporations; restricted credit corporation loans to farmers and stockmen while excluding canners, packers, commission merchants, and cooperatives; decided that loans could be made only for refinancing and for the cost of seed, cultivation, harvesting, and marketing; and, to avoid competition with private lenders, set the interest rate on RACC loans at a minimum of 7 percent. [50]

The Agricultural Credit Division could also loan funds to banks, agricultural credit corporations, and livestock loan companies, which could then reloan the RFC money to marketing corporations selling agricultural products. The administration had concluded that commodity prices were deflated because the normal distributors and consumers of commodities could not get credit to make initial purchases from farmers; consequently, the demand for the products as well as the prevailing price level was down. If distributors could acquire the credit necessary to purchase supplies from farmers, then demand would revive and adequate prices would be restored. The key to the problem was the same as that for industrial production: the supply of credit. [51] President Hoover and the RFC board believed that the agricultural depression was a product of the rural credit crisis. The administration believed that after harvesting their crops debt-ridden farmers, severely pressed by current expenses, had to sell their commodities in glutted markets at low prices. [52]

The Agricultural Credit Division had one objective: to increase the supply of credit to individual farmers and intermediate lending institutions. The Regional Agricultural Credit Corporations, through their loans to individual farmers, would fill the void left by overcautious rural banks. Farmers with funds to pay off current expenses would be under no financial pressure to sell their crops in glutted, postharvest markets; and commodity prices would begin to return to normal levels. Also, RFC loans to financial intermediaries would provide marketing corporations and consumer industries, particularly cotton textiles, with the credit they needed to make normal purchases of raw materials and commodity products; that too would stimulate demand and raise prices. [53]

Unfortunately, the Agricultural Credit Division never fulfilled the hopes of either the administration or the agrarian community. McCarthy and Hovey were discouraged because farmers did not apply for RACC loans. The farmers complained that the 7 percent interest rate was exorbitant — under no circumstances would they accept funds at those prices. Consequently, the RFC never increased the capital of the RACCs beyond the initial $36 million authorized by the Emergency Relief and Construction Act. By the November elections, the Agricultural Credit Division had financed only $5 million in loans by the Regional Agricultural Credit Corporations. [54]

The RFC encountered similar problems in its loans to intermediate financial institutions. Private financial institutions refused to cooperate with the Agricultural Credit Division, because, reluctant to compete with other private lenders, the division charged 6-7 percent on its loans. Bankers felt the rates were excessive — agricultural prices were too low and too unstable to guarantee investment and make the risk of reloaning government funds worthwhile. Since the RFC would not guarantee the loans, bankers would not carry the risk themselves. President Hoover and the RFC board were disappointed. Late in November, Atlee Pomerene threatened that unless the program soon received their cooperation the RFC would bypass private institutions and make direct loans to farmers, marketing organizations, and industries. But, the bankers remained uncooperative. Although negotiations took place for $50 million loans to the Cotton Stabilization Corporation and to the government of China for the purchase of American cotton, high interest rates of the RFC scuttled both deals. During 1932 the Agricultural Credit Division loaned a paltry $1,500,000 to private financial institutions. The division was a failure. [55]

Despite the lift the administration experienced in August, the Emergency Relief and Construction Act doomed the President to political defeat. The Self-Liquidating Division and the Agricultural Credit Division had been woefully inadequate, and the Emergency Relief Division, even though it released most of its allocation, further embarrassed the administration because of the controversy with Pinchot. The RFC relief programs reinforced the public's disgust for the President. Henry Rainey's warning came true.

The RFC relief programs failed for several reasons. The magnitude of the depression brought circumstances beyond the President's control. Complex engineering problems created frustrating delays for the Self-Liquidating Division, and the $300 million relief appropriation seemed inadequate to the RFC board after the first wave of applications arrived. These circumstances hurt the President by negating the impact of the

RFC. Both the President and the Board of Directors had overestimated the flexibility of the self-liquidating program and underestimated the extent of the nation's relief needs. President Hoover had promised too much. When the RFC failed to redeem that promise, the public abandoned him.

Economic miscalculation also characterized RFC relief programs. Although there was no danger of competing with private banks, the administration set interest rates on RFC loans unreasonably high, killing the desire of many legitimate borrowers to apply. They also mistakenly assumed that demand for agricultural loans on the part of the textile industries and marketing corporations was high while arguing that the cautious attitude of bankers was responsible for the continuing slide in commodity prices. Again the administration was concerned only with the supply dimension of the crisis; in reality, the need for credit by textile industries and marketing corporations was limited by the general instability of the entire economy and low consumer demand.

To a lesser extent American Individualism inhibited RFC relief work, if only because it helped make the program so controversial. The President and the RFC board unanimously agreed that if the RFC supplanted public and private relief agencies, the loyalties of the poor would shift from local groups to the federal government and the Washington bureaucracy would dominate yet another area of social and economic power. They insisted on releasing funds only as a last resort, after a maximum contribution from local institutions. But if the administration was ideologically pure, its leaders were politically naive. While they conscientiously distributed relief funds, they constantly warned against the dangers of their actions and reiterated their misgivings about the program. By preaching American Individualism they left themselves open to criticism; anyone could blame the inadequacies of their program on their philosophy. Pinchot's criticisms of the RFC illustrated the danger of this.

The RFC relief programs did establish important precedents and create an administrative momentum leading directly to the New Deal. The Self-Liquidating Division was a forerunner of the Public Works Administration (PWA) of the New Deal. In February 1933 the administration began to consider important changes in the Self-Liquidating Division. Harvey Couch appeared before the Senate Committee on Banking and Currency and asked Congress to permit the RFC to undertake a much broader building program that was concerned not with the redemption of loans but with the creation of new jobs for the unemployed. Such an amendment would permit the RFC to make loans on projects that were not fully secured or might not be completely self-liquidating.[56] During the famous "One Hundred Days" of the New Deal, Congress created the Public Works Administration as a direct extension of the Self-Liquidating Division of the RFC. On June 16, 1933, all RFC authority to make loans for public works was transferred to Harold Ickes and the PWA. Throughout 1933 and 1934 Harvey Couch assisted Ickes in administering the program. Couch transferred all his own records to the PWA and even allowed some of the RFC clerical personnel in the Self-Liquidating Division to move over to the new agency.[57] The PWA immediately assumed control of the construction projects the RFC had begun and relied heavily on the appraisals of pending projects already completed by the Self-Liquidating Division engineering staff.[58] Thus a large measure of credit for the origin of the Public Works Administration must go to the RFC and the Hoover administration for the precedent they established and the institutional momentum they initiated.

The Emergency Relief Division of the RFC also provided President Franklin Roosevelt with a model during the early days of his administration. The frustration experienced by many governors and liberal congressmen over RFC relief loans generated several attempts to amend the Emergency Relief and Construction Act in the lame duck session of the 72d Congress. Senator Wagner led the assault by sponsoring a bill to double the $300 million relief appropriation, to eliminate the requirement that states be completely destitute before federal assistance could be given, and to discontinue one-month loans.[59] Senators Costigan and La Follette supported Wagner's legislation but insisted that the RFC distribute the money as grants rather than loans.[60] Because of White House hostility and the difference of opinion over the grant provision, the Congress failed to pass the bill before the inauguration of Roosevelt.

But during the "One Hundred Days" that followed, Congress created the Federal Emergency Relief Administration. The FERA received $500 million to carry on the work begun by the RFC under the Emergency Relief and Construction Act. By mid-May 1933 the RFC had distributed the $300 million, and Fred Croxton urged Roosevelt to nominate an administrator for the new FERA so that more funds could be granted during May and June. After Roosevelt selected Harry Hopkins as administrator, the FERA took up where the RFC Emergency Relief Division left off. It drew on the services of staff personnel who had worked in the Emergency Relief Division, and the administrator's funds came from the RFC. The FERA relied extensively on the state and local relief agencies that the RFC had ordered the states to organize in 1932 as a prerequisite for government loans. Like the Emergency Relief Division, Hopkins left the main burden of administration to the states. He required that all FERA work projects had to be public rather than private, all recipients of relief had to be destitute, and no project worker could replace an already employed worker. Hopkins drew heavily on the information and area studies the Emergency Relief Division had collected during 1932-1933.[61] During 1933 the FERA spent the entire RFC grant of $500 million and succeeded where the Emergency Relief Division of the RFC had failed.[62] But a distinct line of continuity linked the Emergency Relief Division with the Federal Emergency Relief Administration.

Also, the RFC Agricultural Credit Division paved the way for the Commodity Credit Corporation. The principle of federal price support assistance had been firmly established in 1929 when Congress passed the Agricultural Marketing Act and created the Federal Farm Board. The Federal Farm Board had intended to support farm prices by making loans to cooperatives and stabilization corporations for the purchase of staple crops. The Emergency Relief and Construction Act sought to supplement the Farm Board by providing for RFC loans to rural banks and marketing associations. Although only $1.5 million was loaned under the RFC program, it did join with the Agricultural Marketing Act of 1929 in setting the precedent for federal loans to support farm prices.[63] In October 1933 President Roosevelt took advantage of that precedent and founded the Commodity Credit Corporation as an affiliated corporation of the RFC; the Commodity Credit Corporation replaced the private institutions the RFC had tried to work through in 1932 and 1933.[64] Under the New Deal arrangement the RFC loaned money to the Commodity Credit Corporation, which then reloaned it to bankers, businessmen, and farmers. The Commodity Credit Corporation also assumed fiscal responsibility for the $1.5 million the RFC had loaned under the old program. The Agricultural Credit Division of the RFC now directed the RFC fiscal relationship with the Commodity Credit Corporation, which was a logical extension of the work of the RFC Agricultural Credit Division during the Hoover administration.[65]

In light of RFC activities under the Emergency Relief and Construction Act, it is obvious that the Hoover administration played an important role in the development of twentieth century American public policy. Despite its failure to end poverty and revive the economy, the Reconstruction Finance Corporation established important precedents in banking, unemployment, relief, and agriculture. Unfortunately for President Hoover, history's memories for accomplishments is far clearer than its recollection of precedents. He should not be remembered as the man who followed Calvin Coolidge into the White House, but as the man who preceded Franklin Roosevelt.

8

Final Collapse

ALTHOUGH the relief activities of the RFC captured the public's attention during the fall and the winter of 1932/33, the most important objective of the Hoover administration remained that of financial reconstruction. Administration officials considered the RFC relief programs as artificial tools designed to relieve suffering, prevent social instability, and blunt political criticism until the bank reconstruction loans finally stimulated a complete recovery. But despite RFC programs under the Emergency Relief and Construction Act, suffering had increased, social instability had intensified, and political criticism had become even more severe. Unfortunately, the RFC bank reconstruction program would similarly fail and ultimately bring the nation close to financial ruin.

Back in August the RFC financial record had seemed quite impressive. To banks and trust companies, the corporation had authorized loans totaling $853,496,289 and had actually advanced $706,591,780. To assist the money market in general, the RFC had approved a total of $264,366,933 and advanced $228,051,573 to various railroads. Building and loan associations had received $80,310,984 of an $87,638,738 commitment. To various insurance companies, the RFC had promised $75,193,200 and had forwarded $59,433,319. Finally, the corporation had offered $83,846,000 to hundreds of mortgage loan companies and had advanced a total of $80,485,998. Compared to previous peacetime efforts by the federal government, it was a remarkable achievement. Including its loans to Federal Land banks, joint stock land banks, livestock loan companies, agricultural credit corporations, and credit unions, the RFC had authorized $1,410,026,518 in loans and had advanced $1,180,441,982.[1] These totals did not include expenditures under the Emergency Relief and Construction Act.

The administration felt optimistic about its work. In August 1932 the collective opinion of the RFC Board of Directors was more positive than at any time since March. Ogden Mills claimed that the RFC had saved the banks of the United States, and had begun to restore the faith of many bankers:[2]

The cumulative effect of all our efforts at last began to tell. The strain under which all have labored for many long months was relieved. The blind fear which had led men to doubt our ability to survive disappeared. Whatever disappointments and setbacks might be experienced in recovery from the business depression, the financial panic had been definitely overcome. The national credit had been made secure, the integrity of the dollar was no longer open to question.[3]

Although some of this new faith was election rhetoric, several more tangible reasons helped the administration believe that the worst was over.

President Hoover thought that the new Democratic majority on the RFC board would negate some of the criticism the corporation had been receiving from Congress. He hoped that the removal of Meyer as chairman would dim the prevailing view of the RFC as a tool of Wall Street, and with Atlee Pomerene and Charles Miller personal relationships on the board were more cordial in August than ever before.[4] New leadership also meant new energy and higher morale.

Moreover, the general economic climate of the late summer inspired confidence. Ever since the Chicago liquidity crisis in June, financial indicators had improved considerably. The number of bank failures dropped from 151 in June to 131 in July, 85 in August, and 67 in September. Deposits of Federal Reserve member banks increased from $24,712,000,000 in July to $25,292,000,000 in October. Member banks had reduced their borrowings from Federal Reserve banks to the lowest point in a year while building up their reserve balances to approximately $2.5 billion, the highest level since June 1931.[5] Securities prices increased from an average of thirty-four in June to fifty-eight in October, railroad prices jumped from fourteen in June to thirty-five in September, and utilities values increased from fifty-five to ninety-one during the same period. Also, applications by banks for RFC loans had drastically declined—in July the board evaluated about fifty applications per day, but in October they received only seventeen per day. Although Pomerene and Miller suspected that some banks were reluctant to apply for RFC loans because of the initiation of publication of RFC transactions, they also believed that fewer banks needed assistance.[6] In October the administration was further encouraged because for the first time repayments on previous loans exceeded the amount the RFC had distributed to banks.[7]

Another reason for optimism was that late in July Congress had passed the Home Loan Bank Act; and with $125 million in capital from the RFC, the new Home Loan banks began to discount the home mortgages of building and loan associations. The administration believed the banks would liquefy the market for mortgages and revive the construction industry.[8] In the late summer of 1932, Hoover and the administration believed they had finally stabilized the money market by eliminating bank and railroad suspensions.[9] Their confidence was restrained, but their feelings of success and relative security were daily becoming stronger.

But they were still worried about bank credit. Although the corporation had brought bank failures under control, industrial recovery had not followed. The RFC directors still believed that businessmen throughout the country were demanding bank credit to expand production and were confident enough about the economic future to assume new debts.[10] But the administration saw that commercial loans had declined from $20,622,544,000 to $10,895,374,000 between 1928 and 1932 and bankers had replaced commercial loans with more liquid U.S. government securities.[11] The Hoover administration realized that these investment policies left the RFC impotent. Without increases in commercial credit and industrial production, RFC loans would actually become class actions on behalf of the financial community.[12] Because interest rates were at their lowest point in history,[13] the administration was convinced that bankers were just being too conservative.[14] For their part, bankers replied that they were only being prudent with depositors' money and the RFC was overestimating the number of eligible borrowers and the demand for credit. Nevertheless, the administration was still convinced that a relaxation of the credit crisis would eventually bring the depression to an end.[15]

The new campaign to increase commercial credit had begun quietly when Hoover had first interviewed Pomerene about his appointment to the RFC. In describing that meeting on July 24, 1932, Pomerene recalled,

The President said that many of the banks were failing to perform their duties to their clientele and to aid industry and that, if we could not bring about a change for the better in the next four to five months, the country would be a financial loss.[16]

Hoover had believed then that a degree of financial stability had been achieved, and during the remaining six months of his administration, he had committed the RFC to a more important objective: convincing private bankers to expand the volume of their commercial loans.

To outline that objective, Hoover sponsored a conference of the Federal Reserve Banking and Industrial committees. As usual, he resorted to the analogue of war to introduce the program, announcing that the conference would "organize a concerted program of action along the whole economic front."[17] He went on to say that "the major financial crisis of the depression has been overcome, but the war is not over."[18] The avowed purpose of the meetings was to express confidence in the banking structure and convince bankers of the need to expand their commercial lending. On August 26, the committees met in Washington to discuss ways of coordinating credit relations between bankers and businessmen. Throughout the day a parade of Treasury, Federal Reserve, and RFC officials argued that financial stability had now been restored by the government, thus shifting the burden of responsibility to private business — bankers should put aside their liquidity fears and increase their loans to businessmen.[19] In a speech to the National Radio Forum on August 29, Jesse Jones summarized the sentiment of the conference:

There has been too much reluctance on the part of banks, trust companies, insurance companies, etc., to borrow for the purpose of relending, not alone from the R.F.C. but from any source. Most banks have been endeavoring to get as liquid as possible, some of them too much so for the public good.[20]

Unfortunately, the optimistic program of the RFC was tragically short-lived. During the peak of the fall election campaign, Ogden Mills remarked,

Wouldn't things be much worse if every bank was closed and the savings of 40,000,000 depositors tied up and no credit facilities available? Wouldn't they be much worse if the assets of our great fiduciary institutions . . . were completely frozen; if all values were temporarily frozen from lack of a market. [21]

Mills, unaware, had accurately portrayed what the country's financial condition would shortly become. The RFC not only failed to stimulate an increase in commercial credit but was premature in its belief that financial stability had been restored. Immediately following the conference of the Banking and Industrial committees, a series of minor banking crises which undermined the prevailing optimism developed in several western states and then in the Midwest. It was a repetition of the crisis in June — throughout the early spring the RFC board had confidently assumed that bank failures had been brought under control, but in June the crisis in Chicago had dashed their assumptions. Throughout the late fall and the winter of 1932/33, the RFC moved from crisis to crisis, losing its prestige in the process and presiding over the collapse of the American banking system.

In August a panic developed in Boise, Idaho. Idaho banks had suffered from serious declines in mineral, lumber, and agricultural industries; delinquencies on bank loans were common. Early in the month the Boise City National Bank suspended, initiating a run on banks throughout the Boise Valley and in eastern Oregon. The pressure was acute at the First National Bank of Idaho in Boise, and on August 31 it closed.[22] Nine of the bank's affiliates had to close as well.[23] On September 2 several other banks in central Idaho declared moratoriums restricting withdrawals. [24] For the Hoover administration it was a serious problem, threatening to snowball into a regional financial crisis, so the RFC intervened. After the $90 million loan to the Central Republic Bank in Chicago which had failed to save the bank, the RFC board realized that even massive loans could not save banks on the verge of total insolvency. The administration wanted to provide Idaho with a permanent solution to its difficulties.[25] After weeks of careful examination, the RFC decided that four small banks would have to be placed in receivership; the corporation then loaned $2 million to the First National Bank, and on November 1 the bank and its affiliates reopened.[26]

The Idaho crisis was immediately followed by a crisis in Nevada on November 1 when the state governor, Fred Balzar, declared a banking holiday. The Wingfield banking chain, which controlled twelve of Nevada's forty-one banks, possessed more than 65 percent of all the deposits in the state and more than 75 percent of all commercial loans. The Reno National Bank, center of the chain and largest bank in the state, served as the financial agent for the state's public funds.[27] The Nevada economy had also suffered under the impact of the depression. Both livestock and mineral prices had dropped precipitously, stagnating the entire economy. In addition to the general deterioration of their assets, Nevada banks suffered when livestock raisers, with virtually no market for their stock, defaulted on loan repayments. In 1932 the Wingfield chain lost $3.5 million through defaults on agricultural loans.[28]

As pressures mounted on the state's banks, their only recourse was the Reconstruction Finance Corporation. The RFC board realized that the Wingfield chain was in serious condition and if it folded a panic might spread throughout the West. They also feared that state funds deposited in the Reno National Bank would be jeopardized if the bank failed;[29] consequently, the RFC had loaned $5,170,000 to the Wingfield chain earlier in 1932.[30] But it was not enough. In October the Wingfield chain informed state banking officials that suspension was imminent. On October 30 Governor Balzar flew to Washington, D.C., and met with President Hoover and the RFC board, begging them to save the Nevada banking system. After careful consideration the RFC refused to make more loans, and Balzar immediately declared a holiday to protect the state's other banks.[31] Throughout November negotiations with the RFC continued. Finally, the corporation agreed to make more loans to the Wingfield banks if the chain could attract $500,000 in new capital. But no major private investors were interested in supplying it. The RFC then refused to throw good money after bad and the holiday continued. On December 14, 1932, the Wingfield chain formally suspended and federal and state banking authorities quickly assumed control of the institutions.[32]

The Midwest displayed a disturbing instability as well. During the last quarter of the year, simultaneously with the banking difficulties in the West, 140 banks that had received RFC loans failed. Seventy-nine of the banks were in seven north central and plains states: Minnesota, Wisconsin, Iowa, Missouri, Kansas, Nebraska, and South Dakota. For the RFC board such a concentration of failures, particularly among banks which had received assistance from the RFC, was especially frustrating. It also was concerned that instability in those states might spread into Chicago or Detroit, triggering a nationwide banking crisis.[33]

The onset of financial difficulties in the West and Midwest revived administration doubts about the general strength of the banking system, and several economic indicators declined later in the year. In October securities prices weakened, wiping out the late summer gains,[34] and the number of bank failures began to climb. In October 102 banks suspended, in November 95, and in December 100.[35] These statistics did not compare with those of 1931, but they were unsettling. Equally frightening, applications for RFC loans, which had declined to 462 in November, climbed to 633 in December.[36] Depositors throughout the country responded to fact and rumor by withdrawing their funds from banks. During the last quarter of 1932, the banking system sustained a loss of over $300 million in deposits, further dissipating its ability to survive a renewal of the 1931 liquidity crisis.[37]

It had become obvious to Hoover, the RFC, and Congress that the corporation's statutory authority would have to be extended. The President's hope that the RFC would serve only as an emergency measure ebbed in the face of new economic problems. Hoover and the RFC board began to worry that even after eleven months the RFC had not substantially assisted the economy. Hundreds of million of loan dollars were still outstanding by December 31, and the RFC was deeply engaged in its relief and employment projects. More and more it began to appear that the corporation's life might be of indefinite duration, and it would be much more difficult for the government to withdraw from the situation than it had been to invade it.[38]

More than anything else Hoover had hoped to contain RFC power and limit its tenure, but the vast dimensions of the depression had forced him to expand the corporation's scope, and now, to extend its life. His convictions about survival instincts of bureaucracies were confirmed. By December the RFC employed over 4,000 people nationwide, had authorized loans of $1,623,704,844, and had advanced $1,427,603,122. Banks and railroads had received $850,822,060 and $284,311,271, respectively. Building and loan associations had accepted $93,933,114, while insurance companies received $68,037,618. Mortgage loan companies had been granted loans of $88,332,020.[39] The RFC had expanded far beyond original expectations even though administration officials had assumed in January 1932 that most of its appropriated funds would not have to be used. Now the President found it impossible to dismantle the Reconstruction Finance Corporation. His hopes for an early end to the depression had been premature, and on December 8, 1932, he exercised his option and extended the authority of the RFC beyond its one-year limit to include January 1934.[40]

It was a fortuitous decision; although the administration did not yet realize it, the banking system was heading into an absolute liquidity crisis. Severe problems plagued the financial structure. Most banks in rural areas were still undercapitalized; over 57 percent of the state bank failures in Michigan, for example, were concentrated in banks with $50,000 or less.[41] Even the largest banks were no longer immune to the crisis; as panic put pressure on small banks, it was translated into increased pressures on larger banks. Eroded assets and frightened depositors afflicted both large and small institutions.[42]

The entire system balanced precariously on the foundation of public confidence. As the weaknesses of a bank became public knowledge, runs on the bank's affiliates or neighboring institutions often developed and eventually the banks of a whole region could be affected. Any breach in public confidence in any area could lead to a run on the entire system. The banks were not liquid enough or sound enough to meet such a challenge.

The continuing decline in the securities markets impaired bank assets until in thousands of cases the value of their assets fell below their liabilities. If withdrawal pressures increased, bankers had to liquidate their assets at depressed values. Not until new investment restored their capital structures could these institutions become really solvent. But the reputation of banks as profitable investments had long since declined. Most bank directors and stockholders were unwilling to invest in their own banks; the public was similarly reticent.[43] President Hoover and the RFC ultimately decided to permit federal investment in private banks, but their decision came too late to save the system.[44]

Many banks also had difficulties because of their RFC loans. The RFC requirements that loans be "fully and adequately secured" severely restricted the corporation's ability to help troubled banks, and the RFC was able to help only those basically sound enterprises that needed temporary liquidity.[45] On the surface the corporation's record was impressive. During 1932 thousands of banks had needed and received RFC assistance; many would have failed otherwise. Approximately 10 percent of all banks receiving RFC loans failed anyway. For weaker banks the strict conditions of an RFC loan offered no solutions, and collateral requirements often forced banks to deposit their most liquid assets as security for advances.[46] These banks were then completely unprepared for the crisis that developed in February 1933.

The directors of the RFC believed they had no choice but to protect corporation resources by cautiously distributing the funds. With over $40 billion in deposit liabilities, the banking system dwarfed the capabilities of the RFC. At best, the corporation could only hope to deal with isolated situations and prevent regional panic. But this conservatism brought more criticism from the financial community. The administration was at a loss to deal with the bankers' charge that the RFC was too stingy with its funds.[47] An editorial in *Business Week* contained some caustic remarks:

What is the RFC?

Is it a pawnshop, or a fire department? If it is a pawnshop in which necessitous borrowers are compelled to hock assets worth two or three times the amount of the loan, we are opposed to it. . . . We see no reason why the government should be engaged in a careful pawnbroking enterprise, niggling over security, haggling over interest, competing with other lenders.

Is the RFC a fire department? If so, what is the idea in counting out the buckets of water?[48]

Such criticism seemed unfair to the administration. By December 31, 1932, the RFC had already authorized loans totaling $1,623,704,844. Its total appropriation under Section 5 of the original RFC act had only been $2 billion. The board directors could not see that the corporation had been unfair or stingy; they had loaned most of the money Congress had given them. Still, bankers accused them of being too conservative and of trying to protect their assets from the effects of the depression. They argued that the RFC was guilty of tunnel vision, of too often acting as bank examiners evaluating collateral for loans, and of ensuring that the corporation was not burdened with frozen assets. It was a distressing irony. While the government blamed bankers for being stingy with their commercial loans, the bankers accused the government of being too liquidity-conscious!

Commercial banks, savings banks, and insurance companies were still threatened by the condition of the railroads. The RFC board had originally hoped that temporary loans to the railroads would improve the value of their securities and strengthen the portfolios of financial institutions. During 1932 the corporation authorized loans of $337,435,093 to help railroads meet their operating expenses and fixed charges.[49] These loans had already brought severe criticism because many felt that the money had provided relief only to railroad executives and eastern bankers. These charges were largely true. The railroad loans had been ineffectual because the roads were victims not only of the industrial depression but of competition from pipelines and trucks. Not until 1940 would railroad revenue revive sufficiently to meet expenses. In the first seven months of 1932 the roads failed to meet their fixed charges by $160 million. Worse yet, while their total fixed obligations for 1932 were $181 million, they would mount to $295 million in 1933 and to a staggering $370 million in 1934.[50]

The problem was insurmountable. By 1931 the total funded debt of Class I steam railroads in the United States exceeded $10 billion and required hundreds of millions of dollars in service payments each year. At the same time railroad revenue declined from $896 million in 1929 to $134 million in 1931.[51] The railroads could not carry the burden, and they turned to the RFC.

But even the $337 million the RFC authorized in 1932 was not enough because revenues did not recover. Government loans only transferred the debt from private creditors to the RFC and increased its size, permitting some roads to postpone bankruptcy while perpetuating their weak financial structures. The Hoover administration was dealing with symptoms rather than causes; like its loans to banks, the corporation's railroad program did not see the real problems of declining revenue, increased competition, and burdensome debt structures.[52]

The RFC railroad program was a dismal failure. Of the total $337 million authorized in 1932, $280,274,000 went to only fifteen lines and ten of these ultimately filed for bankruptcy or judicial readjustment of their debts. Only five survived the depression and the RFC loans unscathed.[53] The combination of bankruptcies and chronic revenue deficits bred severe skepticism in the money markets, and railroad bonds continued to decline in value. In January 1932 the average price of railroad securities was thirty-seven. It dropped to fourteen in June, revived to thirty-five in September, and dropped again to twenty-six in December.[54] Despite $337 million in authorized loans and $284 million in actual advances, the RFC had not improved the railroad bond market. This deflationary spiral intensified the pressure on bank investment portfolios and aggravated the nation's financial difficulties. Railroad bonds remained frozen and unmarketable assets.

Finally, Federal Reserve policies in 1932-1933 contributed to the banking system's unpreparedness for a severe liquidity crisis. Throughout 1932 Federal Reserve officials had considered the RFC responsible for strengthening the banking system. Once the corporation had restored confidence by ending bank suspensions and railroad instability, lenders would use the funds that Federal Reserve open market operations had provided them to increase credit. When commercial credit did not increase in 1932, Federal Reserve officials blamed the RFC for not restoring banker confidence. Unfortunately, as Elmus Wicker demonstrated, "there was a failure of an overwhelming majority of the governors of the Federal Reserve Banks and members of the Federal Reserve Board to understand how open market operations could be used to counteract recessions and depressions."[55] In the face of the accumulation of excess reserves in New York and Chicago, the Open Market Policy Conference and the Federal Reserve Board decided on January 4, 1933, not to permit the total value of government securities holdings to exceed $1,851,000,000. They also decided to peg the maximum volume of excess reserves at $500 million, fearing that further purchases of government securities would increase excess reserves and lead to a suspension of interest payments on demand deposits that would certainly stimulate more hoarding. But in February 1933 the nation underwent a major liquidity panic, and the Federal Reserve's refusal to provide needed funds proved disastrous.[56]

By January 1933 the banking system was ready to collapse. The administration had gradually become pessimistic, defensive, and frustrated because the problems they faced in 1933 mirrored the problems of 1932. Massive RFC loans had failed to restore the health of the banking system. Several new political controversies in 1933 further weakened the banking system.

The final crisis for the RFC actually began in December when Congress convened for its lame duck session. Because of renewed economic decline and the controversies surrounding RFC relief programs, progressive Republicans and liberal Democrats intensified their attacks on the corporation. Senators La Follette and Couzens reopened the Senate Manufactures Committee hearings on relief and severely criticized RFC policies.[57] Senator Wagner also believed that the corporation had been negligent in its unemployment relief program and began writing legislation to change radically the RFC approach to the crisis.[58] Senator Norris had called for a major investigation of the RFC in December, and early in February Representative Hamilton Fish of New York asked Congress to investigate all businesses that had gone into receivership after accepting RFC assistance.[59] Senator Cordell Hull of Tennessee demanded that Congress investigate the corporation's agricultural loans and force the RFC to lower its interest rates to 4 percent.[60] At the very time that the Association of Railway Executives was asking for unlimited and unsecured RFC loans, Senator Couzens began an investigation to terminate all further RFC railroad loans.[61] Combined with the hostile attitudes of many businessmen, these criticisms brought on a rapid degeneration of morale on the RFC board early in 1933.

Compulsory publication of all RFC loans also assumed new importance in 1933. The Emergency Relief and Construction Act required the RFC to submit a monthly list of all borrowers to Congress, beginning with its August loans. Senator Joseph Robinson had promised the administration that the report would not be released to the press until Congress was in session, but John Nance Garner pressured South Trimble, the clerk of the House, into releasing the report in August.[62] Following the publication, the number of loan applications dropped precipitously. Although the board realized that the upturn in the economy partially explained the decline in applications, they worried that some bankers might be reluctant to apply for loans, since the public might interpret their application as a sign of weakness.[63] Throughout 1932 the RFC carried on a running battle with Congress concerning publication, but Trimble continued to release monthly reports.[64]

The administration fears were actually unjustified at that time. In August 1932 the first publication occurred, and the number of bank closings did not increase. During September only sixty-five banks failed, the smallest monthly total since March.[65]

But early in 1933 the situation had changed, since the election campaign of 1932 and the famous "interregnum" further weakened the banking system and made publication more significant. Throughout the campaign Democrats severely criticized the RFC and the banking system in general; during the process public faith in the system declined.[66] The interregnum did nothing to shore up public confidence; on the contrary, the political battle waged by Hoover and Roosevelt between November and March made matters worse. Hoover attempted to secure firm commitments from Roosevelt on a wide range of issues, including the balanced budget, the gold standard, and the foreign debt. Roosevelt remained completely neutral, refusing to sanction a repudiated program. Rumors about the future of the monetary system were rampant during the first two months of 1933.[67]

Into that climate of fear, rumor, and criticism came the congressional decision in January 1933 requiring the RFC to publish a list of loans made between February 2 and July 31, 1932, the period not covered by the Emergency Relief and Construction Act.[68] Again, no rash of failures accompanied the publication, but the issue raised questions in the public mind. If bankers and RFC officials so fiercely resisted publication, the public surmised there must be something to worry about. In an economy where the slightest change in public confidence could endanger the whole banking system, the controversy surrounding the publication of RFC loans contributed materially to public fear and consequently to the weakness of the banking system.[69]

Eventually, the RFC had to abandon its hope of increasing commercial credit. In the late summer of 1932, the board had believed that the liquidity crisis was over,[70] and the accumulation of excess reserves had strengthened Hoover's assumption that the banks were too frequently using RFC loans to liquefy themselves rather than to loosen up credit.[71] He had even threatened in November 1932 to undercut the banks by asking for congressional approval for direct RFC loans to business.[72] But by the end of the year optimism was turning into depression,[73] particularly in the face of the growing evidence of financial instability and irrationality in the banking system.[74] Instead of attempting to increase credit, the RFC reverted to its original goal of preventing bank failures because the state of crisis was persisting.

The first sign of serious regional instability appeared in Iowa. During the last two weeks of December and the first week of January several important Iowa banks closed, including the American Trust Company of Davenport. To stop the failures before they reached the major banks in Des Moines, the governor of Iowa declared a banking moratorium on January 20, 1933.[75]

At the same time several other important banks throughout the country, all recipients of RFC loans in 1932, experienced renewed difficulties. Late in January the Bank of America and Trust Company of Memphis, Tennessee, requested a loan of $13 million to meet the demands of its depositors. The governor of Tennessee, who feared that the failure of the bank would trigger a statewide panic, personally intervened with the RFC. The corporation granted the loan and the bank survived.[76] At the other end of the state in Knoxville, the East Tennessee National Bank and the Fidelity Bankers Trust Company both suffered runs by depositors and appealed to the RFC for help. Because their collateral was insufficient, the corporation refused the loan. Both banks teetered on the verge of failure.[77]

The problems in Tennessee and Iowa affected other banks in that part of the country. On January 25 the Pioneer Trust Company of Kansas City suspended and a wave of withdrawals engulfed the whole section. Great pressures were placed on the city's largest bank, the Fidelity National. It possessed over five hundred correspondents, two hundred of which would automatically close if it failed. The panic in Kansas and Missouri was complete. On January 25 the bank had over $31 million in deposits; $6 million were withdrawn during the next five days. Governor Hamilton of the Federal Reserve District of Kansas City intervened, arguing that the closing of the Fidelity National Bank would be a major financial disaster for his district. The RFC quickly evaluated the bank and authorized a loan of $7.5 million, but the damage had already been done. In January the number of bank suspensions climbed to 242, the highest monthly total in RFC history.[78]

Early in February another grave situation developed in New Orleans with the important Hibernia Bank and Trust Company. Severe runs for deposits had begun late in January and the bank was not liquid enough to meet the demand. Senator Huey Long appeared before the corporation and requested a loan of $20 million for the bank, claiming that its correspondents reached all the way into Arkansas, Tennessee, and Texas and made it a key financial institution for the entire South. The board agreed to dispatch a team of special RFC examiners to New Orleans, but on February 4 the governor of Louisiana declared a banking holiday to stop the runs that had quickly expanded over the entire state. The RFC then granted the loan. National concern over the condition of the banking system had intensified.[79] Within the RFC board serious apprehension about the depth of the crisis developed — an apprehension that would soon become pessimism, panic, and ultimately, a sense of helplessness.

In February an important monetary event occurred when large-scale withdrawals began. Although in late January there was no increase in the total volume of money in circulation, funds did begin to shift toward the healthier money markets in New York and Chicago. The public distrusted individual banks rather than the entire system, even though general skepticism was becoming stronger. The banks losing the cash were compelled to borrow on their sound assets from the RFC, convert their assets into cash at severely depressed prices, and draw on their balances at stronger banks — thereby placing them in jeopardy as well.[80] The banking system could not tolerate another major regional crisis.

The final blow came in mid-February when the two largest banks in Detroit closed. Detroit was particularly vulnerable to the financial crisis because of its dependency on the production of cars. The automobile industry was a barometer of the national economy. In the late 1920s two large holding companies, the Guardian Detroit Union Group and the Detroit Bankers' Company, were formed and came into control of dozens of important banks throughout the state. Both holding companies had become intimately related to the automobile companies in Detroit; and both had invested heavily in the securities markets during the twenties, borrowing depositor funds for some purchases and using their own stock as collateral. With the collapse of the stock market, both bank groups suffered from serious weaknesses in their capital structures.[81]

Early in January 1933 Lynn Talley of the RFC Examining Division visited Detroit to investigate rumors circulating about the city's banking situation. He thought that the Detroit Bankers' Company could survive, but he found the Guardian Detroit Union Group hopelessly insolvent. He returned to Washington and suggested an RFC loan to enable the Union Guardian Trust Company, largest bank of the Guardian Detroit Union Group, to pay off its depositors. On January 24, Ernest C. Kanzler, head of the Guardian Detroit Union Group, went to Washington and formally requested RFC assistance.[82]

The RFC board immediately dispatched John McKee, its leading bank examiner, and several assistants to Detroit to evaluate the condition of the Union Guardian Trust Company. The Hoover administration was convinced that if the Guardian Detroit Union Group failed, a chain reaction of failures would spread through Michigan and precipitate a nationwide panic. Earlier (in December) the RFC had tentatively approved a loan of $18 million to the Union Guardian Trust Company. McKee now decided that a total loan of $65 million from the RFC would be necessary to guarantee the survival of the Guardian Detroit Union Group.[83]

The RFC board tentatively agreed to grant the loan even though the actual loan value of the mortgage assets submitted as collateral amounted to only $37 million. The decision reflected administration concern, for the corporation was willing to absorb a paper loss of nearly $30 million to underwrite the assets of the Union Guardian Trust Company.[84]

The RFC plans, however, were upset by the criticisms of liberals, progressives, and extremists of several types. Father Coughlin, the populistic demagogue then popular as a radio commentator, accused Detroit bankers of intentionally conspiring to create a crisis as a means of attracting emergency government capital.[85] Senator Couzens, longtime critic of RFC railroad loans, argued that the federal government had no business loaning money to insolvent banks.[86] John T. Flynn, a liberal critic of the RFC and the Hoover administration, similarly attacked the whole idea of government loans to troubled Michigan banks, charging that Secretary of Commerce Roy Chapin (former head of the Hudson Motor Company) had illegally used his cabinet post to influence RFC decisions in favor of Detroit banks.[87]

The Board of Directors realized immediately that a large loan to the Guardian Detroit Union Group involving a $30 million paper loss would raise the liberal ire and bring on another major controversy resembling the Dawes crisis of June 1932. Instead, the board decided that $50 million, of which the RFC would loan $36 million, might save the Union Guardian Trust Company. That still left a $14 million deficit. The board expected the Guardian Detroit Union Group to either raise enough cash or subordinate enough deposits to cover the $14 million deficit and wanted them to raise $5 million for a new mortgage company to absorb their weaker assets.[88]

On February 9 President Hoover entered the negotiations and met with Senators Couzens and Arthur Vandenberg of Michigan, Undersecretary of the Treasury Arthur Ballantine, Ogden Mills, Roy Chapin, and Charles Miller. Couzens still opposed any RFC loan exceeding the value of the collateral and threatened to denounce it as a class action on behalf of the rich.[89] President Hoover presented his plan to Couzens and the rest of the group. Edsel Ford had agreed to subordinate a $7.5 million deposit in the Union Guardian Trust Company, and General Motors and Chrysler had offered to deposit $1 million each in the banks. Hoover then asked Couzens for a personal commitment of $1 million. At that point, the traditional rivalry between Henry Ford and Couzens complicated the proposal. Ford was a major stockholder in the Union Guardian Trust Company and Couzens refused to bail out his old enemy.[90]

On Saturday, February 11, President Hoover breakfasted with executives from General Motors, Chrysler, and Hudson; explained to them the situation; and asked them to return to Detroit and privately raise the remaining $4.5 million needed for the Guardian Detroit Union Group. Hoover sent Arthur Ballantine and Roy Chapin to Detroit to coordinate the plan.[91]

On February 12 Charles Miller of the RFC visited with Hoover and informed him that the General Motors, Chrysler, and Hudson executives had been able to raise only $825,000. Hoover's only option then was to ask Henry Ford not only to continue to subordinate the $7.5 million deposit but also to put up the additional $4.5 million in capital for the Union Guardian Trust Company. Late that evening Hoover telephoned Ford and proposed the idea, but Ford refused to commit any more money to the Union Guardian. He did agree to meet the following day with Roy Chapin and Arthur Ballantine.[92]

On February 13, with Hoover, Miller, and Mills keeping in touch over the telephone, Chapin and Ballantine met with Henry and Edsel Ford. The whole situation was annoying Henry Ford, and he argued that Couzens was trying to force him alone to support the whole Detroit financial structure. Ford refused to commit any new capital to the Union Guardian Trust Company, withdrew his offer to subordinate the $7.5 million deposit in the company, and said he would withdraw his $25 million deposit from the First National Bank of Detroit, the largest bank in the state and the central institution of the Detroit Bankers' Company. Chapin, Ballantine, Miller, Mills, and Hoover all pleaded with Ford, hoping to convince him of the national implications of his decision. But with characteristic stubbornness, Ford refused to yield even though the failures of the Union Guardian Trust Company and the First National Bank of Detroit were imminent.[93]

With no other choice, the RFC shifted its attention to the First National Bank of Detroit and the Detroit Bankers' Company. Because of the failure of the Guardian Detroit Union Group that would come with the suspension of the Union Guardian Trust Company and the upcoming withdrawal of $25 million in cash from the First National Bank, the officers of the Detroit Bankers' Company estimated they would need up to $200 million in cash to remain open. They applied to the RFC for a loan of $100 million, hoping to be able to raise the remainder by liquidating some of the company's better assets. But the RFC was unwilling to pour such a huge sum into such a desperate situation, particularly after concluding that the First National Bank of Detroit could not be saved. On February 13 the Union Guardian Trust Company and the First National Bank of Detroit suspended operations, and their respective groups also closed. The next day Governor Comstock declared a statewide eight-day moratorium on all banking activities.[94]

The Michigan moratorium aggravated the national dilemma. The movement of funds from weak to strong banks increased and direct withdrawals increased astonishingly, particularly in New York, Chicago, and Cleveland. In the first week following the Michigan holiday, the amount of money in circulation increased by $150 million. The crisis came in the final week of February when banks lost over $730 million in deposits. On March 1 the volume of money in circulation totaled $6.72 billion, an increase of over $1 billion since the first of the year. When it became evident that the RFC was unable to cope with such massive drains on thousands of banks, state after state arranged some form of restrictions on withdrawals.[95]

During the remaining two weeks of the Hoover administration, the RFC tried unsuccessfully to deal with a dizzying array of confusing and critical banking situations. Almost immediately after the onset of the holiday in Michigan, the banks of Cleveland experienced severe pressures from depositors. Both the Cleveland Trust Company and the Union Trust Company were in serious trouble, and RFC examiners began evaluating their assets in anticipation of a large loan. At the same time, the corporation continued to work on the crisis in Detroit, still trying to attract new investment capital and create a separate mortgage company to write off the poorer assets. They also considered the use of clearinghouse scrip to liquefy the city's economy.[96] The Baltimore Trust Company also appealed to the RFC for assistance during the last two weeks of February, but on February 24 Governor Ritchie of Maryland had to declare a three-day holiday.[97] The panic had gotten out of control, and the RFC was virtually helpless.

By February 23 all Indianapolis banks went on a restriction of 5 percent on withdrawals. On February 27, the Ohio governor declared a voluntary holiday and Arizona restricted withdrawals. And on March 1-2 Arizona, California, Idaho, Kentucky, Minnesota, Mississippi, Nevada, Oklahoma, Oregon, Tennessee, Texas, Utah, Washington, Wisconsin, Georgia, and New Mexico began bank holidays. Withdrawal restrictions were imposed in Iowa, Nevada, Nebraska, New Jersey, Pennsylvania, Vermont, West Virginia, Colorado, and North Carolina.[98] By March 3 only the banks in the largest financial centers were still open without restrictions, until on inauguration morning the governors of New York and Illinois closed the banks of New York City and Chicago.[99] The financial system had collapsed, and the worst fears of the Hoover administration had been realized. Despite nearly $2 billion in RFC loans in less than fourteen months to an incredible variety of private financial institutions, state relief commissions, local political subdivisions, and farmers, the economy had ceased to function by March 4, 1933.[100]

The work of the Reconstruction Finance Corporation during the administration of Herbert Hoover had been unprecedented in scope. As chief executive, Hoover had exerted more control over the national economy than any other peacetime president in American history. Under his direction the RFC had become deeply involved in banking, public works, agriculture, unemployment relief, and general finance— commitments from which the federal government would never really extricate itself. But on March 4, 1933, Herbert Hoover was a portrait in irony: he had done more than any other individual in United States history in an effort to end the depression, yet on leaving the White House he was the most unpopular man in the country. Despite all the loans, all the speeches, all the criticisms, and all the hopes, he and the Reconstruction Finance Corporation had failed.

9

Emergency Banking Act of 1933

ON March 4, 1933, the "war" finally ended for Herbert Hoover, and it appeared that he had lost — politically, economically, and historically. The banking system was in a state of ruin, and American citizens were confused and frightened about the future. Businessmen and workers, conservatives and liberals, and Republicans and Democrats had grown frustrated with Hoover's leadership, his philosophy, and his fears. Thirteen million people were unemployed, and throughout the country there was poverty and suffering that had not existed since the hard times of 1893. Hoover's own disappointment and pessimism reflected the national mood; he left Washington knowing that most Americans were glad to see him go.

In contrast, Roosevelt entered the White House with confidence that he would be able to deal with the crisis. His confidence was remarkable considering the lack of proposals he had for reconstructing the banking system. Though most Americans were unaware of it, the Hoover administration had not left them helpless; the New Deal's swift response to the financial panic was generally possible only because the Hoover administration had already paved the way for the Emergency Banking Act of 1933.

The New Deal ultimately brought about the reconstruction of the banking system, and the administration of Herbert Hoover had presided over its collapse. But March 4, 1933, was not a complete break with the past, and the New Deal was not the antithesis of Hoover's policies. In many ways the Hoover administration served as the bureaucratic forerunner of the New Deal, especially in terms of the Reconstruction Finance Corporation. The bank reconstruction program as embodied in the Emergency Banking Act demonstrated a measure of continuity between the administrations of Herbert Hoover and Franklin D. Roosevelt. Just as RFC relief, construction, and agricultural programs developed into the Federal Emergency Relief Administration, the Public Works Administration, and the Commodity Credit Corporation, the New Deal's financial reconstruction policies originated in the Hoover presidency.

The Emergency Banking Act passed by Congress on March 9 consisted of five titles, three of them especially important. Title I formally legalized Roosevelt's decision to declare a national banking holiday. Title

II permitted the comptroller of the currency to appoint a conservator with powers of receivership over all national banks threatened with suspension, and it permitted the conservator to subordinate certain depositor and stockholder interests to reorganize those banks. Title III authorized the Reconstruction Finance Corporation to purchase the preferred stock or capital notes of banks and trust companies to provide them with long-term investment funds and relieve them of short-term debts to the RFC. These first three titles were critical for the banking system. Title IV permitted Federal Reserve banks to discount previously ineligible assets and to issue new Federal Reserve notes on the basis of those assets as a means of ending the currency shortages in certain areas of the country. It proved to be of little use after the banking holiday because of the surprising return of hoarded currency to the banks. Title V appropriated $2 million to implement the Act. [1]

Although the Emergency Banking Act was passed after Hoover left the White House, complete credit for Titles I, II, and III cannot be given to the New Deal. The ideas for the national banking holiday, the bank conservation procedures, and the RFC preferred stock buying program were formulated during the final weeks of the Hoover administration. Although these reforms were not passed then because of economic confusion and political controversy, it is important to remember that the New Dealers only institutionalized the reforms after the fact.

Title I of the Emergency Banking Act formally legalized what Roosevelt had already done in declaring a bank holiday by authorizing him to restrict banking operations whenever he believed the nation was threatened with a serious liquidity crisis. But the concept of a national holiday did not originate with the New Deal. As early as 1918 Milton Elliott, then a legal counsel for the Federal Reserve Board, speculated about the future and expected that at some time the federal government might find it necessary to abandon the gold standard or at least to embargo the export of gold. He discussed his ideas with Walter Wyatt of the Federal Reserve Board staff, who suggested making some minor amendments to the Trading with the Enemy Act of 1917 to authorize the president to impose such an embargo during financial emergencies.[2] In January 1932, during the liquidity crisis preceding the establishment of the Reconstruction Finance Corporation, Ogden Mills and President Hoover considered declaring a national banking holiday or some other form of moratorium to relieve the crisis. In June during the crisis in Chicago, Mills again considered the idea and consulted with Adolph Miller, Walter Wyatt, and Eugene Meyer. Fortunately for Mills, the crises of January and June eased under the impact of massive RFC loans and made such extraordinary action unnecessary. In the fall of 1932, Mills approached Wyatt about the constitutionality of a national banking holiday, and Wyatt explained to him the amendments he had added to the Trading with the Enemy Act.[3]

As financial conditions worsened in January and February 1933, the administration began to realize that the year-old program of RFC loans was inadequate and a more dramatic move by the federal government would be necessary to restore financial stability. In addition to considering the measures that eventually became Titles II and III of the Emergency Banking Act, the idea of a national banking holiday again surfaced in the minds of Mills and other administration officials.[4] With the banking system collapsing, the need to break the cycle of panic and forced liquidation had become imperative. By the third week of February, George Harrison of the Federal Reserve Bank of New York and Walter Wyatt were urging Hoover to impose some form of national banking moratorium, using the authority of the Trading with the Enemy Act. Mills believed the holiday would provide the nation with a breathing spell—a period of relative stability when Congress and the administration could formulate legislation to deal with the crisis.[5] But at that point Hoover looked on the idea as only a last resort. He doubted the constitutionality of a banking holiday and hoped that other alternatives, such as a federal guarantee of bank deposits, the issuance of clearinghouse certificates, more RFC loans, and new purchases of government securities by the Federal Reserve banks, would make a moratorium unnecessary.[6]

However, none of those alternatives worked out. Senator Carter Glass informed Hoover that, considering the mood of most Democrats in Congress, federal legislation guaranteeing bank deposits was extremely unlikely.[7] The use of clearinghouse certificates was bitterly opposed by the Federal Reserve Board directors; they felt it would circumvent the Federal Reserve banks and nullify much of the banks' effectiveness.[8] The idea of further RFC loans was similarly discredited. By the end of February the corporation was being deluged with applications for loans; banks throughout the country were turning to the RFC as their last resort.[9] Many, such as the Cleveland Trust Company, were even demanding that the RFC make loans up to 90 percent of the face value of their collateral. But the RFC had been rendered completely impotent by the breadth of the crisis; it did not possess the resources to rescue thousands of banks and trust companies simultaneously.[10] Finally, the President failed to stimulate expanded Federal Reserve open market operations. By late February the personal relationship between Mills and Meyer was strained. Mills and Hoover wanted the Federal Reserve banks to purchase another $100 million in government securities to counter increases in foreign exchange rates. But consistent with the policy they had established in January, the board refused, maintaining that further purchases would not relieve the crisis. Mills was incensed and frightened about the impact their decision would have on liquidity-conscious bankers throughout the country.[11]

The President then had to reconsider the wisdom of declaring a national banking holiday. On February 22 he wrote to the Federal Reserve Board, asking their opinion about the severity of the crisis and "what, if any, further authority should be obtained."[12] The board met on February 22-23 to consider the request but was unable to reach any conclusions. Meyer answered Hoover's letter with an ostrichlike refusal to make any commitments. With the banking system of the United States collapsing around them, the board replied to the President:

> While some of the recent developments are disturbing, and many proposals as to ways and means of dealing with them are being made, the Board feels it is essential in times like these that every suggestion be carefully weighed and considered from the point of view of whether, if adopted, it would accomplish the results sought, or whether it would be likely to bring even greater disturbance and make worse the situation that it is designed to correct.
>
> At the present moment the Board does not desire to make any specific proposals for additional measures or authority, but it will continue to give all aspects of the situation its most careful consideration.[13]

On February 28 the President asked the board to evaluate three approaches to the crisis: should the government (1) guarantee the deposits of national banks, (2) create a system of clearinghouse associations to issue scrip, or (3) ignore the crisis and let the private banking community work itself out of the situation without federal assistance?[14] On the evening of February 28 the Federal Reserve Board again met to consider Hoover's proposals, and invited the RFC board to join them. They again failed to reach a consensus about how to approach the crisis.[15] On March 1 the board continued to evaluate Hoover's proposals and finally drafted a letter on March 2 rejecting both the plan for issuing clearinghouse scrip and for guaranteeing bank deposits.[16] Hoover considered the board almost criminally passive throughout the entire crisis.[17]

On Thursday, March 2, the President faced the final alternative of declaring a bank holiday after receiving an opinion from Attorney General DeWitt Mitchell that a moratorium under the authority of the Trading with the Enemy Act, though feasible, was of questionable legality. Mitchell told Hoover that before declaring such a holiday, they should secure the approval of President-elect Roosevelt with a promise that he would immediately convene Congress in a special session to ratify the declaration. Only then would Mitchell confirm the constitutionality of the declaration. Buoyed by Mitchell's opinion, Mills urged Hoover to request another advisory meeting of the Federal Reserve Board.[18]

The President drafted a letter to the Federal Reserve Board outlining Mitchell's opinion and asked if he should declare a banking holiday. Late in the evening of March 2, the Federal Reserve Board met with Ogden Mills and Comptroller of the Currency Francis Awalt to consider Hoover's proposal. At the meeting Mills announced that Hoover agreed with the attorney general; having exhausted all other alternatives, he was prepared to declare a moratorium on withdrawals and gold shipments from March 3 to March 5, providing Roosevelt would promise to convene Congress immediately to ratify the declaration and to pass the emergency legislation that the administration was preparing. Without that assurance, Hoover would not take such a constitutionally dubious step. The meeting at the Federal Reserve Board offices lasted into the early morning hours of March 3, and the board finally agreed to the holiday. Walter Wyatt drafted a tentative proclamation closing the banks, gave one copy to Mills, and forwarded several others to the White House. Wyatt and Mitchell then prepared a holiday proclamation in the form of a joint congressional resolution in case Congress would pass the bill before adjourning on March 3.[19]

Throughout Friday, March 3, into the early hours of Saturday negotiations over the holiday continued between the two administrations. Mills, in constant touch with incoming Secretary of the Treasury William Woodin, repeatedly urged him to speak with Roosevelt about the holiday.[20] Late in the evening of March 3, Adolph Miller of the Federal Reserve Board visited with the President-elect and left him several copies of the proclamation. The negotiations were in vain. Roosevelt argued that Hoover, already possessing sufficient authority under the Trading with the Enemy Act to declare the holiday, did not need his approval. Roosevelt offered to support Hoover in declaring a holiday to last through noon on March 4 but refused to approve publicly the declaration of a three-day holiday and to pass emergency legislation.[21] President Hoover then decided on March 3 not to declare a moratorium unless Roosevelt reconsidered.[22]

But the pressure mounted on Hoover to declare the holiday regardless of Roosevelt's position. Mills insisted that Hoover disregard Roosevelt and impose the moratorium anyway.[23] The Federal Reserve Board and the Federal Reserve banks of New York and Chicago urged him to close the banks immediately to save them from total disaster.[24] President Hoover, frustrated with the temporizing attitudes of the Federal Reserve Board and with what he considered the criminal inflexibility of the New Dealers, held to his position: there would be no holiday without Roosevelt's prior approval.[25]

Mills then turned his attention away from the national holiday and instead concentrated on closing those financial centers still open on March 4 so as to effectively create a national banking holiday without a presidential proclamation.[26] With the assistance of Harrison in New York and Eugene M. Stearns, chairman of the Federal Reserve Bank of Chicago, Mills convinced the state governors to declare holidays in Illinois, New York, Massachusetts, New Jersey, Iowa, and Pennsylvania.[27] By the time of the inauguration the banking system of the United States, for all intents and purposes, had closed.

On Sunday, March 5, following inaugural festivities, a series of conferences were held by the new administration to consider the emergency. Along with a large number of prominent bankers, congressmen, and New Deal officials, William Woodin asked several members of the Hoover administration to participate. Ogden Mills, Arthur Ballantine, and Francis Awalt, played especially prominent roles in formulating reconstruction policies. With complete concurrence from Hoover's associates, the conference agreed to declare a national banking holiday. Wyatt then produced a copy of the proclamation that he and former Attorney General Mitchell had drafted and Hoover had approved.

Wyatt had the proclamation examined by new Attorney General Homer Cummings, and on March 6, 1933, President Roosevelt signed it and formally declared the moratorium. On March 9 Title I of the Emergency Banking Act formally legalized it.[28]

Title II of the Emergency Banking Act dealt with the problem of reorganizing the thousands of closed banks throughout the United States. Although this dilemma was most acute after the declaration of the holiday, the Hoover administration had been concerned about the procedures for reorganizing the thousands of banks that had closed since 1930. Throughout 1932 the office of comptroller of the currency encountered problems in getting unanimous agreement from depositors and stockholders — even a small minority of depositors or stockholders could delay reorganization plans by refusing to subordinate their interests. To reorganize the closed banks efficiently, some means of mandatory control by the federal government over national bank depositors and stockholders had to be developed and the requirement of almost unanimous consent had to be eliminated. Francis Awalt was particularly concerned about the problem, and in 1932 he began to explore alternatives to traditional procedures.[29]

At the same time Mills and Meyer, despite their personal antagonisms, began urging Hoover to abandon the idea of clearinghouse scrip in favor of another approach. Both Mills and Meyer believed that issuing scrip was anachronistic, since it circumvented the Federal Reserve system. Instead, they asked Hoover to consider an idea brought to their attention by Secretary of State Henry Stimson. Under this proposal, the comptroller of the currency would have the authority to evaluate and isolate the free assets of any national bank. He could then force depositors and stockholders alike to subordinate the exact amount of any deficiency that had developed. The bank would have to issue a certificate of obligation to each depositor for his share of the deficiency, guaranteeing that the profits of the bank would be credited and paid to each depositor until his losses had been recovered.[30] Awalt considered the idea a perfect solution to his problem. Between February 14 and 17, Awalt and Wyatt drafted a bill permitting the comptroller to declare bankrupt any closed national bank and appoint a conservator to initiate reorganization or liquidation procedures. They sent a copy of the bill to Mills for his consideration. Mills liked the idea and forwarded it to the President.[31]

Hoover was reluctant to approach Congress with the bank conservation bill; he feared it could not be maneuvered through Congress during the last few days of the lame duck session, and Senators Glass and Robinson confirmed his fears. It was too close to the end of the old administration and the advent of the new to expect Congress to support the measure.[32] The President also feared that if the bill did pass Congress it might precipitate an even more severe banking panic, particularly in New York and Chicago where, at least in mid-February, the situation was still under control. His fears were probably unfounded. But he refused to push the Bank Conservation Act in the last two weeks of February.[33]

Hoover's deliberations on the Bank Conservation Act mirrored his approach to the bank holiday. By March 2 he realized that the Bank Conservation Act was probably the only way of successfully reorganizing the thousands of closed and closing banks. Hoover linked the idea of the national holiday with the Bank Conservation Act. A national holiday without some effective means of reorganizing closed banks would be foolish, while the Bank Conservation Act would be useless unless a holiday protected the thousands of banks that were still solvent. Hoover and Mills used this approach in asking Roosevelt to approve the holiday and to convene Congress in special session on March 6 to pass the Bank Conservation bill. Roosevelt had refused to cooperate. Once again Herbert Hoover had come to accept a startling innovation in public policy, but only when it was too late for his own administration to implement the idea or to receive any credit for originating it.[34] The Bank Conservation Act was incorporated into the Emergency Banking Act as Title II during the first two days of the New Deal.

Title III of the Emergency Banking Act concerned the power of the Reconstruction Finance Corporation. Throughout 1932 it was increasingly obvious that the real problem for many banks was not simply the need for temporary liquidity but the need to improve their capital structures. Hoover and the RFC board realized that troubled banks had to raise more capital to counteract the deflation of their assets. But private subscriptions to bank capital had all but ceased. The obvious weaknesses of the banking system frightened the public in 1932, and the rumors of widespread scandal in bank administration compounded its skepticism. In the Nevada crisis, as well as in the crises in Chicago, Detroit, Kansas City, and New Orleans, the RFC had urged the banks to raise more capital in addition to seeking more government loans. But the banks had been singularly unable to attract enough new money. A void existed that could be filled only by the federal government. Hoover contemplated such an idea with little enthusiasm, since direct federal investment in private banks contradicted a main tenet of American Individualism—government loans and RFC relief programs were regrettable necessities, but to make the federal government a stockholder in the banking system was worse.

As early as February 1932 Franklin W. Fort, former congressman from New Jersey and president of the Lincoln National Bank of Newark, urged administration officials to permit government purchases of the preferred stock of banks and trust companies. President Hoover was skeptical of the proposal, but he referred Fort to John W. Pole, then comptroller of the currency. Hoover had no intention of giving the federal government such authority as long as the RFC appeared to be successful, but he was willing to keep the proposal in mind as an emergency measure. Fort talked to Pole, but the idea lay dormant during April and May when the administration believed that short-term RFC loans would restore stability.[35]

After the summer crisis in Chicago, the talk of government investment in private banks became more urgent. During the spring and summer of 1932 Harrison and Young of the Federal Reserve Bank of New

York began urging Hoover to consider the proposal; most banks, they told him, had capital as well as liquidity problems. Hoover agreed. But Harrison and Young wanted to permit the RFC to make direct purchases of the preferred stock of troubled, private banks. The President was reluctant.[36] During the June crisis, the ideas of Fort, Harrison, and Young began to receive the cautious approval of Couch and McCarthy of the RFC board. Dawes, Meyer, Jones, and Bestor, and later Miller, Pomerene, and Cowles, remained skeptical, regarding it as a drastic step to be taken only after regular RFC loans had obviously failed. Hoover still sided with the skeptics, but his opinion was gradually shifting.[37]

The idea of goverment investment in the banking system received a boost from the President in August 1932 when he named Franklin Fort to head the newly created Federal Home Loan bank system, an important position in the President's recovery program.[38] Hoover's faith in Fort had grown immeasurably, and from that new position of power Fort continued to advocate direct RFC investment in banks and trust companies. Now, however, his credibility was increased—Fort was no longer an outsider making suggestions but a member of an administration team trying to rebuild the financial structure.

As the banking situation deteriorated late in 1932 and early in 1933, the idea of government investment appeared increasingly reasonable. An inverse relationship existed between the Reconstruction Finance Corporation and the idea of government investment. As the traditional policies of the RFC appeared less and less adequate, the alternative of government investment became more legitimate. In December Meyer was converted to the idea, and began suggesting that either the Federal Reserve banks or the RFC invest in the preferred stock of banks and trust companies. In the meantime, Awalt had become comptroller of the currency and he enthusiastically favored the plan. Later in January Fort and Awalt ultimately convinced Miller of the RFC board of the importance of the plan. Under the combined pressure of Fort, Miller, Harrison, Young, Meyer, McCarthy, Couch, and Awalt, the President became more favorably disposed. Mills, Pomerene, and Jones were still skeptical, but Hoover nevertheless directed Fort, Awalt, and Walter Wyatt to draft a bill permitting national banks to issue preferred stock and the RFC to purchase it when necessary.[39]

In February, with most of the administration favoring the bill, Mills invited Melvin Traylor of the First National Bank of Chicago to discuss it with Hoover, Fort, Awalt, and himself. Traylor enthusiastically supported the idea, and agreed to meet with Senator Glass to discuss the possibilities of maneuvering the bill through Congress. Mills now favored the idea. Glass warned them that like the bank conservation bill, the chances of approving the bill were nil, and he did not want even to introduce it. Consequently, Awalt and Wyatt simply retained copies of the bill in their files.[40] Again, the administration had come to favor the right measure at the wrong time. After the inauguration, the bill became Title III of the Emergency Banking Act.[41]

Fortunately, the power of some important officials in the Hoover administration continued after the inauguration of Roosevelt. They had written the legislation for the banking holiday, the bank reorganization procedures, and the preferred stock purchase plan. During the interregnum, William Woodin had developed a deep respect and close working relationship with Mills, Ballantine, and Awalt.[42] These men had all been partly responsible for the collapse of the banking system and had played decisive roles in the development of the reconstruction legislation. They participated in all the discussions held by the new administration between March 4 and March 9 and worked closely with Roosevelt, Woodin, Homer Cummings, Adolph Berle, and Raymond Moley. For two reasons their roles in the new administration were decisive. They had already developed three specific approaches to the crisis, while the New Dealers had no concrete suggestions for dealing with it. The old officials impressed the new with their understanding of the crisis. These officials also had worked for years with Wyatt, Goldenweisar, and Meyer of the Federal Reserve Board. Wyatt personally had drafted the three bills the Hoover administration had created to deal with the banking collapse. The force of the Federal Reserve system stood behind the proposals of Mills, Ballantine, and Awalt. On March 7, after several meetings with Woodin, President Roosevelt, Goldenweisar, Secretary to the Federal Reserve Board Chester Morrill, and Adolph Berle, the old Hoover associates specifically proposed the Emergency Banking Act as a follow-up to the banking holiday. Woodin asked Wyatt and Ballantine to draft the final piece of legislation. Wyatt created an omnibus measure that included the legislation he had already written declaring a banking holiday, creating a bank conservation program, and authorizing the RFC to invest in the preferred stock of troubled banks.[43]

On Thursday, March 9, 1933, Roosevelt convened Congress in special session and introduced the Emergency Banking bill. Within a matter of hours the bill was law.[44] During the next two weeks, the New Dealers reopened 12,756 banks, 69 percent of the 18,290 banks that had been operating before the holiday.[45] Public confidence revived, and by the end of March nearly $1 billion of hoarded money had returned to the banking system.[46] During the remainder of 1933, only 221 banks closed, reassuring the public that the nearly 13,000 banks and trust companies that had reopened were sound.[47] Not since the mid-1920s had the national mood been more positive.

During these reopening procedures, the Reconstruction Finance Corporation began its program of investing in private banks. By April 27, 1934, the corporation had purchased nearly $1.1 billion of preferred stock in over 6,500 banks, and by September the RFC owned stock in nearly half the nation's banks. With a 25 percent increase in securities values over 1933 levels, the capital structures of commercial banks throughout the country improved substantially.[48] Bank deposits by December totaled more than $44 billion — an increase of more than $7 billion over the holiday levels.[49] Only 61 failures of licensed commercial banks occurred in 1934, and in 1935 only 32 more closed.[50] Not until June 1935 did the RFC discontinue the preferred stock program, after assisting nearly 6,800 banks with over $1.3 billion in new government capital.[51] At last the banking system had recovered. Stability and hope replaced the pessimism and faltering cautiousness of the Hoover years.

The origins of the Emergency Banking Act have been obscured by the generally favorable coverage historians have given the first months of the Roosevelt administration. But behind the scenes of this earliest New Deal drama, the Hoover administration had tried desperately to cope with the economic disaster and had eventually developed the tools that restored stability to the money markets. Because of political difficulties with an impatient lame duck Congress, economic confusion about stimulating a more serious banking panic, and misgivings about delegating too much power to the federal government, the Hoover administration postponed their three proposals. By the time they were willing to push the ideas aggressively, it was too late. As Secretary of State Henry Stimson recalled in his diary, President Hoover was unwilling "to make his last days in office an admission of bankruptcy."[52]

To be sure, credit for declaring the banking holiday and passing the Emergency Banking Act cannot be given to Herbert Hoover; it was the New Deal that ultimately revived the banking system. But it is important to remember that the Emergency Banking Act, while the first major proposal of the New Deal, was also the last major proposal of the Hoover administration—proof that the President and his advisors were still in touch with reality and able to view the crisis clearly.

10

Hoover and the RFC:
A Perspective

THE four years in the White House were a personal tragedy for Herbert Hoover. Americans were experiencing the most debilitating depression in their history, and Hoover's name became almost a curse to most people. Eighteen months passed between the creation of the National Credit Corporation in September 1931 and Hoover's departure from the White House in March 1933. During that time, he established the Reconstruction Finance Corporation and presided over its precedent-shattering activities. No other president in American history had created such a powerful agency or injected the federal government so deeply into national affairs. But because the RFC failed to ease the depression, it played the central role in the political ordeal of Herbert Hoover.

One overwhelming problem that inhibited RFC effectiveness was the chronic inability of Hoover administration leaders to estimate accurately the severity of the economic decline. They assumed in good faith that the economy was structurally sound and the depression was only a temporary crisis of confidence. The RFC loans did not repair capital structures of financial institutions and as a result only temporarily postponed the collapse of the system. Administration leaders did not fully understand the seriousness of the railroad dilemma; the RFC dealt with symptoms rather than causes and ultimately failed to rescue the railroad bond market. In the matter of relief, the administration, underestimating the extent of the nation's problems, appeared parsimonious, creating an image of the RFC that reinforced the public's distaste for the President.

In addition to underestimating the severity of the depression, the Hoover administration employed several faulty economic assumptions. The administration believed that the central dilemma for the economy involved the supply of instead of the demand for credit. Businessmen in the absence of demand were unwilling to increase production; instead, they consistently tried to eliminate indebtedness and build up cash surpluses.[1] Hoover and the RFC board did not realize that bankers were as liquidity-conscious as businessmen. There was no "trickle-down" of government funds because financial executives, rather than commit themselves to new commercial loans, preferred to maintain large amounts

116

of nonearning cash reserves at Federal Reserve banks.[2] This situation led to another miscalculation: the desire to set interest rates on RFC loans far above prevailing money market rates to guarantee that the federal government would not be competing with private financial institutions. But competition for the government's loans did not exist. As a result, RFC interest rates and loan terms placed heavy burdens on recipients and priced other institutions out of the market completely.

Severe political difficulties also limited RFC effectiveness. From the beginning, the Reconstruction Finance Corporation was criticized by both liberals and conservatives; compromise between these competing interests was seemingly impossible. While bankers and Federal Reserve officials attacked the RFC for not loaning enough money and for loaning it under usurious terms, the Interstate Commerce Commission, progressive Republicans, and liberal Democrats accused it of lending too much to the business community and too little to the poor. By March 1933, the corporation had loaned nearly $2 billion through its various programs, but virtually no one was satisfied with its performance because it had not fulfilled its objectives.

Political difficulties prevented the administration from achieving more permanent successes. By the end of Hoover's term, for example, the Emergency Relief Division of the RFC dispensed most of its original $300 million, but the controversy with Gifford Pinchot made it appear as if the RFC had done little to relieve the suffering of the unemployed. During congressional maneuvering over the Reconstruction Finance Corporation Act and the Emergency Relief and Construction Act, the President requested the authority for the RFC to make direct loans to business and industry; in both instances, progressives and liberals in Congress rejected the proposal. (Not until June 19, 1934, after repeated requests from both Jesse Jones and President Roosevelt, did Congress finally permit the RFC to make commercial loans directly to businessmen.[3]) In the case of the national banking holiday, the Bank Conservation Act, and the RFC preferred stock purchase program, political problems with Congress during the closing weeks of the Hoover administration eliminated any hope of passing an emergency banking act.

The ordeal of Herbert Hoover, however, transcended these concrete problems with the RFC; his own political philosophy contributed substantially to his personal crisis. No other president of the twentieth century has understood and feared the potential of the bureaucratic state as much as Hoover. He was always reluctant to initiate new programs and preferred to leave most responsibilities in the hands of private interest groups and local governments. But until recently most historians treated Hoover as a doctrinaire ideologue unwilling to make use of the federal government, blaming American Individualism and Hoover's rigid personality for the inability of the RFC to come to terms with the Great Depression. This has been grossly unfair.

The RFC failed to reconstruct the banking system and ease the relief crisis not because of American Individualism, but because the administration underestimated the depth of the economic disaster, employed faulty economic theories, and constantly became embroiled in bitter political controversies. The real problem with American Individualism was that it made Hoover *appear* unwilling to use the powers of the federal government. Instead of supporting the Reconstruction Finance Corporation Act from the beginning, he tried to use the National Credit Corporation as an alternative. Instead of supporting a federal relief program from the beginning, he waited until the Emergency Relief and Construction Act conformed to his expectations; and then, even as he equitably and efficiently distributed money, he preached of the dangers of the federal government. He was the victim of his own rhetoric. Instead of declaring a bank holiday, or reforming bank reorganization procedures, or permitting the RFC to purchase the preferred stock of troubled banks, he waited until it was too late to pass the legislation before the inauguration of Franklin Roosevelt. Because of American Individualism it appeared as if Hoover opposed all RFC programs. But time after time he had been willing to abandon important features of American Individualism to "defeat" the depression. He rarely received credit for the Reconstruction Finance Corporation Act, the Emergency Relief and Construction Act, and the Emergency Banking Act; but once he agreed to the need for these measures, he supported all three with the hope that they would end the crisis.[4] American Individualism, though playing a role in RFC problems, does not explain the failure of the Hoover administration to end the depression—other, more concrete problems account for that. Hoover's political philosophy, rather than justifying RFC programs, seemed to contradict them. When the programs failed it was easy to blame the philosophy. American Individualism did not destroy RFC effectiveness; it was simply the wrong rhetoric at the time.

To concentrate exclusively on the shortcomings of the Reconstruction Finance Corporation and the Hoover administration is a disservice. For the first time in American history, the federal government had accepted direct responsibility for controlling the business cycle. Under the authority of the Emergency Relief and Construction Act of 1932, the RFC assumed the responsibility for maintaining the quality of life in the United States until the economy revived. The federal government would never be able to abandon these commitments. Later American presidents would only expand on that foundation.

The work of the RFC during 1932 and early 1933 served as a model for the New Deal. During its first fourteen months, the RFC underwrote the private money market in an attempt to revitalize the nation's credit machinery. Historians have tended to ignore the central role played by government credit agencies during the early New Deal. The National Recovery Administration (NRA) and the Agricultural Adjustment Administration (AAA) were important attempts to relieve suffering and revive the flaccid economy; at the same time a quiet expansion of RFC efforts to liquefy the money markets occurred. Between 1933 and 1935 the New Dealers expanded RFC authority and also created the Farm Credit

Administration, the Federal Farm Mortgage Corporation, the Production Credit Corporations, the Banks for Cooperatives, the Federal Credit Unions, the Federal Deposit Insurance Corporation, the Home Owners Loan Corporation, the Federal Housing Administration, the Commodity Credit Corporation, and the First and Second Export-Import Banks.[5] The New Dealers were just as concerned with the need to restore solvency to the private money market as the Hoover administration had been; but while Hoover concentrated that entire effort in one agency, Roosevelt permitted several agencies to handle the program.

The forces of bureaucratic inertia also generated several direct RFC legacies to the New Deal. In both principle and form, a direct line of administrative continuity existed between the RFC and the Federal Emergency Relief Administration, the Public Works Administration, the Commodity Credit Corporation, and the Emergency Banking Act of 1933. These programs were descendants of the Reconstruction Finance Corporation.

Under the administration of Herbert Hoover, the RFC had established important precedents and had released $2 billion to a cash-starved economy. Under any other set of circumstances, the president would have been able to take pride in those accomplishments. Economic recovery, the one achievement that would have rendered Hoover's presidency meaningful, was elusive. The RFC was never able to stop deflation, revive production, or increase employment. And while Hoover publicly worried about the future substance and structure of American Individualism, seventy million fellow citizens worried more about tomorrow night's meal or next month's rent. The stark immediacy of their needs rendered Hoover's fears irrelevant and eventually transformed his nightmares into reality. Ultimately, President Hoover's greatest enemy was his own vision.

Some men live life as purists—never compromising their ethical standards for any objective and often remaining proud despite overwhelming failure. Others live lives of expediency—sacrificing principles to more immediate ends. But Herbert Hoover occupied a unique and tragic position in American history: he sacrificed his personal philosophy to objectives that he could never achieve. He was left with neither his means nor his ends. But he bequeathed to the United States a legacy of analytical precedents, administrative agencies, and apocalyptic visions that has endured far beyond his political tenure. Unfortunately, history has forgotten his achievements and focused instead on his failures. The United States has never really understood him nor, for that matter, ever really appreciated him.

N O T E S

Abbreviations

COHR: Columbia Oral History Research Office
FDRML: Franklin D. Roosevelt Memorial Library
HHPL: Herbert Hoover Presidential Library
NA: National Archives
OF: Official File
OH: Oral History
PP: Presidential Papers
PPP: Post-Presidential Papers
RG: Record Group
SF: Subject File

PREFACE

1. See Eugene Lyon, *Herbert Hoover* (Garden City, N.Y., 1964); Harold Wolfe, *Herbert Hoover: Public Servant and Leader of the Loyal Opposition* (New York, 1956); and David Hinshaw, *Herbert Hoover: American Quaker* (New York, 1950).

2. See Richard Hofstadter, *The American Political Tradition,* pp. 279-310; Arthur M. Schlesinger, Jr., *The Crisis of the Old Order, 1919-1933; Albert U. Romasco, The Poverty of Abundance;* Gerald D. Nash, "Herbert Hoover and the Origins of the Reconstruction Finance Corporation," pp. 455-68; John Kenneth Galbraith, *The Great Crash, 1929;* and John D. Hicks, *Republican Ascendancy, 1919-1933* (New York, 1960).

3. See Carl Degler, "The Ordeal of Herbert Hoover," pp. 563-83; Harris G. Warren, *Herbert Hoover and the Great Depression;* Ellis W. Hawley, "Herbert Hoover, the Commerce Secretariat, and the Vision of an 'Associative State,' " pp. 116-40; Joan Hoff Wilson, *Herbert Hoover. Forgotten Progressive;* Craig Lloyd, *Aggressive Introvert;* Martin Fausold and George Mazuzan, eds., *The Hoover Presidency;* and J. Joseph Huthmacher and Warren I. Susman, eds., *Herbert Hoover and the Crisis of American Capitalism* (Cambridge, Mass., 1973).

CHAPTER ONE

1. Bernard Bailyn, *The Ideological Origins of the American Revolution,* pp. 55-61, 79-84; Sidney Fine, *Laissez-Faire and the General Welfare State,* pp. 3-23.

2. Bray Hammond, *Banks and Politics in America from the Revolution to the Civil War,* pp. 659-70.

3. Ibid., pp. 326-29.

4. Ibid., pp. 443-45. For a view that brings into serious question the effectiveness of the Second Bank of the United States as a centralizing influence on the financial system, see

Peter Temin, "The Economic Consequences of the Bank War," pp. 257-74; and Peter Temin, *The Jacksonian Economy.*

5. Hammond, *Banks and Politics,* pp. 451-57.

6. *New York Times,* 27 Apr. and 23 May 1930; Jack Dublin, *Credit Unions,* p. 149; Gerald Fischer, *The American Banking Structure,* p. 110; Raymond J. Saulnier, *Industrial Banking Companies and Their Credit Practices,* p. 2; John Lintner, *Mutual Savings Banks in the Savings and Mortgage Markets* (Boston, 1948), p. 49; Josephine Ewalt, *The Savings and Loan Story, 1930-1960,* p. 26.

7. Fischer, *American Banking Structure,* p. 201.

8. Paul Trescott, *Financing American Enterprise,* p. 5.

9. Ibid., p. 110; also Lynn Muchmore, "The Banking Crisis of 1933," p. 631.

10. Paul Studenski and Herman E. Krooss, *Financial History of the United States,* p. 303.

11. Raymond W. Goldsmith, *Financial Intermediaries in the American Economy Since 1900,* pp. 74-75; Shephard Clough, *A Century of American Life Insurance* (New York, 1946), pp. 374-75; Lintner, *Mutual Savings Banks,* p. 49; Ewalt, *Savings and Loan Story,* pp. 6-9.

12. John Kenneth Galbraith, *The Great Crash, 1929,* pp. 7-12.

13. Ibid., pp. 13-23; also Goldsmith, *Financial Intermediaries,* pp. 74-75.

14. Galbraith, *Great Crash,* pp. 53-54, 183-84; Hugh Bullock, *The Story of Investment Companies* (New York, 1959), pp. 40-42; Benjamin Beckhart, *The New York Money Market, Vol. 3. Uses of Funds* (New York, 1932), pp. 181-85.

15. See Lintner, *Mutual Savings Banks,* pp. 216-22; J. Carroll Moody and Gilbert C. Fite, *The Credit Union Movement,* p. 128; Clough, *Century of Life Insurance,* pp. 306-8; R. J. Saulnier, *Urban Mortgage Lending by Life Insurance Companies,* pp. 12-13; Ewalt, *Savings and Loan Story,* pp. 6-9; and American Bankers' Association, *The Earning Power of Banks* (New York, 1939), pp. 242-45.

16. American Bankers' Association, *Changes in Bank Earning Assets,* p. 18; Beckhart, *New York Money Market,* vol. 3, pp. 242-45.

17. American Bankers' Association, *Bank Earning Assets,* p. 12; George Soule, *Prosperity Decade,* p. 155; Beckhart, *New York Money Market,* vol. 3, pp. 128-34; Robert Sobel, *The Great Bull Market,* pp. 115-16.

18. Beckhart, *New York Money Market,* vol. 3, pp. 128-34.

19. American Bankers' Association, *Bank Earning Assets,* p. 14.

20. Ibid., pp. 14-15.

21. Marcus Nadler, Sipa Heller, and Samuel Shipman, *The Money Market and Its Institutions* (New York, 1955), pp. 181-82; Benjamin Beckhart, James G. Smith, and William Brown, *The New York Money Market,* vol. 4, p. 390; Sobel, *Great Bull Market,* pp. 51-54; Cedric B. Cowing, *Populists, Plungers, and Progressives,* p. 187; Elmus R. Wicker, *Federal Reserve Monetary Policy, 1917-1933,* pp. 43-44.

22. Wicker, *Federal Reserve Monetary Policy,* pp. 85-86, 102, 107, 126; Lester V. Chandler, *American Monetary Policy, 1928-1941,* pp. 83-89.

23. Margaret Myers, *Financial History of the Unites States,* pp. 301-5.

24. Wicker, *Federal Reserve Monetary Policy,* pp. 118, 123, 127-28, 140.

25. Galbraith, *Great Crash,* pp. 34-36; Studenski and Krooss, *Financial History,* pp. 331-39; David C. Elliott, "The Federal Reserve System, 1914-1929," in *The Federal Reserve System,* ed. Herbert V. Prochnow (New York, 1960), pp. 310-15; Wicker, *Federal Reserve Monetary Policy,* pp. 129, 135-36, 143.

26. Wicker, *Federal Reserve Monetary Policy,* pp. 142-43.

27. J. M. Daiger, "Confidence, Credit, and Cash," pp. 283-86; Charles Collins, *Rural Banking Reform,* pp. 67-68; *Commercial & Financial Chronicle,* 27 Nov. 1930.

28. "The House of Jesse," *Fortune,* p. 46; Muchmore, "Banking Crisis of 1933," pp. 639-40.

29. Daiger, "Confidence, Credit, and Cash," pp. 283-85; Trescott, *Financing American Enterprise,* pp. 199-203.

30. Eugene Burris, "A Plan to Stabilize Credit," pp. 40-41.

31. Mark W. Potter, "The Railway Situation," 23 Apr. 1931, unpublished manuscript, NA, RG 40, Department of Commerce; Franklin Snow, "The Railroads Again Become a

Problem,'' *Commerce and Finance* 20(14 Jan. 1931):58; Samuel O. Dunn, ''Railroads Still in Dump,'' *Forbes* 28(1 Sept. 1931):45.

32. *New York Times,* 7 Jan. 1932; Grenville Clark, ''Memorandum as to the Proposed President's Committee on the Transportation System,'' 13 Oct. 1931, unpublished manuscript, NA, RG 40, Department of Commerce; U.S., Congress, Senate, Subcommittee of the Committee on Banking and Currency, *Hearings on S. 1,* pp. 94-100.

33. *Commercial & Financial Chronicle,* 22 Nov. 1930; Milton S. Friedman and Anna Jacobsen Schwartz, *The Great Contraction, 1929-1933,* pp. 12-19.

34. Friedman and Schwartz, *Great Contraction,* pp. 19-20.

35. Lewis C. Solmon, *Economics* (New York, 1972), inside cover table.

36. Eugene Meyer, ''From Laissez-Faire with William Graham Sumner to the R.F.C.,'' p. 24; Eugene Meyer, COHR, pp. 614-15.

37. Gerald D. Nash, ''Herbert Hoover and the Origins of the Reconstruction Finance Corporation,'' pp. 456-57; Secretary of the Treasury, *Annual Report, 1919,* pp. 105-6.

38. Nash, ''Hoover and the RFC,'' pp. 458-61; Louis B. Wehle, *Hidden Threads of History,* pp. 71-73.

CHAPTER TWO

1. Quoted in Harris G. Warren, *Herbert Hoover and the Great Depression,* p. 53.

2. William S. Myers and Walter H. Newton, *The Hoover Administration,* p. 118; ''Copy of Prepared Statement Read to the Meeting of Nineteen New York Bankers Held at Secretary Mellon's Apartment, Sunday, October 4, 1931,'' unpublished manuscript, Hoover correspondence, Harrison Papers. For a recent analysis of several phases of Hoover's prepresidential career, see Craig Lloyd, *Aggressive Introvert.*

3. Joan Hoff Wilson, *Herbert Hoover,* p. 47. Also see Richard Hofstadter, *The American Political Tradition,* pp. 283-314; Carl Degler, ''The Ordeal of Herbert Hoover,'' pp. 563-82; Murray Rothbard, *America's Great Depression* (Princeton, 1963), pp. 167-85; and Martin Fausold and George Mazuzan, *The Hoover Presidency.*

4. Herbert Hoover, *The New Day,* p. 5; Herbert Hoover, *American Individualism,* pp. 9, 41-45; Herbert Hoover, *The Ordeal of Woodrow Wilson* (New York, 1958), p. viii; Herbert Hoover, *America's First Crusade,* pp. 76-79.

5. Hoover, *American Individualism,* pp. 32-33.

6. Ibid., pp. 8-11, 51-55, 59-60; also Hoover, *Ordeal of Wilson,* pp. vii-viii, 11; William S. Myers, ed., *The State Papers and Other Public Writings of Herbert Hoover,* vol. 1, p. 399; Herbert Hoover, *The Memoirs of Herbert Hoover,* vol. 2, pp. 101-8, and vol. 1, p. 22; Herbert Hoover, *Further Addresses upon the American Road, 1938-1940,* pp. 4, 42, 60-61, 201, 211; Barry Karl, ''Herbert Hoover and the Progressive Myth of the Presidency,'' unpublished paper, p. 13.

7. Hoover, *American Individualism,* pp. 7-13, 51-60.

8. Quoted in Herbert Stein, *The Fiscal Revolution in America* (Chicago, 1969), pp. 7-8.

9. Hoover, *American Individualism,* pp. 51-53.

10. Herbert Hoover, *The Challenge to Liberty,* pp. 56-60; Hoover, *Memoirs,* vol. 2, p. 71; Hoover, *American Individualism,* pp. 37-38; William Appleman Williams, ''What This Country Needs . . . ,'' pp. 7-9.

11. Hoover, *New Day,* pp. 22-23, 59-60; Hoover, *Memoirs,* vol. 1, pp. 4-7; Hoover, *American Individualism,* pp. 39-44, 57-62.

12. See essay by Ellis W. Hawley in Joseph Huthmacher and Warren I. Susman, eds., *Herbert Hoover and the Crisis of American Capitalism* (Cambridge, 1973), pp. 3-34.

13. Robert H. Wiebe, *The Search for Order, 1877-1920* (New York, 1967), pp. 111-32.

14. Ellis W. Hawley has written the most lucid accounts of Hoover's political philosophy. See ''Herbert Hoover, the Commerce Secretariat, and the Vision of an 'Associative State,' '' pp. 116-40; and ''Herbert Hoover and American Corporatism, 1929-1933'' in Fausold and Mazuzan, *Hoover Presidency,* pp. 101-22.

15. Hoover, *American Individualism,* pp. 41-45, 51-53; Hawley, ''Hoover, Commerce Secretariat,'' pp. 116-40.

16. Hoover, *Memoirs,* vol. 2, pp. 20-23, 63, 169-74; Theodore G. Joslin, *Hoover Off the Record,* pp. 131-33; Hoover, *Memoirs,* vol. 3, p. 97; Hawley, "Hoover, Commerce Secretariat," pp. 116-40.

17. Hawley, "Hoover, Commerce Secretariat," pp. 116-40.

18. Myers, *State Papers,* vol. 2, pp. 14-15.

CHAPTER THREE

1. Theodore Joslin, *Hoover Off the Record,* pp. 131-33; Herbert Hoover to Eugene Meyer, 8 Sept. 1931, and Meyer to Hoover, 9 Sept. 1931, HHPL, PP, SF, Federal Reserve Board.

2. Eugene Meyer, "From Laissez-Faire with William Graham Sumner to the R.F.C.," p. 24.

3. "The House of Jesse," pp. 46-47; Eugene Meyer, COHR, pp. 614-16; Hoover, *Memoirs,* vol. 3, p. 86; Discussion Notes, 26 Oct. 1931, unpublished minutes of meetings of Federal Reserve Bank of New York, Harrison Papers; Adolph Miller to Hoover, 27 Jan. 1931, HHPL, PP, SF, Federal Reserve Board; *Wall Street Journal,* 29 Oct. and 6 Nov. 1931.

4. Meyer, "From Laissez-Faire to the R.F.C.," p. 24; Stanley Klonowski to Hoover, 28 Aug. 1931, HHPL, PP, SF, Federal Reserve Board; Charles Hamlin Diary, 1 Oct. 1931, Hamlin Papers; Henry L. Stimson Diary, 22 Sept. 1931, Stimson Papers.

5. James Couzens to John Nance Garner, 13 Oct. 1931, Couzens Papers; Stimson Diary, 29 Sept. 1931, Stimson Papers; *Wall Street Journal,* 7 Oct. 1931; U.S., Congress, House, Committee on Banking and Currency, *Hearings on H.R. 5060 and H.R. 5116,* pp. 29-30.

6. Hoover, *American Individualism,* pp. 2, 30-31, 47-49; Jackson Reynolds, COHR, pp. 152-53; Hoover, *Memoirs,* vol. 3, p. 86.

7. Meyer, "From Laissez-Faire to the R.F.C.," pp. 23-26; Meyer to Hoover, 18 June 1931, HHPL, PP, SF, Financial Matters; Hoover to Ogden Mills, 1 Oct. 1931, HHPL, PP, SF, Financial, Banking and Bankruptcy.

8. Meyer, COHR, pp. 614-15; *Annalist* 38(11 Dec. 1931):945.

9. Meyer, COHR, p. 614; Hamlin Diary, 8 Oct. 1931, Hamlin Papers.

10. *New York Times,* 5, 6, 7 Oct. 1931.

11. Hoover, *Memoirs,* vol. 3, p. 86; Reynolds, COHR, pp. 151-53; "Copy of Prepared Statement Read to the Meeting of Nineteen New York Bankers Held at Secretary Mellon's Apartment, Sunday, October 4, 1931," unpublished manuscript, Hoover correspondence, Harrison Papers; William S. Myers and Walter H. Newton, *The Hoover Administration,* p. 127. Hoover's attitude toward the revival of the WFC is a controversial matter despite the historical consensus resulting from the article by Gerald Nash, "Herbert Hoover and the Origins of the Reconstruction Finance Corporation," pp. 455-68. Nash, concluding that Hoover bitterly resisted the revival until the last moment, seems to have accepted uncritically Meyer's claims that he, not Hoover, was responsible for the RFC. Manuscript collections at Columbia University and at the Herbert Hoover Presidential Library reveal that the President unquestionably preferred the National Credit Corporation to the revival of the WFC, but he was not an unyielding opponent of the War Finance Corporation. Hoping to preclude calling a special session of Congress and to avoid government intervention, he did opt for the National Credit Corporation, but he also approved immediate drafting of the RFC legislation which was completed later in November. The President was quite willing, though cautious, to support a revival of the War Finance Corporation once the National Credit Corporation had been proven a failure. Nash creates a picture of a blindly reactionary President oblivious to the destruction and the suffering around him. That simply was not the case. See *New York Times,* 7 Oct. 1931; Harrison to Hoover, 7 Oct. 1931, Harrison Papers; Hoover to Harrison, 5 Oct. 1931, HHPL, PP, SF, Financial Matters; Stimson Diary, 5-6 Oct. 1931, Stimson Papers; and *Congressional Record* 75(5 July 1932):14602.

12. John Miller, "The National Credit Corporation," pp. 53-57; "The 57th Annual Convention," *American Bankers' Association Journal* 24(Oct. 1931):191; C. W. Steffler, "Mobilizing to Rout the Forces of the Depression," *Commerce and Banking* 20(14 Oct. 1931):1509; Couzens to C. Lewis, 7 Oct. 1931, Couzens Papers; Hamlin Diary, 7 Oct. 1931,

Hamlin Papers; Stimson Diary, 7 Oct. 1931, Stimson Papers; *Wall Street Journal,* 10 Oct. 1931. There are hundreds of congratulatory messages to Hoover from small bankers and state banking associations all over the United States. For a sampling of these messages, see HHPL, PP, SF, NCC, 1931, folders A-D.

13. Charles Benedict, "What the Hoover Plan Can Accomplish," *Magazine of Wall Street* 49(31 Oct. 1931):16; *Annalist* 38(9 Oct. 1931):577; Paul M. Atkins, "Confidence, Credit, and Cooperation," *Bankers' Magazine* 123(Nov. 1931):617-20; Hoover, *Memoirs,* vol. 3, p. 86; Meyer, COHR, pp. 615-16; Adrian Joyce to Hoover, 22 Oct. 1931, HHPL, PP, SF, Federal Reserve Board; Julius Barnes to Hoover, 25 Oct. 1931, HHPl, PP, SF, Chamber of Commerce; Harrison to Hoover, 7 Oct. 1931, Harrison Papers; Mortimer Buckner to Ogden Mills, 31 Oct. 1931, Mills Papers; Thomas Lamont to Hoover, 20 Nov. 1931, HHPL, PP, SF, Railroads; Louis C. Kurtz to Hoover, 3 Dec. 1931, HHPL, PP, SF, WFC.

14. *Wall Street Journal,* 8 Oct. 1931.

15. "The National Credit Corporation with the New York Trust Company as Agent of the Loan," Debenture Agreement, 15 Oct. 1931, NA, RG 56, Department of the Treasury, NCC; *New York Times,* 18 Oct. 1931; "Certificate of Incorporation of the National Credit Corporation," 13 Oct. 1931, NA, RG 56, Department of the Treasury, NCC.

16. "Plan of Organization of the National Credit Corporation," 14 Oct. 1931, and "National Credit Corporation Board of Directors," unpublished manuscripts, NA, RG 56, Department of the Treasury, NCC; *Wall Street Journal,* 14 Oct. 1931.

17. *New York Times,* 7 Oct. 1931; *Commerical & Financial Chronicle,* 10 Oct. 1931; Atkins, "The National Credit Corporation," p. 68; Roger Leavitt, "The New Credit Corporation Has Renewed Public Confidence," p. 72.

18. *New York Times,* 7 Oct. 1931.

19. Hoover to George M. Reynolds, 6 Nov. 1931, HHPL, PP, SF, Financial Matters, NCC. Folder G in this collection of Hoover Papers includes many telegrams from Hoover and Mills to individual bankers in Federal Reserve districts urging them to move forward with the National Credit Corporation.

20. Buckner to Ogden Mills, 26 Oct. 1931, NA, RG 56, Department of the Treasury, NCC; Mills to Walter Frew, 30 Oct. 1931, Mills Papers. Also see unpublished and untitled memorandum by Buckner, 30 Oct. 1931, NA, RG 56, Department of the Treasury, Secretary's File; *Wall Street Journal,* 28, 30 Oct. 1931.

21. *New York Times,* 7 Nov. 1931.

22. *New York Times,* 9 Nov. and 19 Dec. 1931.

23. *Federal Reserve Bulletin* 17(Dec. 1931):665; *Wall Street Journal,* 9 Nov. 1931.

24. Buckner to Theodore Joslin, 17 Nov. 1931, and George M. Reynolds to Hoover, 4 Nov. 1931, HHPL, PP, SF, Financial Matters, NCC.

25. *Federal Reserve Bulletin* 17(Dec. 1931):665; Donald B. Colton to Walter H. Newton, 28 Dec. 1931, HHPL, PP, SF, Financial Matters, NCC; H. E. Beeke to Hoover, 25 Nov. 1931, HHPL, PP, SF, WFC.

26. *New York Times,* 19 Dec. 1931 and 1, 7, 11 Jan. 1932.

27. *Federal Reserve Bulletin* 17(Dec. 1931):665; *Wall Street Journal,* 1 Jan. 1932.

28. Meyer, COHR, pp. 615-16; *Wall Street Journal,* 4-7 Dec. 1931; Stimson Diary, 24 Nov. 1931, Stimson Papers; Hamlin Diary, 17 Dec. 1931, Hamlin Papers.

29. *New York Times,* 8 Dec. 1931.

30. Buckner to Hoover, 19 Dec. 1931, HHPL, PP, SF, Financial Matters, NCC.

31. *Congressional Record* 75(11 Jan. 1932):1659-60; U.S., Congress, Senate, *Hearings on S. 1,* pp. 71-83.

32. *Commercial & Financial Chronicle,* 5, 26 Mar. 1932; Angus W. McLean to Carter Glass, 29 Oct. 1931, Glass Papers; *Congressional Record* 75(11 Jan. 1932):1671; "House of Jesse," pp. 46-47.

33. Albert U. Romasco, *The Poverty of Abundance,* pp. 87-91, 181-82; Harris G. Warren, *Herbert Hoover and the Great Depression,* pp. 140-42; Nash, "Hoover and R.F.C.," pp. 455-68.

34. E. P. Adler to Hoover, 21 Nov. 1931, and Harvey Couch to Lawrence Richey, 30 Dec. 1931, HHPL, PP, SF, Financial Matters, NCC.

35. William S. Ryland to Hoover, and W. P. O'Neal to Hoover, 2 Jan. 1932, HHPL, PP, SF, Financial Matters, NCC; Mills to James R. Garfield, 9 June 1932, Mills Papers; *New*

York Times, 29 Mar., 2, 23 Apr., 24 May, 4 June, 20 Aug., 25 Oct. 1932, and 21 Dec. 1934; S. Lowman to Margaret Carrody, 21 July 1932, NA, RG 56, Department of the Treasury, NCC. In March 1932 the National Credit Corporation went into liquidation, and by December it had repaid 90 percent of its obligations. It nominally existed until July 1934 when it repaid the last of its debts and formally closed.

36. Harrison to Hoover, 7 Oct. 1931, Harrison Papers.

37. *Commercial & Financial Chronicle,* 24 Oct. 1931; Grenville Clark, "Memorandum as to the Proposed President's Committee on the Transportation System," 13 Oct. 1931, unpublished manuscript, NA, RG 40, Department of Commerce.

38. *Commercial & Financial Chronicle,* 12 Dec. 1931 and 11 June 1932; *Federal Reserve Bulletin* 17(Dec. 1931):665; U.S., Congress, Senate, *Hearings on S. 1,* p. 225; Thomas Lamont to Hoover, 20 Nov. 1931, and M. D. Lorenz to M. Hastings, 23 Oct. 1931, HHPL, PP, SF, Railroads; Hamlin Diary, 2 Dec. 1931, Hamlin Papers.

39. "Emergency Pool to Help Banks May Serve to Stop Deflation," pp. 5-6; U.S., Congress, House, *Hearings on H.R. 5060 and H.R. 5116,* pp. 31-32; Couzens to Fay Horton, 10 Oct. 1931, Couzens Papers.

40. See, for example, H. E. Beeke to Hoover, 25 Nov. 1931, HHPL, PP, SF, WFC.

41. Louis C. Kurtz to Hoover, 3 Dec. 1931, HHPL, PP, SF, WFC.

42. U.S., Congress, Senate, *Hearings on S. 1,* p. 77; *Annalist* 38(9 Oct. 1931):577; *Wall Street Journal,* 29 Jan. 1932; *Bank and Quotation Record,* 9 Nov. 1931; Meyer, COHR, pp. 615-16.

43. S. E. Harris, "Banking and Currency Legislation, 1932," pp. 547-48; U.S., Congress, Senate, *Hearings on S. 1,* pp. 176-77; Guy Houston to Henry Rainey, 27 Apr. 1931, Rainey Papers.

44. U.S., Congress, Senate, *Hearings on S. 1,* p. 68; *Wall Street Journal,* 29 Jan. 1932; Hoover, *Memoirs,* vol. 3, p. 97.

45. Donald B. Colton to Walter Newton, 28 Dec. 1931, HHPL, PP, SF, Financial Matters, NCC.

46. *New York Times,* 28 Jan. 1932.

47. Hoover, *Memoirs,* vol. 3, pp. 86, 97-98.

CHAPTER FOUR

1. *New York Times,* 5, 26 Jan. 1932.

2. Richard Teeling to David Walsh, 1 Feb. 1932, NA, RG 234, RFC, Administrative SF, Closed Banks; *New York Times,* 26 Jan. 1932; Jesse Jones, *Fifty Billion Dollars,* p. 15; Hoover to George Harrison, 26 Apr. 1932, Hoover Correspondence, Harrison Papers; Charles Hamlin Diary, 30 Nov. 1931, Hamlin Papers; Hoover, *Memoirs,* vol. 3, pp. 107-8, 148-49; William S. Myers and Walter H. Newton, *The Hoover Administration,* pp. 157-58; *Annalist* 38(25 Dec. 1931):1025-26; Willard M. Kiplinger, "Indirect Relief," pp. 349-52; Theodore M. Knappen, "The Irony of Big Business Seeking Government Management," pp. 386-88.

3. Speech to American Acceptance Council, 25 Jan. 1932, Speech File, Mills Papers; *Wall Street Journal,* 16 Oct. 1931; *Washington Post,* 16 Jan. 1932; Adolph Miller to Hoover, 27 Jan. 1932, HHPL, PP, SF, Federal Reserve Board.

4. In a speech to the New York State Bankers' Association, Assistant Secretary of the Treasury Arthur Ballantine made exactly that argument. Speech File, 8 Jan. 1932, Mills Papers; also see Discussion Notes, 29 Mar. 1932, Harrison Papers.

5. *New York Times,* 23 Jan. 1932; Hoover, *Memoirs,* vol. 3, pp. 148-49; Rexford G. Tugwell, *The Brains Trust,* pp. 13-17, 96, 145, 314; U.S., Congress, House, *Hearings on H.R. 5060 and H.R. 5116,* p. 66; E. A. Goldenweisar, "Notes on Credit Policy in 1932," 7 Jan. 1932, unpublished manuscript, Goldenweisar Papers.

6. Lawrence R. Klein, *The Keynesian Revolution,* p. 38; Henry W. Spiegel, *The Growth of Economic Thought,* pp. 583-85; Robert Lekachman, *A History of Economic Ideas,* pp. 358-59; Jacob Oser, *The Evolution of Economic Thought* (New York, 1963), pp. 285-88; R. G. Hawtrey, *The Art of Central Banking* (London, 1932), pp. 167-68.

7. Eugene Meyer, COHR, pp. 617-18.

8. Paul Shoup to Hoover, 5 Jan. 1932, HHPL, PP, SF, Financial Matters.

9. *New York Times,* 17, 19, 20-22 Dec. 1931, 5-11 Jan. 1932; Myers and Newton, *Hoover Administration,* pp. 157-63; Lawrence H. Chamberlain, *The President, Congress and Legislation,* pp. 289-90.

10. C. D. Cass to Walter Newton, 18 Dec. 1931, HHPL, PP, SF, RFC; *Wall Street Journal,* 21-24 Dec. 1931; *Annalist* 38(11 Dec. 1931):945; *New York Times,* 23 Feb. 1932; U.S., Congress, Senate, *Hearings on S.1,* pp. 15, 77, 94, 99-100, 129-130, 160, 225-27; *Congressional Record* 75(5 Jan. 1932):1343; "The Reconstruction Finance Corporation," pp. 207-8; J. M. Daiger, "What the R.F.C. Means to Every Business Man," pp. 20-22; "Need We Fear Inflation," p. 449; Morris Edwards, "What the Reconstruction Plan Means to Your Bank," *American Bankers' Association Journal* 24(Feb. 1932):489-90.

11. *Congressional Record* 75(11 Jan. 1932):1742.

12. *Wall Street Journal,* 7 Jan. 1932; *Congressional Record* 75(13 Jan. 1932):1924.

13. *Congressional Record* 75(11 Jan. 1932):1350; *New York Times,* 7 Jan. 1932; Chamberlain, *President, Congress and Legislation,* pp. 290-92.

14. Speech File, 15 Jan. 1932, Wagner Papers.

15. See "Resolution Adopted by the Conference of Governors of the Federal Reserve Banks Held Monday, January 11, 1932," unpublished manuscript, RFC File, Federal Reserve Board (Board Records).

16. Robert Wagner to forty-seven New York bankers, 6 Jan. 1932, Wagner Papers.

17. Preston S. Krecker, "The Securities Markets," p. 139; *New York Times,* 21 Dec. 1931, and 5, 6, 19, 20 Jan. 1932; U.S., Congress, Senate, *Hearings on S. 1,* pp. 9, 42-45, 78-85, 162; *Wall Street Journal,* 10 Dec. 1931; U.S., Congress, House, *Hearings on H.R. 5060 and H.R. 5116,* pp. 20-35.

18. *New York Times,* 6 Jan. 1932. Also see final report of Senate Subcommittee on Banking and Currency on changes made in S. 1, 5 Jan. 1932, NA, RG 56, Department of the Treasury, RFC File.

19. *Congressional Record* 75(11 Jan. 1932):1665-1772; *New York Times,* 9 Dec. 1931; Jones, *Fifty Billion Dollars,* p. 520; Hoover, *Memoirs,* vol. 3, pp. 107, 148-49, 169; *Annalist* 38(25 Dec. 1931):1025-26; Meyer, COHR, pp. 619-20.

20. *Washington Post,* 8-11 Jan. 1932; Joseph Robinson to Bernard Baruch, 17 Jan. 1932, Baruch Papers; *New York Times,* 9 Jan. 1932.

21. *New York Times,* 12 Jan. 1932.

22. Robinson selected Harvey Couch of Pine Bluff, Arkansas, while Garner named Jesse Jones of Houston, Texas. See Hoover, *Memoirs,* vol. 3, p. 107.

23. *Wall Street Journal,* 7 Dec. 1931, and 12 Jan. 1932; Lawrence Richey to Hoover, 23 Jan. 1932, HHPL, PP, SF, RFC; *Congressional Record* 75(11 Jan. 1932):1658-59, 1682-86; *New York Times,* 11 Jan. 1932.

24. *Congressional Record* 75(11, 15 Jan. 1932):1705, 2081; "Borrowing Billions to Turn the Tide," pp. 7-8.

25. "The President's Reconstruction Finance Corporation," *Congressional Digest* 11(Jan. 1932):55; RFC, *Quarterly Report for February 2 to March 31, 1932,* p. 2.

26. Hoover, *Memoirs,* vol. 3, p. 108; *Nation* 134(10 Feb. 1932):154; Theodore M. Knappen, "Can These Men Bring Back Prosperity," pp. 522-23.

27. Hoover, *Memoirs,* vol. 3, p. 108; Knappen, "Can These Men," pp. 522-23.

28. Ibid; also *Who Was Who in America, 1961-1968,* p. 82.

29. Hoover, *Memoirs,* vol. 3, p. 108; *Nation* 134(10 Feb. 1932):154; Knappen, "Can These Men," p. 523; *Chicago Tribune,* 28 Jan. 1932.

30. *Who Was Who in America, 1897-1942,* pp. 264-65; Knappen, "Can These Men," p. 556.

31. Hoover, *Memoirs,* vol. 3, p. 108; *Nation* 134(10 Feb. 1932):154; Knappen, "Can These Men," pp. 555-56.

32. Ibid; also *Who Was Who in America, 1951-1960,* p. 568.

33. Meyer, COHR, pp. 627-29; *New York Times,* 23-31 Jan. and 1-7 Feb. 1932.

34. Jones, *Fifty Billion Dollars,* p. 514.

35. Meyer, COHR, pp. 627-29.

36. RFC, *Custodian Bulletin No. 1,* p. 1.

37. Ibid.

38. *Washington Post,* 16 Jan. 1932; WFC, *Third Annual Report* (1921), p. 1; George Cooksey to Mills, 11 Mar. 1932, Mills Papers.

39. WFC, *First Annual Report* (1919), pp. 1, 3-4; Meyer, COHR, p. 617; Working Papers Relating to Records of RFC, Interoffice Communication No. 22, 2 Feb. 1944, NA, RG 234, RFC, Secretarial Division.

40. WFC, *First Annual Report* (1919), p. 1; *Who Was Who in America, 1951-1960,* p. 87; *New York Times,* 3 Feb. 1932.

41. *Who Was Who in America, 1951-1960,* pp. 101, 411; *Who Was Who in America, 1942-1950,* p. 523; RFC, Minutes 1(9 Feb. 1932):62.

42. Working Papers, Interoffice Communication No. 22, 2 Feb. 1944, and "Functional Organization Charts," 18 Mar. 1932, NA, RG 234, RFC, Secretarial Division.

43. WFC, *Fourth Annual Report* (1922), p. 2; RFC, *Quarterly Report for February 2 to March 31, 1932,* pp. 1-2; "RFC Loan Agencies and Managers," 7 Feb. 1932, unpublished manuscript, Jones Papers.

44. Meyer, COHR, pp. 627-29; "Number of Personnel," unpublished manuscript, HHPL, PP, SF, RFC, History.

45. *Washington Post,* 23 Jan. 1932. Also see Arthur Schlesinger, Jr., *The Age of Roosevelt,* vol. 2, p. 431.

46. RFC, *Special Loan Agency Bulletin No. 1* (1932), p. 1; WFC, Minutes 9(24 Sept. 1921):193; Winston P. Wilson, *Harvey Couch,* p. 146.

47. *Congressional Record* 75(11 Jan. 1932):1703.

48. The domestic history of the United States during World War I has been one of the most neglected periods in American historiography. For two generations of American scholars, the progressive period ended in 1917 and the 1920s began in 1919. The two wartime years of transition, between 1917 and 1919, until recently have been ignored by historians, who consequently have failed to explain governmental policies during the 1930s as in part a function of the war. In reality, the bureaucratic apparatus established to supervise and coordinate the operation of the wartime economy later served as a model for both the Republican and Democratic approaches to the Great Depression. William Leuchtenberg, "The New Deal and the Analogue of War" (*Change and Continuity in Twentieth Century America,* edited by John Braeman) argued that during the thirties Americans symbolized and interpreted the depression in terms of the war. In addition to using the metaphor of war to describe the depression, the New Dealers drew on the experience of World War I economic mobilization in an attempt to cope with the economic decline. The War Industries Board, the War Trade Board, the Railroad Administration, the Fuel Administration, the Food Administration, and the War Labor Board all helped destroy many laissez-faire assumptions and generated national economic planning during the New Deal. Herbert Hoover participated in that use of the analogue of war during his administration.

49. William S. Myers, ed., *The State Papers and Other Public Writings of Herbert Hoover,* vol. 1, p. 559.

50. *New York Times,* 6 Jan. 1932; "President Hoover's Special Message," *Congressional Digest* 11(Jan. 1932):54.

51. Myers, *State Papers,* vol. 2, p. 112.

52. See speech by Mills to Federal Reserve Banking and Industrial committees, 26 Aug. 1932, Speech File, Mills Papers.

53. Meyer, COHR, pp. 619-20.

54. Myers, *State Papers,* vol. 1, pp. 417, 557, 559, 565, 576, 583, 620; Myers, *State Papers,* vol. 2, pp. 14-18, 108-9, 112, 128, 137-38, 270, 296-97, 317, 389.

55. Myers, *State Papers,* vol. 2, p. 317.

56. Knappen, "Irony of Big Business," p. 386.

CHAPTER FIVE

1. RFC, *Loan Agency Bulletin No. 1* (1932), p. 1; Jesse Jones to M. H. Gossett, 17 Mar. 1932, Jones Papers; RFC, *Loan Agency Bulletin No. 8* (1932), p. 1.

2. For an example of techniques and regulations employed by RFC local loan agencies,

see Minutes of the Advisory Committee of the Atlanta Loan Agency, 5 Feb. 1932, NA, RG 234, RFC, Secretarial Division. In particular, see information about loans to People's First National Bank of Quitman, Georgia, and the loan to the Bank of Hopeville, Hopeville, Georgia.

3. RFC, Minutes 2(17 Mar. 1932):647; RFC, *Loan Agency Bulletin No. 1*, p. 1; *Wall Street Journal*, 3, 5, 9 Mar., and 1, 10, 22 Apr. 1932.

4. Daniel Wing to Charles Dawes, 25 Mar. 1932, Dawes Papers; Charles Hamlin Diary, 3, 5 Mar. 1932, Hamlin Papers.

5. William Hayes, "Government and the Banking Business," pp. 437-42.

6. Richard Teeling to David Walsh, 1 Feb. 1932, NA, RG 234, RFC, Administrative SF; Jackson Reynolds, COHR, p. 142; James Warburg, COHR, pp. 64-65; Discussion Notes, Federal Reserve Bank of New York, 16 Aug. 1931, Harrison Papers.

7. Hoover, *Memoirs*, vol. 3, pp. 115-20; *New York Times*, 11, 12, 18, 23, 27 Feb. 1932; Hamlin Diary, 11 Feb. 1932, Hamlin Papers; *Congressional Record* 75(27 Feb. 1932):4223-24.

8. William S. Myers, ed., *The State Papers and Other Public Writings of Herbert Hoover*, vol. 2, pp. 110-11; also see Citizens' Reconstruction Organization file in HHPL, PP, SF, Hoarding.

9. RFC, Minutes 1 (3 Feb. 1932):23, (21 Feb. 1932):120; Paul Shoup to Hoover, 5 Jan. 1932, HHPL, PP, SF, Financial Matters.

10. RFC, *Quarterly Report for October 1 to December 31, 1932*, Table 13; RFC, Minutes 1(23-29 Feb. 1932).

11. Arthur Hyde to Dawes, 21 Apr. 1932, Dawes Papers; RFC, Minutes 3(26 Apr. 1932):868-69.

12. *New York Times*, 28 Feb. 1932.

13. RFC, *Quarterly Report for February 2 to March 31, 1932*, p. 1; Reynolds, COHR, pp. 155-56; *New York Times*, 25, 31 Mar. 1932.

14. *Wall Street Journal*, 16 Apr. 1932; *Washington Post*, 11, 23, 25 Mar. 1932; Willard M. Kiplinger, "The Reconstruction Workshop," *American Bankers' Association Journal* 24(Apr. 1932):619.

15. William Wallace Atterbury, "A Brighter Outlook for the Railroads," *American Bankers' Association Journal* 24(Feb. 1932):500-501; *Commercial & Financial Chronicle*, 6 Aug. 1932.

16. ICC, *46th Annual Report* (1932), pp. 12-13; *New York Times*, 19-29 Mar. 1932; "Rail Relief," *Magazine of Wall Street* 49(Apr. 1932):708; *Washington Post*, 19, 20, 26 Mar. 1932; *Commercial & Financial Chronicle*, 9 Apr. 1932; *Wall Street Journal*, 22 Mar. 1932; "Railroad Loan Policy Draws Critics' Fire," p. 6; "Railroad Loans," unpublished manuscript, HHPL, PP, SF, RFC; James Couzens to Atlee Pomerene, 13 Aug. 1932, in RFC, Minutes 7(18 Aug. 1932):856-57.

17. *Congressional Record* 75(29 Mar. 1932):6989, (30 Mar. 1932):7102-5.

18. *Congressional Record* 75(28 Mar. 1932):6906-7.

19. *Wall Street Journal*, 1-2 Apr. 1932; *Washington Post*, 2 Apr. 1932; "Railroad Loan Stirs Up the Senate," p. 44.

20. U.S., Congress, House, Committee on Ways and Means, *Extract from Hearings on Payment of Adjusted Compensation Certificates*, 72d Cong., 1st sess., 1932, p. 353.

21. *Commercial & Financial Chronicle*, 6 Aug. 1932.

22. U.S., Congress, Senate, Subcommittee of the Committee on Banking and Currency, *Hearings on S. J. Res. 245*, p. 1.

23. Atlee Pomerene to Dawes, 25 Apr. 1932, Dawes Papers; *Washington Post*, 22, 28 Apr. 1932.

24. J. T. Flynn, "Bailing Out the Van Swerigans," pp. 279-80.

25. Josephus Daniels to Bernard Baruch, 17 June 1932, and Senator Elmer Thomas to Baruch, 30 Mar. 1932, Baruch Papers; Elsie Robinson to George Cooksey, ? Oct. 1932, NA, RG 234, RFC, General Correspondence File, Treasury Department; W. Yale Smiley to Walter Newton, 17 May 1932, HHPL, PP, SF, Business Conditions; Senator James J. Davis to Herbert Hoover, 19 Apr. 1932, HHPL, PP, SF, RFC; Bradley Nash, OH, HHPL, pp. 65-66.

26. *New York Times*, 8 Apr. 1932.

27. Hamlin Diary, 2 Apr. 1932, Hamlin Papers; *New York Times*, 19 Mar. 1932; *Wall Street Journal*, 12 Mar. 1932; "Intelligent Rail Relief," *Magazine of Wall Street* 50(14 May 1932):72.

28. Jesse Jones, *Fifty Billion Dollars*, pp. 84, 517-19; Eugene Meyer, COHR, p. 676; Winston P. Wilson, *Harvey Couch*, pp. 145, 156-57; Atlee Pomerene to Dawes, 25 Apr. 1932, Dawes Papers; Dawes to Butler Hare, 23 May 1932, and Ralph Hore to Hoover, 25 May 1932, NA, RG 234, RFC, Administrative SF; Eugene Meyer to Hiram Johnson, 1 June 1932, in RFC, Minutes 5(1 June 1932):3; Meyer to Charles McNary, 1 Apr. 1932, in RFC, Minutes 3(1 Apr. 1932):4-5; Hamlin Diary, 1 Mar. and 7 June 1932, Hamlin Papers; *Chicago Tribune*, 7 June 1932; Stanley Reed, OH, HHPL, p. 8.

29. *Wall Street Journal*, 3 Feb. 1932; Henry L. Stimson Diary, 18 Dec. 1931, Stimson Papers.

30. RFC, *Loan Agency Bulletin No. 1*, p. 1; Joseph Chapman to Dawes, 3 May 1932, Dawes Papers; RFC, Minutes 3(9 Apr. 1932).

31. RFC, Minutes 4(17 May 1932), 5(28 June 1932), 6(18 July 1932).

32. *Commercial & Financial Chronicle*, 23 Jan. 1932; Richard Teeling to David Walsh, 1 Feb. 1932, NA, RG 234, RFC, Administrative SF; Charles Richardson to Charles H. Toll, 27 Apr. 1932, HHPL, PP, SF, Financial, Banking and Bankruptcy; E. G. Buckland to Dawes, 19 Apr. 1932, Ray R. Karraker to Dawes, 25 Apr. 1932, and Daniel Wing to Dawes, 25 Mar. 1932, Dawes Papers.

33. George Seay to H. Parker Willis, 22 Dec. 1931, Federal Reserve Board Records, RFC File 033.03; Hamlin Diary, 18 Dec. 1931, Hamlin Papers.

34. Hamlin Diary, 15 Sept. and 7 Oct. 1931, and 23 May 1932, Hamlin Papers.

35. George Seay to H. Parker Willis, 22 Dec. 1931, Federal Reserve Board Records, RFC File 033.03; Federal Reserve Board, Minutes 19(17 May 1932):403-4; Hamlin Diary, 11 Jan. 1932; E. A. Goldenweisar, "Notes on Credit Policy in 1932," 7 Jan. 1932, unpublished manuscript, Goldenweisar Papers; Discussion Notes, 21 Jan. 1932, Harrison Papers.

36. American Bankers' Association, *Changes in Bank Earning Assets*, pp. 7-8, 13-14, 36-38; *Federal Reserve Bulletin* 21(Dec. 1935):803; *Wall Street Journal*, 8 Mar. 1932; *Chicago Tribune*, 1, 14 June 1932.

37. Lester V. Chandler, *American Monetary Policies, 1928-1941*, pp. 192-99.

38. Discussion Notes, 18 Feb., 30 June, and 7, 11, 14 July 1932, Harrison Papers; Harrison to Hoover, 22 Apr. 1932, HHPL, PP, SF, Federal Reserve Board.

39. Hamlin Diary, 1 Sept. 1932, Hamlin Papers; "To Bankers: Loosen Up Credit," p. 22.

40. Ogden Mills to Guy Emerson, 12 Mar. 1932, Mills Papers; Discussion Notes, 24 Mar. 1932, Harrison Papers; Harrison to Hoover, 22 Apr. 1932, Hoover to Harrison, 26 Apr. 1932, and Harrison to Hoover, 3 May 1932, Harrison Papers; *New York Times*, 26 Jan. and 3 May 1932; Jones, *Fifty Billion Dollars*, p. 15; *Washington Post*, 12 Apr. 1932; *Congressional Record* 75(22 June 1932):13705; *Wall Street Journal*, 29 Apr. 1932; John D. C. Weldon, "Will Business Recovery Follow Banking Improvement," *Magazine of Wall Street* 49(18 Apr. 1932):778-80; Goldenweisar to Theodore Joslin, 11 Apr. 1932, and Joslin to Hoover, 23 May 1932, HHPL, PP, SF, Federal Reserve Board.

41. *Washington Post*, 21 May 1932; *Commercial & Financial Chronicle*, 31 May 1932; James H. Douglas, Jr., OH, HHPL, p. 13; Hamlin Diary, 17, 21, 23 May 1932, Hamlin Papers.

42. *Wall Street Journal*, 8 June 1932; Hamlin Diary, 15 June and 5, 28 July 1932, Hamlin Papers.

43. Stimson Diary, 16 May 1932, Stimson Papers; Hamlin Diary, 2 Dec. 1931, Hamlin Papers.

44. *Chicago Tribune*, 7 June 1932; Hamlin Diary, 1 Mar. and 18 June 1932, Hamlin Papers; Reynolds, COHR, p. 97; Hoover, *Memoirs*, vol. 3, pp. 170-71.

45. *New York Times*, 21 Sept. 1932.

46. *Federal Reserve Bulletin* 19(Dec. 1933):745.

47. *Congressional Record* 75(28 Jan. 1932):2877-79; RFC, Minutes 5(27 June 1932):1017-26; *Chicago Tribune*, 25-28 June and 2 July 1932; *Commercial & Financial Chronicle*, 2 July 1932; Hoover, *Memoirs*, vol. 3, pp. 170-71; Wilson, *Harvey Couch*, pp. 160-

61; Jones, *Fifty Billion Dollars,* pp. 74-78; *Wall Street Journal,* 3 Feb. 1932; Stimson Diary, 27 June 1932, Stimson Papers.

48. RFC, Minutes 8(23 Sept. 1932):974-76.

49. *New York Times,* 21 Sept. 1932.

50. Hoover, *Memoirs,* vol. 3, p. 161; RFC, *Quarterly Report for July 1 to September 30, 1932,* p. 1.

51. *Chicago Tribune,* 2, 3, 10, 12, 19, 20, 22 June 1932; *New York Times,* 28-29 June, 16 Sept., and 5 Nov. 1932; *Congressional Record* 75(22 June 1932):13706-7; Marie H. Hunter to Hoover, 21 June 1932, HHPL, PP, SF, RFC; RFC, Minutes 5(8 June 1932):251; Henry Allen to Theodore Joslin, 16 July 1932, HHPL, PP, SF, RFC; *Wall Street Journal,* 2 July 1932; "Mr. Dawes Borrows $80,000,000," *Labor,* 5 July 1932, p. 1; Willard M. Kiplinger, "Indirect Relief," 87(June 1932):349.

52. Charles Miller to Walter Newton, 10 Aug. 1932, NA, RG 234, RFC, White House Correspondence; RFC, Minutes 4(3 May 1932):59-60; "The Crisis and the RFC," speech by Ogden Mills, 19 Aug. 1932, Speech File, Mills Papers; D. C. Elliott to Arthur Ballantine, 23 Aug. 1932, HHPL, PP, SF, RFC.

53. RFC, *Quarterly Report for January 1 to March 31, 1933,* Table 7; *Congressional Record* 75(7 July 1932):14799.

54. See RFC, *Quarterly Report for January 1 to March 31, 1933,* Table 7; *Financial Age* 65(16 Jan. 1932):45-57. These figures were compiled by comparing the 210 largest banks listed in *Financial Age* with the list of all individual RFC loans granted in 1932. See RFC, Index to Minutes 1(1932):656-1246, NA, RG 234, RFC, Secretarial Division.

55. RFC, *Quarterly Report for April 1 to June 30, 1932,* Table 7.

56. *New York Times,* 15 May 1932; Hamlin Diary, 6, 12, 19 July and 1 Sept. 1932, Hamlin Papers.

CHAPTER SIX

1. For an analysis of the idea of progress in the late nineteenth century, see David W. Noble, *The Paradox of Progressive Thought* (Minneapolis, 1958).

2. Hoover, *American Individualism,* pp. 32-33.

3. William S. Myers, ed., *The State Papers and Other Public Writings of Herbert Hoover,* vol. 1, p. 384.

4. Herbert Hoover, *The Ordeal of Woodrow Wilson* (New York, 1958), p. 147.

5. Hoover, *America's First Crusade,* pp. 1-2.

6. Hoover, *Ordeal of Woodrow Wilson,* pp. 94-95.

7. Ibid., p. 147.

8. Hoover, *Further Addresses, 1938-1940,* p. 202.

9. Hoover, *Memoirs,* vol. 2, p. 28.

10. "Chronology of Important Economic and Financial Events," unpublished manuscript, HHPL, PP, SF, Chronology.

11. Myers, *State Papers,* vol. 1, p. 557.

12. Roger Daniels, *The Bonus March,* pp. 67-89. For an excellent revisionary account of the Bonus March, see Donald J. Lisio, *The President and Protest.* Also see U.S., Congress, Senate, Subcommittee of the Committee on Manufactures, *Hearings on S. 4592, Federal Cooperation in Unemployment Relief,* 72d Cong., 1st sess., 1932, part 2.

13. Daniels, *Bonus March,* pp. 67-89; "How the Cities Stand," p. 71.

14. Fred Croxton to Harvey C. Couch, 26 Feb. 1932, Croxton Papers.

15. Daniels, *Bonus March,* pp. 80-89; *Proceedings of the National Conference of Social Work,* pp. 11-27, 72-79.

16. "The Policies and Actions of the Hoover Administration in Respect to the Depression," unpublished memorandum from Hoover to Walter Newton, 27 Jan. 1934, Newton Papers; *Wall Street Journal,* 2 May 1932; Henry L. Stimson Diary, 17 May 1932, Stimson Papers. A sampling of thousands of demands by labor unions, social workers, the unemployed and businessmen for some form of federal relief assistance can be found in two

sources: HHPL, PP, SF, RFC, Box 275, and "Relief and Construction Act, 1932" File, Wagner Papers.

17. *Washington Post,* 2-3, 16 Feb. 1932.

18. *New York Times,* 17 Feb. 1932; *Congressional Record* 75(16 Feb. 1932):3911-14.

19. *Washington Post,* 7-12 May 1932.

20. *Congressional Record* 75(17 Feb. 1932):4113; Wagner Speech File, 15 Feb. and 14 Mar. 1932, Wagner Papers; *Wall Street Journal,* 11 May 1932; *Washington Post,* 7-12 May 1932. For an analysis of the 1932 federal relief controversy written from the perspective of the Democratic Congress, see Jordan A. Schwarz, *The Interregnum of Despair,* pp. 142-78.

21. *New York Times,* 14 May 1932. For a discussion of the willingness of bankers to lend funds see Eugene Meyer to Hoover, 23 July 1932, HHPL, PP, SF, Federal Reserve Board; and Charles Hamlin Diary, 14, 23 July 1932, Hamlin Papers.

22. Bernard Baruch to Joseph Robinson, 7 Mar. 1932, Robinson to Baruch, 16, 22 Apr. 1932, Baruch to Hoover, 11 Apr. 1932, and Baruch to Cordell Hull, 10 May 1932, Baruch Papers; *New York Times,* 12 May 1932.

23. *Washington Post,* 13 May 1932; "Statement Issued by President Hoover for Unemployment Relief after a White House Conference with Senators Robinson and Watson," 12 May 1932, unpublished manuscript, HHPL, PP, SF, RFC.

24. *Wall Street Journal,* 13 May 1932; Robinson to Baruch, 12, 16 May 1932, and Baruch to Arthur Krock, 16 May 1932, Baruch Papers; *Washington Post,* 12 May 1932.

25. *Commercial & Financial Chronicle,* 14 May 1932; Arthur Ballantine to Lawrence Richey, 15 June 1932, HHPL, PP, SF, Financial Matters, Banking; Paul Shoup to Hoover, 1 July 1932, HHPL, PP, SF, Railroads; *Chicago Tribune,* 8 July 1932. Also see the notation President Hoover made in an early draft of the Emergency Relief and Construction Act calling for RFC loans to industry, HHPL, PP, SF, RFC, Legislation.

26. *Washington Post,* 14 May 1932.

27. *New York Times,* 15 May 1932.

28. Robinson to Baruch, 16 May 1932, Baruch Papers; *New York Times,* 14-15 May 1932; *Wall Street Journal,* 24 May 1932.

29. Rexford G. Tugwell, *The Brains Trust,* p. 315; *Washington Post,* 20 May 1932; *Wall Street Journal,* 23 May 1932.

30. Baruch to Robinson, 13 June 1932, Baruch Papers; Jesse Jones, *Fifty Billion Dollars,* p. 520; *Wall Street Journal,* 28 May 1932; William Allen White to Henry Allen, 29 May 1932, White Papers; Stimson Diary, 27 May, 1932, Stimson Papers.

31. *New York Times,* 21, 23, 26 May 1932; *Wall Street Journal,* 28 May 1932; Hamlin Diary, 30-31 May 1932, Hamlin Papers; Hoover to Herbert J. Crocker, 22 May 1932, HHPL, PP, SF, RFC.

32. *Congressional Record* 75(31 May 1932):11596-98; *New York Times,* 1 June 1932; Hoover, *Memoirs,* vol. 3, pp. 153-54.

33. *Washington Post,* 6 June 1932; William S. Myers and Walter H. Newton, *The Hoover Administration,* p. 152; *New York Times,* 6-9 June 1932. Also see unpublished copy of minutes of the Rapidan Conference, 5-6 June 1932, HHPL, PP, SF, RFC.

34. *Congressional Record* 75(7 June 1932):12197-244, (10 June 1932):12513-30; *Washington Post,* 24 June 1932; Robinson to Baruch, 21 June 1932, Baruch Papers; *Wall Street Journal,* 18 June 1932.

35. *New York Times,* 26 June and 1-5, 9 July 1932; Robinson to Baruch, 7 July 1932, Baruch Papers; Myers, *State Papers,* vol. 2, pp. 222-26; *Wall Street Journal,* 28-29 June 1932.

36. *New York Times,* 7 July 1932.

37. *Congressional Record* 75(11 July 1932):15040-41; Myers, *State Papers,* voi. 2, p. 233; *Washington Post,* 12 July 1932; RFC, Minutes 6(5 July 1932):70-71; U.S., Congress, Senate, Committee on Banking and Currency, *Hearings on S. 4632, S. 4727, and S. 4822, Bills Relating to Federal Loans to Aid Unemployment,* 72d Cong., 1st sess., 1932, pp. 3-11. For more traditional, anti-Hoover views of the origins of the Emergency Relief and Construction Act, see Schwarz, *Interregnum of Despair,* pp. 170-73; Arthur M. Schlesinger, Jr., *The Age of Roosevelt,* vol. 1, pp. 240-41; Albert U. Romasco, *The Poverty of Abundance,* pp. 222-23; and Harris G. Warren, *Herbert Hoover and the Great Depression,* pp. 204-7.

38. *Congressional Record* 75(12 July 1932):15096-98; *Commercial & Financial Chronicle,* 23 July 1932; Hamlin Diary, 9-14, 22 July 1932, Hamlin Papers; *Wall Street Journal,* 13, 18 July 1932.

39. RFC, *Loan Agency Bulletin No. 34* (1932), p. 1.

40. Eugene Meyer, COHR, p. 676; William Tyler Page to Walter H. Newton, 25 July 1932, and John Miller to Hoover, 15 July 1932, HHPL, PP, SF, RFC; RFC, Minutes 1(29 Feb. 1932):419-20, 6(14 July 1932), 500-502; Jones, *Fifty Billion Dollars,* p. 82; George R. Cooksey to Hoover, 14 July 1932, NA, RG 234, RFC, White House Correspondence.

41. RFC, Minutes 7(17 Aug. 1932):801.

42. *Congressional Record* 75(8, 9 July 1932):14821, 14957.

43. Myers, *State Papers,* vol. 2, pp. 236-37.

44. *Washington Post,* 22 July 1932.

45. *Reconstruction Finance Corporation Act as Amended and Provisions of the Emergency Relief and Construction Act of 1932* (Washington, D.C., 1932), pp. 1-4.

46. Hoover to Henry Steagall, 8 July 1932, NA, RG 234, RFC, Administrative SF; Stimson Diary, 18 July 1932, Stimson Papers; Hoover, *Memoirs,* vol. 3, p. 168.

47. Hamlin Diary, 6, 12, 19 July and 1 Sept. 1932, Hamlin Papers; *Wall Street Journal,* 28 July 1932.

48. Hoover, *Memoirs,* vol. 3, p. 168; Jones, *Fifty Billion Dollars,* p. 521.

49. *Wall Street Journal,* 28 July 1932; Jones, *Fifty Billion Dollars,* p. 521; *Who Was Who in America, 1897-1942,* p. 980.

50. Jones, *Fifty Billion Dollars,* p. 521; *Who Was Who in America, 1942-1950,* p. 373; Discussion Notes, 7 July 1932, Harrison Papers.

51. *Who Was Who in America, 1942-1950,* p. 131; *Chicago Tribune,* 24 June 1932; Jones, *Fifty Billion Dollars,* p. 521.

52. Discussion Notes, 7 July 1932, Harrison Papers; "R.F.C. Goes Democratic," p. 6.

53. Myers, *State Papers,* vol. 2, pp. 273-74.

54. *Wall Street Journal,* 18 July 1932.

55. *Wall Street Journal,* 12 July 1932.

CHAPTER SEVEN

1. See untitled and unpublished memorandum written by Hoover to Atlee Pomerene, 12 Aug. 1932, HHPL, PP, SF, RFC; Winston P. Wilson, *Harvey Couch,* pp. 150-55.

2. *New York Times,* 31 July 1932; B. M. Miller to George R. Cooksey, 29 July 1932, NA, RG 234, RFC, Records Relating to Emergency Relief to the States (Emergency Relief).

3. *Wall Street Journal,* 11 Aug. 1932; *New York Times,* 2 Sept. 1932.

4. Wilson, *Harvey Couch,* p. 143; Roger Lambert, "Hoover and the Red Cross in the Arkansas Drought of 1930," p. 6; Gail S. Murray, "Forty Years Ago: The Great Depression Comes to Arkansas," *Arkansas Historical Quarterly* 29(Winter 1970); 305-8.

5. "Employment Conditions and Unemployment Relief," pp. 493-95.

6. "Legal and Financial Tangles Delay Jobs on RFC Projects," p. 22.

7. Harvey Couch, *Financing the Construction of Self-Liquidating Public Works Projects through the Reconstruction Finance Corporation,* p. 7; Jesse Jones to Thomas Connally, 19 Dec. 1932, Jones Papers.

8. Couch, *Financing,* p. 7; Jones to Carter Glass, 25 Sept. 1932, Glass Papers.

9. Hoover to Pomerene, 18 Aug. 1932, NA, RG 234, RFC, White House Correspondence; *New York Times,* 5 Aug. 1932; RFC, Minutes 10(3 Nov. 1932):148-51; "Housing and Slum Clearance," pp. 10-11; "RFC and Housing," p. 673.

10. "Sabotage and the R.F.C.," *New Republic* 72(12 Oct. 1932):223-24.

11. *Washington Post,* 10 Oct. 1932.

12. RFC, Minutes 9(6 Oct. 1932):197-200; J. R. Knowland to Lawrence Richey, 10 Oct. 1932, HHPL, PP, SF, RFC; Wilson, *Harvey Couch,* pp. 147-50.

13. Paul Y. Andersen, "Buying California for Hoover," p. 392.

14. *Washington Post,* 27 Nov. 1932.

15. "RFC, To Make Jobs Quickly, Asks for More Small Projects," *Business Week,* 2 Nov. 1932, p. 22.

16. U.S., Congress, Senate, Committee on Banking and Currency, *Hearings on S. 5336,* pp. 105-12.

17. RFC, Minutes 9(6 Oct. 1932):197-200.

18. Index to RFC Minutes 1(1932):1391-1401.

19. B. M. Miller to George Cooksey, 29 July 1932, NA, RG 234, RFC, Emergency Relief; *New York Times,* 31 July 1932.

20. RFC, *Emergency Relief Bulletin No. 1* (1932), p. 1. Also see application forms used by the RFC, NA, RG 234, RFC, Emergency Relief, Boxes 1-8.

21. Atlee Pomerene, *An Interpretation of the Relief and Construction Provisions of the Relief and Construction Act of 1932,* pp. 3, 8-9.

22. Ibid., pp. 8-9; also A. J. Cermak to Pomerene, 9 June 1932, NA, RG 234, RFC, Emergency Relief, Illinois; *New York Times,* 28 July 1932; Hoover to William S. Myers, 27 Jan. 1934, Myers Papers.

23. Louis Emmerson to the RFC Board of Directors, 19 July 1932, NA, RG 234, RFC, Emergency Relief, Illinois; *Washington Post,* 28 July 1932.

24. George White to the RFC Board of Directors, 27 July 1932, NA, RG 234, RFC, Emergency Relief, Ohio; Fred Croxton, "Federal Funds Made Available," p. 1, unpublished manuscript, Unemployment Relief and the RFC File, Croxton Papers.

25. Croxton, "Federal Funds Made Available," p. 1.

26. RFC, Minutes 7(6 Aug. 1932):292-93.

27. Clarke Chambers, *Seedtime of Reform,* pp. 195-200.

28. Gifford Pinchot to RFC Board of Directors, 18 July 1932, NA, RG 234, RFC, Emergency Relief, Pennsylvania; RFC, Minutes 7(2 Aug. 1932):58.

29. *Washington Post,* 5 Aug. 1932.

30. Gifford Pinchot, "The Case for Federal Relief," pp. 347-50; U.S., Congress, Senate, *Hearings on S. 4592,* pp. 20-26; U.S., Congress, Senate, Subcommittee of the Committee on Manufactures, *Hearings on S. 5125,* pp. 5-21.

31. RFC, Minutes 7(2 Aug. 1932):58, 7(6 Aug. 1932):292-93.

32. Ibid.

33. RFC, Minutes 7(18 Aug. 1932):896-97.

34. Pinchot to Pomerene, 19 Aug. 1932, NA, RG 234, RFC, Emergency Relief, Pennsylvania.

35. Croxton to Pinchot, 30 Aug. 1932, NA, RG 234, RFC, Emergency Relief, Pennsylvania; U.S., Congress, Senate, *Hearings on S. 5125,* p. 336.

36. *Philadelphia Record,* 21 Sept. 1932; *New York Times,* 21 Sept. 1932; Robert F. Wagner to Pinchot, 20 Sept. 1932, Pinchot Papers. Also see press releases of Governor Pinchot during August and September 1932, Box 2598, Pinchot Papers.

37. *Philadelphia Public Ledger,* 17 Mar. 1932.

38. Pomerene, *Interpretation,* pp. 3, 8-9; *Wall Street Journal,* 16 Sept. 1932.

39. *Washington Post,* 22 Sept. 1932.

40. Pinchot to Pomerene, 24 Sept. 1932, Pinchot Papers; RFC, Minutes 8(27 Sept. 1932).

41. Croxton to Pinchot, 22 Oct. 1932, Pinchot Papers.

42. Transcripts of Board Notes, 28 Oct. 1932, NA, RG 234, RFC, Secretarial Division; *Philadelphia Public Ledger,* 29 Oct. 1932; RFC, Minutes 10 (4 Nov. 1932):215-19.

43. Pomerene to Pinchot, 8 Nov. 1932, Pinchot Papers.

44. Pinchot to Edward Costigan, 8 Nov. 1932, Pinchot Papers.

45. Croxton, "Federal Funds Made Available," p. 1.

46. See acceptance letters from Governor George White for RFC loans, NA, RG 234, RFC, Emergency Relief, Ohio, Boxes 76-80.

47. U.S., Congress, Senate, *Hearings on S. 5125,* pp. 304-8.

48. Arthur Hyde to Charles Dawes, 22 Mar. 1932, Dawes Papers; RFC, *Quarterly Report for October 1 to December 31, 1932,* Table 13.

49. RFC, Minutes 7(1 Aug. 1932):1-6; RFC, *Quarterly Report for April 1 to June 30, 1934,* Table 6.

50. RFC, *Regional Agricultural Credit Corporation Bulletin No. 1* (Washington, D.C., 1932), p. 1; RFC, Minutes 8(8 Sept. 1932):289-90; RFC, *Special Loan Agency Bulletin* (1932), p. 1.

51. "Three-Way Recovery Drive Centers on Commodity Rise," p. 3.

52. See speech by Pomerene to New England Council of Governors, 17 Nov. 1932, Pomerene Papers.

53. "Three-Way Recovery Drive," p. 3.

54. Pomerene to Charles McNary, 18 Oct. 1932, in RFC, Minutes 9(18 Oct. 1932):916-18; *Chicago Tribune*, 4 Nov. 1932; *Nashville Tennessean*, 27 Jan. 1932; RFC, *Quarterly Report for April 1 to June 30, 1934,* Table 6.

55. See speech by Pomerene to New England Council of Governors, 17 Nov. 1932, Pomerene Papers; Index to RFC Minutes 1(1932):1247-49; Transcripts of Board Notes, 28 Oct. 1932, NA, RG 234, RFC, Secretarial Division; RFC, Minutes 11(18 Dec. 1932):374-78; RFC, *Quarterly Report for January 1 to March 31, 1933,* pp. 5-10. Also see press releases of RFC, 8 Dec. 1932, HHPL, PP, SF, RFC.

56. U.S., Congress, Senate, Committee On Banking and Currency, *Hearings on S. 5336,* pp. 105-12; *Wall Street Journal,* 4 Feb. 1933; *Washington Post,* 28 Nov. and 20 Dec. 1932.

57. Charles Haydock, *The National Industrial Recovery Act and the Reconstruction Finance Corporation,* pp. 3-4; Jones to W. C. Bell, 23 Oct. 1933, Jones Papers.

58. Harold Ickes, *Back to Work* (New York, 1935), pp. 47, 58-61.

59. U.S., Congress, Senate, *Hearings on S. 5336,* p. 1.

60. U.S., Congress, Senate, *Hearings on S. 5125,* p. 1.

61. RFC Board of Directors to A. H. Vandenberg, 13 Mar. 1933, in RFC Minutes 14(13 Mar. 1933):846-48; U.S., Congress, Senate, *Hearings on S. 5336,* p. 8; William F. McDonald, *Federal Relief Administration and the Arts,* pp. 15-16, 25-26; Robert Sherwood, *Roosevelt and Hopkins,* p. 46; Searle F. Charles, *Minister of Relief,* p. 29; Russell Kurtz, "American Relief Caravan," pp. 11-12; Croxton to Louis Howe, 15 May 1933, FDRML, OF 643, RFC. Also see area studies completed by RFC staff personnel in Hopkins Papers, Box 41.

62. RFC, *Quarterly Report for October 1 to December 31, 1933,* Table 7.

63. RFC, *Quarterly Report for April 1 to June 30, 1933,* pp. 4-5; RFC, *Quarterly Report for October 1 to December 31, 1940,* pp. 6-8.

64. RFC, *Quarterly Report for January 1 to March 31, 1933,* pp. 5-10.

65. U.S., Congress, House, *Document No. 449, Summary of the Activities of the Commodity Credit Corporation through June 30, 1939,* 76th Cong., 1st sess., 1939, pp. 1-2; Jesse Jones to Roosevelt, 16 Oct. 1933, FDRML, OF 643, RFC; RFC, *Quarterly Report for October 1 to December 31, 1940,* Table 13.

CHAPTER EIGHT

1. RFC, *Quarterly Report for July 1 to September 30, 1932,* Table 13.

2. Speech at Toledo, Ohio, 26 Oct. 1932, Mills Papers.

3. *Wall Street Journal,* 5 Oct. 1932.

4. *Wall Street Journal,* 28 July 1932; Charles Hamlin Diary, 8 Mar. 1933, Hamlin Papers.

5. *New York Times,* 4 Jan. 1933; *Federal Reserve Bulletin* 21(Dec. 1935):803, 19(Dec. 1933):745.

6. *Federal Reserve Bulletin* 18(Dec. 1932):759; "Weekly Review of Economic Conditions," 17 Sept. and 1 Nov. 1932, NA, RG 234, RFC, Statistical Division; *Wall Street Journal,* 23 Sept. 1932.

7. "R.F.C. Begins to Collect," p. 192.

8. *New York Times,* 23 July 1932.

9. *Wall Street Journal,* 16 Aug. 1932; Hamlin Diary, 15 June, 5, 28 July 1932, Hamlin Papers; "Government Recovery Program Stimulates Private Economy," *Business Week* 28 Sept. 1932, p. 16; "Weekly Review of Economic Conditions," 1 Oct. 1932, NA, RG 234, RFC, Statistical Division.

10. Hoover to Eugene Meyer, 23 July 1932, HHPL, PP, SF, RFC; Hamlin Diary, 23 July 1932, Hamlin Papers; *New York Times,* 4 Sept. 1932.

11. American Bankers' Association, *Changes in Bank Earning Assets,* pp. 7-8, 13-14, 33-38.

12. "Weekly Review of Economic Conditions," 1 Nov. 1932, NA, RG 234, RFC, Statistical Division.

13. *Wall Street Journal,* 13 Oct. 1932.

14. Meyer to Hoover, 23 July 1932, HHPL, PP, SF, Federal Reserve Board; Discussion Notes, 4 Apr., 12, 16 May, 19 Aug., and 13 Sept. 1932, Harrison Papers.

15. *Commercial & Financial Chronicle,* 19 Mar. 1932; Hamlin Diary, 14 July 1932, Hamlin Papers; *New York Times,* 1 Jan. 1933; Frederick Bradford, "Cash Burdened Corporations," p. 465.

16. See unpublished personal recollection by Atlee Pomerene, 25 July 1932, Pomerene Papers.

17. *Wall Street Journal,* 16 Aug. 1932.

18. *Wall Street Journal,* 27 Aug. 1932. Also see address by Hoover to Banking and Industrial committees, 26 Aug. 1932, HHPL, PP, SF, Federal Reserve Board.

19. "Confidential History of the National Conference of Banking and Industrial Committees," unpublished manuscript, 27-28 July 1932, HHPL, PP, SF, Cabinet, Commerce; Hamlin Diary, 31 Aug. 1932, Hamlin Papers.

20. See speech by Jesse Jones to National Radio Forum, 29 Aug. 1932, HHPL, PP, SF, RFC, History, p. 174.

21. See speech by Mills at Worcester, Mass., 28 Oct. 1932, Speech File, Mills Papers.

22. *New York Times,* 1 Sept. 1932; *Idaho Daily Statesman,* 1 Sept. 1932.

23. *Idaho Daily Statesman,* 1-2 Sept. 1932; "Weekly Review of Economic Conditions," 17 Sept. 1932, NA, RG 234, RFC, Statistical Division.

24. *Idaho Daily Statesman,* 2-3 Sept. 1932.

25. *Idaho Daily Statesman,* 4, 10, 11, 17 Sept. and 18-19 Oct. 1932.

26. *New York Times,* 2 Nov. 1932; "Weekly Review of Economic Conditions," 17 Feb. 1933, NA, RG 234, RFC, Statistical Division; *Idaho Daily Statesman,* 2 Nov. 1932.

27. "Review of Economic Conditions," 5 Apr. 1932, NA, RG 234, RFC, Statistical Division; *New York Times,* 3 July and 2 Nov. 1932; Transcripts of Board Notes, 1 Nov. 1932, NA, RG 234, RFC, Secretarial Division.

28. Transcripts of Board Notes, 1 Nov. 1932, NA, RG 234, RFC, Secretarial Division; "Report on Bank Examinations," 1931-1932, Balzar Papers.

29. RFC, Minutes 6(26 July 1932):1014-15, 6(30 July 1932):177.

30. Federal Reserve Board, Minutes 19(20 July 1932):72. Loan totals can be found in NA, RG 234, RFC, Secretarial Division, Index to RFC Minutes, vol. 1, 1932, by search of references to following names: Reno National Bank, Bank of Nevada Savings and Trust Company, United Nevada Bank, Riverside Bank, Bank of Willis, Henderson Banking Company, First National Bank of Winnemuca, Churchill County Bank, Bank of Sparks, Carson Valley Bank, Virginia City Bank, and Tonopah Banking Corporation.

31. *New York Times,* 2 Nov. and 11 Dec. 1932; *Nevada State Journal,* 1-2 Nov. 1932; Transcripts of Board Notes, 1-2 Nov. 1932, NA, RG 234, RFC, Secretarial Division.

32. *Nevada State Journal,* 19, 21-29 Nov. and 4-6 Dec. 1932; Cecil W. Creel to A. W. McMillen, 6 Dec. 1932, NA, RG 234, RFC, Emergency Relief, Nevada; Transcripts of Board Notes, 31 Jan. 1933, NA, RG 234, RFC, Secretarial Division.

33. The list of banks that failed after receiving RFC assistance can be found in Index to RFC Minutes, vol. 1, 1932, in NA, RG 234, RFC, Secretarial Division.

34. *Federal Reserve Bulletin* 18(Dec. 1932):759.

35. *New York Times,* 4 Jan. 1933.

36. "Weekly Review of Economic Conditions," 26 Nov., 10, 24 Dec. 1932, and 7 Jan. 1933, NA, RG 234, RFC, Statistical Division.

37. *Federal Reserve Bulletin* 21(Dec. 1935):803, 19(Dec. 1933):745.

38. Pomerene to Hoover, 28 Nov. and 6 Dec. 1932, and Morton G. Bogue to Homer Cummings, 23 Nov. 1932, HHPL, PP, SF, RFC; Hamlin Diary, 18 Nov. 1932, Hamlin Papers.

39. "Number of Personnel," unpublished manuscript, HHPL, PP, SF, RFC, History; RFC, *Quarterly Report for October 1 to December 31 , 1932,* Table 13.

40. RFC, *Loan Agency Bulletin #141* (1932), p. 1.

41. Robert G. Rodkey, *State Bank Failures in Michigan* (Ann Arbor, 1935), p. 10.

42. Lynn Muchmore, "The Banking Crisis of 1933," pp. 627-40.

43. Discussion Notes, 6 Aug. 1931, Harrison Papers; Jackson Reynolds, COHR, p. 142; Milton S. Friedman and Anna Jacobsen Schwartz, *The Great Contraction, 1929-1933*, pp. 34-35.

44. See Chapter 9.

45. *New York Times,* 31 Jan. 1932.

46. Daniel Wing to Charles Dawes, 25 Mar. 1932, and Joseph Chapman to Dawes, 3 May 1932, Dawes Papers; G. W. Nerz to Francis Sieberling, 12 May 1932, HHPL, PP, SF, Financial Matters; RFC, Minutes 2(17 Mar. 1932):647.

47. Discussion Notes, 14 July 1932, Harrison Papers; *Wall Street Journal,* 1 Feb. 1933; "The R.F.C. Fails Congress," *National Sphere* 11(Feb. 1933):15-18.

48. "R.F.C.: Pawnbroker or Fire Department," *Business Week,* 1 Mar. 1933, p. 32.

49. *Commercial & Financial Chronicle,* 28 Jan. 1933.

50. "Weekly Report of Economic Conditions," 17 Sept. 1932, NA, RG 234. RFC, Statistical Division; ICC, *Forty-Sixth Annual Report* (1933), p. 5.

51. ICC, *Forty-Fourth Annual Report on the Statistics of Railways in the United States* (1931), p. S-52; ICC, *Forty-Fifth Annual Report on the Statistics of Railways in the United States* (1932), p. S-27; Herbert Spero, *Reconstruction Finance Corporation Loans to Railroads, 1932-1937,* pp. 13-14.

52. Spero, *RFC Loans to Railroads,* pp. 140-43; ICC, *Forty-Sixth Annual Report* (1933), pp. 6-7.

53. *Commercial & Financial Chronicle,* 28 Jan. 1933. Following is a list of major RFC railroad loans during the Hoover administration and the results of those loans. The source for bankruptcy and judicial readjustment information is the *New York Times.*

Railroad	Loan		Date
1. Baltimore and Ohio	$67,125,000	Jud. Read.	9/3/38
2. Pennsylvania	29,500,000		
3. Chicago and Northwest	21,000,000	Bankruptcy	6/28/35
4. New York Central	20,449,000		
5. St. Louis and Southwestern	18,664,000	Bankruptcy	5/17/33
6. New York, Chicago, and St. Louis	18,200,000		
7. Missouri Pacific	17,100,000	Bankruptcy	4/1/33
8. Southern	14,751,000		
9. Wabash	13,335,000	Jud. Read.	6/2/35
10. Erie	13,400,000	Bankruptcy	1/20/38
11. Illinois Central	11,000,000		
12. Boston & Maine	10,000,000	Jud. Read.	1/4/40
13. Rock Island	10,000,000	Bankruptcy	6/8/33
14. St. Louis and San Francisco	8,000,000	Bankruptcy	11/1/32
15. New York, New Haven, and Hartford	7,700,000	Bankruptcy	10/23/35

54. *Federal Reserve Bulletin* 18(Dec. 1932):759.

55. Elmus R. Wicker, *Federal Reserve Monetary Policy, 1917-1933,* p. 195.

56. Ibid., pp. 180-85; also Lester V. Chandler, *American Monetary Policies, 1928-1941,* pp. 217-18.

57. *Washington Post,* 8 Jan. 1933.

58. *Washington Post,* 10 Jan. 1933

59. *Washington Post,* 23 Dec. 1932, and 3 Feb. 1933.

60. *Washington Post,* 8 Feb. 1933.

61. *Washington Post,* 28 Jan. 1933; U.S., Congress, Senate Subcommittee of Committee on Banking and Currency, *Hearings on S. J. Res. 245,* p. 1; U.S., Congress, Senate, Committee on Interstate Commerce, *Hearings on S. 1580,* p. 39; "One Man Show," *Business Week,* 22 Feb. 1933, p. 8; RFC, Minutes 7(18 Aug. 1933):856-57; *Wall Street Journal,* 28 Jan. 1933.

62. *Washington Post,* 18-19 Aug. 1932.

63. Jesse Jones to Carter Glass, 25 Sept. 1932, Glass Papers.

64. RFC, Minutes 8(29 Sept. 1932):1206.

65. *New York Times,* 4 Jan. 1933.

66. Discussion Notes, 20 Feb. 1933, Harrison Papers.

67. Arthur Ballantine, "When All the Banks Closed," p. 134; James Warburg, COHR, p. 67; Discussion Notes, 20 Feb. 1933, Harrison Papers; Henry L. Stimson Diary, 28 Feb. 1933, Stimson Papers; William S. Myers, "The True Causes of the Banking Panic of 1933," unpublished manuscript, pp. 1-8, and Hoover to Myers, 26 Apr. 1935, Myers Papers; Hoover to Ogden Mills, 22 Feb. 1933, HHPL, PP, SF, Franklin D. Roosevelt.

68. John J. Blaine to Pomerene, 31 Jan. 1933, NA, RG 234, RFC, General Correspondence File, Congress; RFC, Minutes 12(7 Jan. 1933):272, 12(25 Jan. 1932):1402.

69. "Bank Failures during December, 1932, and January and February, 1933," unpublished manuscript, HHPL, PP, SF, Treasury; RFC, Minutes 13(7 Feb. 1933):420-24.

70. *New York Times,* 5 Oct. 1932.

71. Walter Newton to Pomerene, 12 Oct. 1933, HHPL, PP, SF, RFC.

72. See Copy of Speech, 17 Nov. 1932, Box 17, Pomerene Papers; *Wall Street Journal,* 19 Nov. 1932.

73. "Weekly Review of Economic Conditions," 19 Dec. 1932, NA, RG 234, RFC, Statistical Division.

74. *Washington Post,* 1 Feb. 1933; Pomerene to Arthur W. Dean, 28 Jan. 1933, Pomerene Papers; *Real America* 1(May 1933):36.

75. *Des Moines Tribune,* 21 Jan. 1933.

76. RFC, Minutes 12(24 Jan. 1933):1321.

77. *Nashville Tennessean,* 22-23 Jan. 1933.

78. RFC, Minutes 12(3 Feb. 1933):185-90.

79. RFC, Minutes 13(5 Feb. 1933):347-60; "Review of Economic Conditions," 3 Mar. 1933, NA, RG 234, RFC, Statistical Division; *New Orleans Times-Picayune,* 28 Jan. and 5 Feb. 1933.

80. *Federal Reserve Bulletin* 19(Apr. 1933):209-10.

81. Howard Neville, "An Historical Study of the Collapse of Banking in Detroit, 1929-1933," pp. 45-54, 127-32. For the most detailed account of the Michigan crisis, see Susan Estabrook Kennedy, *The Banking Crisis of 1933,* pp. 77-102.

82. U.S., Congress, Senate, Committee on Banking and Currency, *Hearings on S. J. Res. 84, Resolution to Investigate the Stock Exchange,* 73d Cong., 1st sess., 1934, pp. 4543-53, 4722-23.

83. Ibid., pp. 4728-55, 5561-71, 5617; also Jesse Jones, *Fifty Billion Dollars,* p. 59; RFC, Minutes 6(5 July 1932):66.

84. RFC, Minutes 13(6 Feb. 1933):400-440; U.S., Congress, *Hearings on S.J. Res. 84,* pp. 4720-31, 4560-65.

85. U.S., Congress, *Hearings on S.J. Res. 84,* pp. 5550-54; Charles Coughlin, *Driving Out the Money Changers* (Detroit, 1933), pp. 5-32.

86. Harry Barnard, *Independent Man,* pp. 221-28; Jones, *Fifty Billion Dollars,* pp. 59-62; *Detroit News,* 17 Aug. 1933.

87. John T. Flynn, "The Bankers and the Crisis," pp. 157-59; "Michigan Magic," *Harper's* 167(Dec. 1932):1-11; "Inside the R.F.C.," *Harper's* 168(Jan. 1933):161-68.

88. RFC, Minutes 13(6 Feb. 1933):402-39; Presidential Logs, 6 Feb. 1933, HHPL, PPP, Banking Crisis.

89. Barnard, *Independent Man,* pp. 221-28; Presidential Logs, 9 Feb. 1933, HHPL, PPP, Banking Crisis.

90. *Detroit News,* 17 Aug. 1934; *Detroit Free Press,* 15 Feb. 1933; Reynolds, COHR, pp. 164-65; Ballantine, "When All the Banks Closed," p. 135; Francis G. Awalt, "Recollections of the Banking Crisis of 1933," pp. 351-52; Jones, *Fifty Billion Dollars,* p. 60; Hoover to Harry Barnard, 7 Feb. 1946, HHPL, PPP, General; Presidential Logs, 9 Feb. 1933, HHPL, PPP, Banking Crisis; James Couzens to C. R. Cummings, 27 Dec. 1932, Couzens Papers; Raymond Moley, OH, HHPL, p. 7. For a view of the Detroit crisis more favorable to Senator Couzens, see Barnard, *Independent Man,* pp. 221-28.

91. Presidential Logs, 10-11 Feb. 1932, HHPL, PPP, Banking Crisis; Ballantine, "When All the Banks Closed," pp. 135-36; Awalt, "Recollections," pp. 349-54.

92. Presidential Logs, 12 Feb. 1933, HHPL, PPP, Banking Crisis; Eugene Meyer, COHR, p. 678; RFC, Minutes 13(13 Feb. 1933):821.

93. Presidential Logs, 13 Feb. 1933, HHPL, PPP, Banking Crisis; RFC, Minutes 13(12 Feb. 1933):811-13; Couzens to C. R. Cummings, 6 Mar. 1933, Couzens Papers; Hamlin Diary, 13, 14, 24 Feb. 1933, Hamlin Papers; Ballantine, "When All the Banks Closed," pp. 135-36; Awalt, "Recollections," pp. 350-54; Stimson Diary, 14-15, 17, 21 Feb. 1933, Stimson Papers; Arthur Ballantine and Roy Chapin, "Statement of the Interview with Mr. Henry Ford," 13 Feb. 1933, unpublished manuscript, NA, RG 101, Comptroller of the Currency.

94. *Detroit Free Press,* 15 Feb. 1933; Presidential Logs, 14-15 Feb. 1933, HHPL, PPP, Banking Crisis; Meyer, COHR, p. 678.

95. *Annual Report of the Federal Reserve Board, 1932,* p. 154; *Federal Reserve Bulletin,* 21 (Apr. 1934):251; "Weekly Review of Economic Conditions," 3 Mar. 1933, NA, RG 234, RFC, Statistical Division.

96. Federal Reserve Board, Minutes 20(23-25 Feb. 1933): 232-43; RFC, Minutes 13(15, 18, 21-27 Feb. 1933):980, 1240, 1449, 1524, 1588, 1819, 1845.

97. RFC, Minutes 13(26 Feb. 1933):1787; *Baltimore Sun,* 25 Feb. 1933.

98. "Weekly Review of Economic Conditions," 3 Mar. 1933, NA, RG 234, RFC, Statistical Division.

99. *Federal Reserve Bulletin* 19(Mar. 1933):113-25; Ballantine, "When All the Banks Closed," p. 138; RFC, Minutes 14(4 Mar. 1933):425; Hamlin Diary, 3-4 Mar. 1933, Hamlin Papers.

100. Meyer, COHR, pp. 678-80.

CHAPTER NINE

1, *Washington Post,* 10 Mar. 1933.

2. Francis G. Awalt, "Recollections of the Banking Crisis of 1933," pp. 364-65; Presidential Logs, 2 Mar. 1933, HHPL, PPP, Banking Crisis, "The Last Phase," pp. 25-26.

3. Awalt, "Recollections," pp. 364-65; Charles Hamlin Diary, 13 Oct. 1932, Hamlin Papers.

4. *New York Herald Tribune,* 23 Aug. 1944.

5. Awalt, "Recollections," pp. 364-65; Hamlin Diary, 15, 24 Feb. and 1 Mar. 1933, Hamlin Papers; Raymond Moley, OH, HHPL, pp. 9-10.

6. Presidential Logs, 20 Feb. 1933, HHPL, PPP, Banking Crisis; Hamlin Diary, 15 Feb. 1933, Hamlin Papers; Federal Reserve Board, Minutes 20(1 Mar. 1933):282-84; Moley, OH, HHPL, pp. 9-10, 15-16.

7. Presidential Logs, 15 Feb. 1933, HHPL, PPP, Banking Crisis.

8. Presidential Logs, 14-15 Feb. 1933, HHPL, PPP, Banking Crisis.

9. It has been argued that in the closing months of the Hoover administration, banks were reluctant to borrow from the RFC because of the two publicity incidents in July 1932 and January 1933. See, for example, Milton S. Friedman and Anna Jacobsen Schwartz, *The Great Contraction, 1929-1933,* pp. 28-29. In reality, the number of applications to the RFC for assistance doubled in February over December 1932 levels. Bankers were desperate and the corporation had become their last resort. See, for example, RFC Minutes, vol. 13, 1933, NA, RG 234, RFC, Secretarial Division.

10. Presidential Logs, 23 Feb. 1933, HHPL, PPP, Banking Crisis.

11. Moley, OH, HHPL, pp. 14-15; Hamlin Diary, 14 Dec. 1932 and 26 Jan. 1933, Hamlin Papers; Federal Reserve Board, Minutes 20(27 Feb. 1933):257-58.

12. Hoover to Eugene Meyer, 22 Feb. 1933, HHPL, PP, Federal Reserve Board.

13. Federal Reserve Board, Minutes 20(25 Feb. 1933):245-46.

14. Federal Reserve Board, Minutes 20(1 Mar. 1933):281.

15. Hamlin Diary, 1 Mar. 1933, Hamlin Papers.

16. Federal Reserve Board, Minutes 20(2 Mar. 1933):287-88.

17. For a view of the banking crisis written from the perspective of the Federal Reserve Board, see Elmus R. Wicker, *Federal Reserve Monetary Policy, 1917-1933,* pp. 188-95.

18. Presidential Logs, 2 Mar. 1933, HHPL, PPP, Banking Crisis, "The Last Phase," pp. 25-26; Federal Reserve Board, Minutes 20(2 Mar. 1933):301-2; Hamlin Diary, 2 Mar. 1933, Hamlin Papers.

19. Federal Reserve Board, Minutes 20(2 Mar. 1933):299; *New York Herald Tribune,* 23 Aug. 1944; Hamlin Diary, 2-3 Mar. 1933, Hamlin Papers; Moley, OH, HHPL, pp. 15-16; Federal Reserve Board, Minutes 20(3 Mar. 1933):318-19; Walter Wyatt, "Skeleton Outline," unpublished manuscript, Bank Holiday-1933-Gold, Goldenweisar Papers; Personal Notes, Federal Reserve Board meetings, 2-3 Mar. 1933, Bank Holiday-1933-Gold, Goldenweisar Papers; Awalt, "Recollections," pp. 357-60; Arthur Ballantine, "When All the Banks Closed," p. 138; Eugene Meyer, COHR, p. 674; J. F. T. O'Connor Diary, 11 May 1933, O'Connor Papers.

20. Ogden Mills to Hoover, 2 Mar. 1933, HHPL, PP, SF, Franklin D. Roosevelt; Moley, OH, HHPL, pp. 9-10; *New York Herald Tribune,* 23 Aug. 1944; Henry L. Stimson Diary, 3 Mar. 1933, Stimson Papers; Awalt, "Recollections," pp. 357-58.

21. Stimson Diary, 4 Mar. 1933, Stimson Papers; Hoover to Meyer, 4 Mar 1933, Federal Reserve Board Records, Bank Holiday File; Presidential Logs, 3 Mar 1933, HHPL, PPP, Banking Crisis, "The Last Phase," pp. 28-34.

22. Presidential Logs, 3 Mar. 1933, HHPL, PPP, Banking Crisis, "The Last Phase," pp. 29-34.

23. Presidential Logs, 3 Mar. 1933, HHPL, PPP, Banking Crisis.

24. Hamlin Diary, 3, 8 Mar. 1933, Hamlin Papers; also see resolutions of various Federal Reserve banks favoring declaration of national bank holiday, Federal Reserve Board Records, Bank Holiday File, 3 Mar. 1933.

25. Presidential Logs, 3-4 Mar. 1933, HHPL, PPP, Banking Crisis.

26. Awalt, "Recollections," pp. 359-60.

27. Hamlin Diary, 3, 12 Mar. 1933, Hamlin Papers; Eugene M. Stevens to Hamlin, 11 Aug. 1933, and George Harrison to Hamlin, 15 Aug. 1933, Federal Reserve Board Records, Bank Holiday File; Awalt, "Recollections," p. 360.

28. Awalt, "Recollections," pp. 362-63; Ballantine, "When All the Banks Closed," p. 138; Moley, OH, HHPL, pp. 9-11; Stimson Diary, 5 Mar. 1933, Stimson Papers; Personal Notes, 5 Mar. 1933, Bank Holiday-1933-Gold, Goldenweisar Papers.

29. Awalt, "Recollections," p. 364.

30. Presidential Logs, 14-16 Feb. 1933, HHPL, PPP, Banking Crisis; Stimson Diary, 15, 17, 21 Feb. 1933, Stimson Papers.

31. Awalt, "Recollections," pp. 363-64; Hamlin Diary, 17, 21 Feb. 1933, Hamlin Papers.

32. Presidential Logs, 14-15 Feb. 1933, HHPL, PPP, Banking Crisis. Also see unpublished manuscripts of Federal Reserve Board meeting of 16 Feb. 1933, Federal Reserve Board Records, Bank Holiday File.

33. Hamlin Diary, 21 Feb. 1933, Hamlin Papers; Presidential Logs, 15 Feb. 1933, HHPL, PPP, Banking Crisis; Moley, OH, HHPL, pp. 9-13.

34. Presidential Logs, 1-3 Mar. 1933, HHPL, PPP, Banking Crisis. Also see the recollections by Atlee Pomerene of a 1937 meeting with Hoover in which Hoover commended early bank reconstruction efforts of New Deal, Box 37, Pomerene Papers.

35. Awalt, "Recollections," pp. 364-65; Franklin W. Fort to Hoover, 7 Feb. 1932, HHPL, PP, SF, Financial Matters; Fort to Meyer, 29 Mar. 1933, HHPL, PP, SF, Federal Reserve Board.

36. Discussion Notes, 30 June 1932, Harrison Papers.

37. Discussion Notes, 7, 11, 14 July 1932, Harrison Papers; Jesse Jones, *Fifty Billion Dollars,* p. 19; Winston P. Wilson, *Harvey Couch,* p. 157.

38. *Washington Post,* 7 Aug. 1932.

39. Discussion Notes, 7 Nov. 1932, Harrison Papers; Franklin W. Fort to Carter Glass, 3 Jan. 1933, HHPL, PP, SF, Financial Matters; Meyer, COHR, pp. 619-23; Jones, *Fifty Billion Dollars,* p. 21; Awalt, "Recollections," pp. 364-66; Stanley Reed, OH, HHPL, p. 9.

40. Awalt, "Recollections," pp. 364-65.

41. Jones, *Fifty Billion Dollars,* p. 21.

42. Raymond Moley, *The First New Deal,* pp. 214-16.

43. *New York Herald Tribune,* 23 Aug. 1944; Moley, OH, HHPL, pp. 9-16; Hamlin Diary, 9, 15, 19 Mar. 1933, Hamlin Papers; Personal Notes, 4-6 Mar. 1933, Bank Holiday-1933-Gold, Goldenweisar Papers; Stimson Diary, 4, 5, 28 Mar. 1933, Stimson Papers;

Ballantine, "When All the Banks Closed," p. 138; Meyer, COHR, p. 674; Henry Bruere, COHR, pp. 159-60; Jackson Reynolds, COHR, pp. 170-72; Ogden Mills to George Dayton, 15 Sept. 1933, Mills Papers; Awalt, "Recollections," pp. 366-71; Presidential Logs, 5 Mar. 1933, HHPL, PPP, Banking Crisis.

44. *New York Times,* 10 Mar. 1933.

45. "Weekly Review of Economic Conditions," 18 Mar. and 4 Apr. 1933, NA, RG 234, RFC, Statistical Division. Melvin Traylor, president of First National Bank of Chicago, told J. F. T. O'Connor, newly appointed comptroller of the currency, that the banking situation was calmer among depositors following the reopening than it had been in years. See O'Connor Diary, 16 May 1933, O'Connor Papers.

46. "Weekly Review of Economic Conditions," 4 Apr. 1933, NA, RG 234, RFC, Statistical Division.

47. *Annual Report of the Comptroller of the Currency for 1933* (Washington, D.C., 1934), pp. 662-63.

48. RFC, *Quarterly Report for July 1 to September 30, 1934,* Table 6.

49. *Federal Reserve Bulletin* 20(Nov. 1934):733, 763.

50. Gerald Fischer, *The American Banking Structure,* p. 225.

51. RFC, *Quarterly Report for October 1 to December 31, 1938,* Table 6.

52. Stimson Diary, 4 Mar. 1933, Stimson Papers.

CHAPTER TEN

1. Frederick Bradford, "Cash Burdened Corporations," pp. 465-66.

2. Elmus R. Wicker, *Federal Reserve Monetary Policy, 1917-1933,* pp. 176-78; Lester V. Chandler, *American Monetary Policies, 1928-1941,* pp. 233-39. For a brief analysis of the problem from the perspective of a monetary economist, see George Morrison, *Liquidity Preferences of Commercial Banks.*

3. *New York Times,* 11 Feb., 7, 16-17, 20 Mar., 15, 29 Apr., 8 May, and 9, 17, 22 June 1934; Jesse Jones to Duncan Fletcher, 7 May 1934, FDRML, OF 706, Credit; Jesse Jones to Fletcher, 14 Mar. 1934, and Jones to Franklin Roosevelt, 18 Mar. 1934, FDRML, OF 643, RFC; J. F. T. O'Connor Diary, 26 June 1934, O'Connor Papers; Jones to Fletcher, 21 Mar. 1934, NA, RG 234, RFC, White House Correspondence.

4. For an example of the negative interpretation of Hoover's position on each of these measures, see Gerald D. Nash; "Herbert Hoover and the Origins of the Reconstruction Finance Corporation," p. 468; Jordan A. Schwarz, *The Interregnum of Despair,* pp. 162-63; Harris G. Warren, *Herbert Hoover and the Great Depression,* pp. 291-92.

5. American Bankers' Association, *Government Lending Agencies.*

BIBLIOGRAPHY

Manuscript Collections

Berkeley, Calif. University of California. J. F. T. O'Connor Papers.
Charlottesville, Va. University of Virginia. Carter Glass Papers.
Evanston, Ill. Northwestern University. Charles Dawes Papers.
Hyde Park, N.Y. Franklin D. Roosevelt Memorial Library.
   Harry Hopkins Papers.
   Franklin Roosevelt Papers.
Kent, Ohio. Kent State University. Atlee Pomerene Papers.
New Haven, Conn. Yale University. Henry Stimson Papers.
New York. Columbia University. George Harrison Papers.
Princeton, N.J. Princeton University.
   Bernard Baruch Papers.
   William Myers Papers.
Washington, D.C. Federal Reserve Board Papers.
Washington, D.C. Library of Congress.
   James Couzens Papers.
   E. A. Goldenweisar Papers.
   Charles Hamlin Papers.
   Jesse Jones Papers.
   Ogden Mills Papers.
   Gifford Pinchot Papers.
   William Allen White Papers.
Washington, D.C. Georgetown University. Robert Wagner Papers.
Washington, D.C. National Archives.
   Records Group 40. Department of Commerce.
   Records Group 56. Department of the Treasury.
   Records Group 101. Comptroller of the Currency.
   Records Group 234. Reconstruction Finance Corporation.
West Branch, Ia. Herbert Hoover Presidential Library.
   Fred Croxton Papers.
   Herbert Hoover Papers.

Oral Histories

These oral histories are unpublished manuscripts of interviews conducted with the individuals under the auspices of the libraries.

New York. Columbia University Oral History Research Office.
  Eugene Meyer.
  Jackson Reynolds.
  James Warburg.
West Branch, Ia. Herbert Hoover Presidential Library.
  James H. Douglas, Jr.
  Raymond Moley.
  Bradley Nash.
  Stanley Reed.

Newspapers

Baltimore Sun	*Nevada State Journal*
Chicago Tribune	*New Orleans Times-Picayune*
Commercial & Financial Chronicle	*New York Herald Tribune*
Des Moines Tribune	*New York Times*
Detroit Free Press	*Philadelphia Public Ledger*
Detroit News	*Philadelphia Record*
Idaho Daily Statesman	*Wall Street Journal*
Nashville Tennessean	*Washington Post*

Government Publications

Washington, D.C. Federal Reserve Board. *Annual Reports,* 1930-1933. *Federal Reserve Bulletins,* 1931-1933.
  Interstate Commerce Commission. *Annual Reports*, 1930-1933.
  Reconstruction Finance Corporation. *Circulars*, 1932-1933. *Custodian Bulletins*, 1932-1933. *Emergency Relief Bulletins*, 1932-1933. *Loan Agency Bulletins*, 1932-1933. *Minutes of the Meetings of the Board of Directors,* 1932-1933. *Monthly Reports,* 1932-1933. *Quarterly Reports,* 1932-1933.
  Secretary of the Treasury. *Annual Reports*, 1919-1921, 1931-1932.
  War Finance Corporation. *Annual Reports*, 1919-1923.

Congressional Publications

Washington, D.C. *Congressional Record*, 1931-1933.
U.S. Congress.
  House. Committee on Banking and Currency. *Hearings on H.R. 5060 and H.R. 5116: Creation of a Reconstruction Finance Corporation.* 72d Cong., 1st sess., 1932.
  Senate. Committee on Banking and Currency. *Hearings on S. 1: Creation of a Reconstruction Finance Corporation.* 72d Cong., 1st sess., 1932.
  Senate. Subcommittee of Committee on Manufactures. *Hearings on S. 4592: Federal Cooperation in Unemployment Relief.* 72d Cong., 1st sess., 1932.
  Senate. Committee on Banking and Currency. *Hearings on S. 4632, S. 4727, and S. 4822: Bills Relating to Federal Loans to Aid Unemployment.* 72d Cong., 1st sess., 1932.
  Senate. Committee on Manufactures. *Hearings on S. 5125: Federal Aid for Unemployment Relief.* 72d Cong., 2d sess., 1933.

Senate. Committee on Banking and Currency. *Hearings on S. 5336: Further Unemployment Relief through the RFC.* 72d Cong., 2d sess., 1933.

Senate. Committee on Banking and Currency. *Hearings on S.J. Res. 245: Joint Resolution to Suspend the Making of Loans to Railroads by the RFC.* 72d Cong., 2d sess., 1933.

Senate. Committee on Banking and Currency. *Hearings on S. 509: Bill to Amend the Emergency Relief and Construction Act of 1932.* 73d Cong., 1st sess., 1933.

Senate. Committee on Interstate Commerce. *Hearings on S. 1580: Bill to Relieve the Existing National Emergency to Interstate Railroad Transportation.* 73d Cong., 1st sess., 1933.

Senate. Committee on Banking and Currency. *Hearings on S.J. Res. 84 and S. 56 and S. 97: Stock Exchange Practices.* 73d Cong., 2d sess., 1934.

Books

American Bankers' Association. *Banking after the Crisis.* New York, 1934.

————. *Changes in Bank Earning Assets.* New York, 1936.

————. *Government Lending Agencies.* New York, 1936.

Anderson, Clay J. *A Half-Century of Federal Reserve Policymaking, 1914-1964.* Philadelphia, 1965.

Bailyn, Bernard. *The Ideological Origins of the American Revolution.* Cambridge, 1967.

Barnard, Harry. *Independent Man: The Life of Senator James Couzens.* New York, 1958.

Beckhart, Benjamin. *The New York Money Market. Vol. 3. The Uses of Funds.* New York, 1932.

Beckhart, Benjamin; Smith, James G.; and Brown, William. *The New York Money Market. Vol. 4. External and Internal Relations.* New York, 1932.

Chamberlain, Lawrence H. *The President, Congress and Legislation.* New York, 1946.

Chambers, Clarke. *Seedtime of Reform: American Social Service and Social Action, 1918-1933.* Ann Arbor, 1967.

Chandler, Lester V. *American Monetary Policies, 1928-1941.* New York, 1971.

Charles, Searle F. *Minister of Relief: Harry Hopkins and the Depression.* Syracuse, N.Y., 1963.

Cochran, Thomas C. *The Great Depression and World War II.* Glenview, Ill., 1968.

Collins, Charles. *Rural Banking Reform.* New York, 1931.

Conkin, Paul. *The New Deal.* New York, 1967.

Couch, Harvey. *Financing the Construction of Self-Liquidating Public Works Projects through the Reconstruction Finance Corporation.* Washington, D.C., 1932.

Cowing, Cedric B. *Populists, Plungers, and Progressives: A Social History* of Stock and Commodity Speculation, 1890-1936. Princeton, 1965.

Daniels, Roger. *The Bonus March: An Episode of the Great Depression.* Westport, Conn., 1971.

Dublin, Jack. *Credit Unions: Theory and Practice.* Detroit, 1966.

Ewalt, Josephine. *The Savings and Loan Story, 1930-1960.* Chicago, 1962.

Fausold, Martin, and Mazuzan, George, eds. *The Hoover Presidency: A Reappraisal.* Albany, 1974.

Fine, Sidney. *Laissez-Faire and the General Welfare State.* Ann Arbor, 1964.

Fischer, Gerald. *The American Banking Structure.* New York, 1968.

Friedman, Milton S., and Schwartz, Anna Jacobsen. *The Great Contraction, 1929-1933.* Princeton, 1967.

Galbraith, John Kenneth. *The Great Crash, 1929.* Boston, 1954.

Gay, George I., and Fisher, H. H. *Public Relations of the Commission for Relief in Belgium: Documents,* 2 vols. Stanford, 1929.

Goldsmith, Raymond W. *Financial Intermediaries in the American Economy since 1900.* Princeton, 1958.

Green, George D. *Finance and Economic Development in the Old South: Louisiana Banking, 1804-1861.* Palo Alto, 1972.

Guilfoyle, James H. *On the Trail of the Forgotten Man: A Journal of the Roosevelt Presidential Campaign.* Boston, 1933.

Hammond, Bray. *Banks and Politics in America from the Revolution to the Civil War.* Princeton, 1957.

Haydock, Charles. *The National Industrial Recovery Act and the Reconstruction Finance Corporation.* Philadelphia, 1933.

Hofstadter, Richard. *The American Political Tradition.* New York, 1960.

Hoover, Herbert. *American Individualism.* New York, 1922.

_____. *The New Day.* Stanford, 1928.

_____. *The Challenge to Liberty.* New York, 1934.

_____. *Further Addresses upon the American Road, 1938-1940.* New York, 1940.

_____. *America's First Crusade.* New York, 1942.

_____. *Further Addresses upon the American Road, 1941-1945.* New York, 1946.

_____. *Addresses upon the American Road, 1945-1948.* New York, 1949.

_____. *Addresses upon the American Road, 1948-1950.* New York, 1951.

_____. *The Memoirs of Herbert Hoover,* 3 vols. New York, 1952.

Jones, Jesse. *Fifty Billion Dollars.* New York, 1951.

Joslin, Theodore. *Hoover Off the Record.* New York, 1934.

Kennedy, Susan Estabrook. *The Banking Crisis of 1933.* Lexington, Kentucky, 1973.

Keynes, John M. *A Treatise on Money.* London, 1930.

Klein, Lawrence R. *The Keynesian Revolution.* New York, 1954.

Lekachman, Robert. *A History of Economic Ideas.* New York, 1959.

_____. *The Age of Keynes.* New York, 1966.

Leuchtenburg, William. *Franklin D. Roosevelt and the New Deal, 1932-1940.* New York, 1963.

Liang, Agnes. *The Banking Structure of the United States in the Twentieth Century.* Washington, D.C., 1952.

Lisio, Donald J. *The President and Protest: Hoover, Conspiracy, and the Bonus Riot.* Columbia, Missouri, 1974.

Lloyd, Craig. *Aggressive Introvert: Herbert Hoover and Public Relations Management, 1912-1932.* Columbus, Ohio, 1973.

Malburn, William P. *What Happened to Our Banks.* Indianapolis, 1934.

McDonald, William F. *Federal Relief Administration and the Arts: The Origins and Administrative History of the Arts Projects of the Works Progress Administration.* Columbus, Ohio, 1969.

Marquis Editors. *Who Was Who in America, 1897-1942,* Chicago, 1942.

———. *Who Was Who in America, 1942-1950.* Chicago, 1950.

———. *Who Was Who in America, 1951-1960.* Chicago, 1960.

———. *Who Was Who in America, 1961-1968.* Chicago, 1969.

Moley, Raymond. *The First New Deal.* New York, 1966.

Moody, J. Carroll, and Fite, Gilbert C. *The Credit Union Movement: Origins and Development, 1850-1970.* Lincoln, Nebraska, 1971.

Morrison, George. *Liquidity Preferences of Commercial Banks.* Chicago, 1966.

Myers, Margaret. *The New York Money Market. Vol. I. Origins and Development.* New York, 1931.

———. *Financial History of the United States.* New York, 1970.

Myers, William S., ed. *The State Papers and Other Public Writings of Herbert Hoover,* 2 vols. New York, 1934.

Myers, William S., and Newton, Walter H. *The Hoover Administration: A Documented Narrative.* New York, 1936.

Nadler, Marcus, and Bogen, Jules I. *The Banking Crisis.* New York, 1933.

National Industrial Conference Board. *The Availability of Bank Credit.* New York, 1932.

Plummer, Wilbur C., and Young, Ralph A. *Sales Finance Companies and Their Credit Practices.* New York, 1940.

Pomerene, Atlee. *An Interpretation of the Relief and Construction Provisions of the Relief and Construction Act of 1932.* Washington, D.C., 1932.

Proceedings of the National Conference of Social Work. Chicago, 1933.

Romasco, Albert U. *The Poverty of Abundance: Hoover, the Nation, the Depression.* New York, 1965.

Saulnier, Raymond. *Industrial Banking Companies and Their Credit Practices.* New York, 1940.

———. *Urban Mortgage Lending by Life Insurance Companies.* New York, 1950.

Saulnier, Raymond; Halenieu, Harold; and Jacoby, Neil H. *Federal Lending and Loan Insurance.* Princeton, 1958.

Schlesinger, Arthur M., Jr. *The Age of Roosevelt. Vol. 1. The Crisis of the Old Order.* Boston, 1957.

———. *The Age of Roosevelt. Vol. 2. The Coming of the New Deal.* Boston, 1959.

Schwarz, Jordan A. *The Interregnum of Despair: Hoover, Congress, and the Depression.* Urbana, 1970.

Shade, William G. *Banks or No Banks: The Money Issue in Western Politics, 1832-1865.* Detroit, 1972.

Sherwood, Robert. *Roosevelt and Hopkins: An Intimate History.* New York, 1948.

Sobel, Robert. *The Great Bull Market: Wall Street in the 1920's.* New York, 1968.

Soule, George. *Prosperity Decade: From War to Depression, 1917-1929.* New York, 1947.

Spero, Herbert. *Reconstruction Finance Corporation Loans to Railroads, 1932-1937.* New York, 1939.

Spiegel, Henry W. *The Growth of Economic Thought.* Englewood Cliffs, N.J., 1971.

Studenski, Paul, and Krooss, Herman E. *Financial History of the United States.* 2d ed. New York, 1963.

Sullivan, Lawrence. *Prelude to Panic: The Story of the Bank Holiday.* Washington, D.C., 1936.

Temin, Peter. *The Jacksonian Economy.* New York, 1969.

Trescott, Paul. *Financing American Enterprise: The Story of Commercial Banking.* New York, 1963.

Tugwell, Rexford G. *The Brains Trust.* New York, 1968.

Upham, Cyril B., and Lamke, Edwin. *Closed and Distressed Banks: A Study in Public Administration.* Washington, D.C., 1934.

Warren, Harris G. *Herbert Hoover and the Great Depression.* New York, 1967.

Wehle, B. Louis. *Hidden Threads of History.* New York, 1953.

Wicker, Elmus R. *Federal Reserve Monetary Policy, 1917-1933.* New York, 1966.

Wilson, Joan Hoff. *Herbert Hoover. Forgotten Progressive.* Boston, 1975.

Wilson, Winston P. *Harvey Couch.* Nashville, 1947.

Young, Ralph A. *Personal Finance Companies and Their Credit Practices.* New York, 1940.

Articles

Andersen, Paul Y. "Buying California for Hoover." *The Nation* 135(26 Oct. 1932):392-93.

Atkins, Paul M. "The National Credit Corporation." *Review of Reviews* 85(Jan. 1932):48-49, 68.

Awalt, Francis G. "Recollections of the Banking Crisis of 1933." *Business History Review* 43(Autumn 1969):347-71.

Ballantine, Arthur. "When All the Banks Closed." *Harvard Business Review* 26(1948):129-43.

"Borrowing Billions to Turn the Tide." *Literary Digest* 112(30 Jan. 1932): 7-8.

Bradford, Frederick. "Cash Burdened Corporations." *American Bankers' Association Journal* 25(Jan. 1933):464-66.

Burris, Eugene. "A Plan to Stabilize Credit." *Bankers' Monthly* 49(Jan. 1932):40-41.

"Credit Expansion Is Now Up To Business and the Banks." *Business Week,* 24 Feb. 1932, pp. 5-6

Daiger, J. M. "Confidence, Credit, and Cash." *Harper's* 166(May 1933): 279-92.

———. "What the R.F.C. Means to Every Business Man." *Forbes* 29(15 Feb. 1932):20-22.

Degler, Carl N. "The Ordeal of Herbert Hoover." *Yale Review* 52(Summer 1963):563-83.

Ebersole, J. F. "One Year of the Reconstruction Finance Corporation." *Quarterly Journal of Economics* 47(May 1933):464-92.

"Emergency Pool to Help Banks May Serve to Stop Deflation." *Business Week,* 14 Oct. 1931, pp. 5-6.

"Employment Conditions and Unemployment Relief." *Monthly Labor Review* 35(Sept. 1932):493-95.

Flynn, John T. "Michigan Magic." *Harper's* 167(Dec. 1932):1-11.

———. "Inside the R.F.C." *Harper's* 168(Jan. 1933):161-68.

———. "The Bankers and the Crisis." *New Republic* 74(22 Mar. 1933):157-59.

———. "Bailing Out the Van Swerigans." *New Republic* 74(19 Apr. 1932):279-80.

"For Public Relief, the R.F.C.; For Industry, Federal Reserve." *Business Week,* 20 July 1932, pp. 3-4.

"Future of the RFC." *New Outlook,* 161(May 1933):11.

Hawley, Ellis W. "Herbert Hoover, the Commerce Secretariat, and the Vision of an 'Associative State.' " *Journal of American History* 61 (June 1974):116-40.

Harris, S. E. "Banking and Currency Legislation, 1932." *Quarterly Journal of Economics* 46(May 1932):546-57.

Hayes, William. "Government and the Banking Business." *Bankers' Monthly* 124(Apr. 1932):437-42.

"The House of Jesse." *Fortune* 21(May 1940):44-50, 122-24, 126, 130-34, 139-40.

"Housing and Slum Clearance." *New Outlook* 161(Nov. 1932):10-11.

"How the Cities Stand." *Survey* 68(15 Apr. 1932):71-75, 92.

Kiplinger, Willard M. "Indirect Relief." *Forum and Century* 87(June 1932):349-52.

Knappen, Theodore. "The Irony of Big Business Seeking Government Management." *Magazine of Wall Street* 49(23 Jan. 1932):386-88.

———. "Can These Men Bring Back Prosperity." *Magazine of Wall Street* 49(20 Feb. 1932):522-24.

Krecker, Preston S. "The Securities Markets." *Commerce and Finance* 21(27 Jan. 1932):139.

Kurtz, Russell. "American Relief Caravan." *Survey* 69(Jan. 1933):11-12.

Lambert, Roger. "Hoover and the Red Cross in the Arkansas Drought of 1930." *Arkansas Historical Quarterly* 29(Spring 1970):1-19.

Leavitt, Roger. "The New Credit Corporation Has Renewed Public Confidence." *Bankers' Monthly* 49(Jan. 1932):72-81.

"Legal and Financial Tangles Delay Jobs on RFC Projects." *Business Week,* 2 Nov. 1932, p. 22.

Leuchtenberg, William. "The New Deal and the Analogue of War." In *Change and Continuity in Twentieth Century America.* Edited by John Braeman. Columbus, Ohio, 1964.

Meyer, Eugene. "From Laissez-Faire with William Graham Sumner to the R.F.C." *Public Policy* 5(1946):5-27.

Miller, John. "The National Credit Corporation." *Investment Banking* 2(2 Dec. 1931):53-57.

"Mobilizing to Rout the Forces of the Depression." *Commerce and Finance* 20(14 Oct. 1931):1509.

Muchmore, Lynn. "The Banking Crisis of 1933: Some Iowa Evidence." *Journal of Economic History* 30(Sept. 1970):627-40.

Nash, Gerald D. "Herbert Hoover and the Origins of the Reconstruction Finance Corporation." *Mississippi Valley Historical Review* 46(Dec. 1959):455-68.

"Need We Fear Inflation." *Magazine of Wall Street* 49(6 Feb. 1932):449-50.

Pinchot, Gifford. "The Case for Federal Relief." *Survey* 67(Jan. 1932):347-50.

Pontecarvo, Guilio. "Investment Banking and Securities Speculation in the Late 1920's." *Business History Review* 23(Summer 1958):166-91.
"Provisions of the Emergency Banking Act." *Congressional Digest* 12 (Apr. 1933):103-4.
"Public Works and the RFC." *New Outlook* 161(Oct. 1932):2-3.
"Railroad Loan Policy Draws Critics' Fire." *Business Week,* 16 Apr. 1932, p. 6.
"Railroad Loan Stirs Up the Senate." *Literary Digest* 113(19 Apr. 1932): 44-45.
"The Reconstruction Finance Corporation." *Commerce and Finance* 21 (10 Feb. 1932):207-8.
"RFC and Housing." *Survey* 68(15 Dec. 1932):676.
"R.F.C. Begins to Collect." *Magazine of Wall Street* 49(10 Dec. 1932):191-92.
"R.F.C. Goes Democratic." *Literary Digest* 114(13 Aug. 1932):6.
Temin, Peter. "The Economic Consequences of the Bank War." *Journal of Political Economy* 76(Mar./Apr. 1968):257-74.
"Three-Way Recovery Drive Centers on Commodity Rise." *Business Week,* 17 Aug. 1932, p. 3.
"To Bankers: Loosen Up Credit." *Forbes* 19(15 Mar. 1932), p. 22.
Williams, William Appleman. "What This Country Needs. . . ." *New York Review of Books* 15(5 Nov. 1970):7-9.

Unpublished Materials

Bee, Clair. "The Reconstruction Finance Corporation." Master's thesis, Rutgers—the State University, 1933.
Carter, John. "The Recovery Program of the Hoover Administration." Master's thesis, University of California, Berkeley, 1936.
Cho, Hyo Won. "The Evolution of the R.F.C." Ph.D. diss., Ohio State University, 1953.
Freidel, Frank. "Hoover and Roosevelt and Historical Continuity." Paper read at centennial meetings of Herbert Hoover Presidential Library Association, Aug. 1974.
Hildebrandt, Donald. "The Reconstruction Finance Corporation." M.B.A. thesis, Ohio State University, 1951.
Karl, Barry. "Herbert Hoover and the Progressive Myth of the Presidency." Paper read at centennial meetings of Herbert Hoover Presidential Library Association, Aug. 1974.
Kemp, Arthur. "Hoover and the Banking Crisis of 1933." Paper read at centennial meetings of Herbert Hoover Presidential Library Association, Aug. 1974.
Neville, Howard R. "An Historical Study of the Collapse of Banking in Detroit, 1929-1933." Ph.D. diss., Michigan State University, 1956.

INDEX